ALSO BY KRISTI COULTER

Nothing Good Can Come from This

EXIT
INTERVIEW

EXIT
INTERVIEW

*The Life and Death of My
Ambitious Career*

Kristi Coulter

MCD  Farrar, Straus and Giroux
New York

MCD

Farrar, Straus and Giroux

120 Broadway, New York 10271

Grateful acknowledgment is made for permission
to reprint the following material:
Lyrics from "Snow Is Gone," composed and written by Josh Ritter,
reprinted by permission of Rural Songs (ASCAP).
Lyrics from "Mirrorball." Words and Music by Ben Watt and Tracey Thorn.
Copyright © 1996 SM Publishing UK Limited. All rights administered by
Sony Music Publishing (US) LLC, 424 Church Street, Suite 1200,
Nashville, TN 37219. International copyright secured. All rights reserved.
Reprinted by permission of Hal Leonard LLC.

Library of Congress Cataloging-in-Publication Data

Names: Coulter, Kristi, 1970– author.

Title: Exit interview : a memoir / Kristi Coulter.

Description: First edition. | New York : MCD / Farrar, Straus and
Giroux, [2023]

Identifiers: LCCN 2023008696 | ISBN 9780374600907 (hardcover)

Subjects: LCSH: Coulter, Kristi, 1970– | Women employees—Biography. |
Amazon.com (Firm)

Classification: LCC HD6053 .C76 2023 | DDC 331.4092—dc23/
eng/20230518

LC record available at https://lccn.loc.gov/2023008696

Our books may be purchased in bulk for promotional, educational, or
business use. Please contact your local bookseller or the Macmillan Corporate
and Premium Sales Department at 1-800-221-7945, extension 5442, or by
email at MacmillanSpecialMarkets@macmillan.com.

www.mcdbooks.com • www.fsgbooks.com

Follow us on Twitter, Facebook, and Instagram at @mcdbooks

1 3 5 7 9 10 8 6 4 2

For Mindy

You can work long, hard, or smart, but at Amazon.com
you can't choose two out of three.

—JEFF BEZOS, 1997 LETTER TO SHAREHOLDERS

Come on girl, it's gonna be alright.
Come on girl, it's never gonna be alright.

—EVERYTHING BUT THE GIRL, "MIRRORBALL"

CONTENTS

PART I: PLUNGED

PART II: BOGGLED

PART III: DROWNED

PART IV: DRY

PART V: GOING, GOING

PART I

PLUNGED

2006–2007

1

IMPLAUSIBILITIES

I can tell people don't believe me when I say my co-workers kept bottles of booze on their desks, or that they sometimes popped beta-blockers before meetings with Jeff Bezos, or that I found out about the Kindle and the drones and Whole Foods on the internet like everyone else. It's hard to swallow that our laptops were sometimes repaired with duct tape, or that my psychiatrist credited Amazon employees for his second home in Hawaii, or that the mere existence of Amazon warehouses could slip my mind for years at a time, never mind what went on inside them or what it might be like to work in one. I learned of Amazon delivery trucks when I saw one broken down on my street. I learned that Amazon was firing people by algorithm by reading Bloomberg. "But you were right there," I've heard, at which times I explain that there's no such thing at Amazon, that it'd be like being *right there* in an ocean or a field of static. That often my only *right there* was whatever had to happen in the next thirty minutes to incite or narrowly avert catastrophe or catapult me into a future I both dreaded and desperately wanted. I can see from people's faces that it's not quite plausible, or that it's plausible but they just don't like it. "You were a good German," a drunk man once said to me, pleased with himself because he thought he was the first. Most improbable of all is when I say parts of it were astounding and fun, that for twelve years Amazon supplied me with a high-grade lunacy I didn't know I needed until I touched it and my ambition bloomed like neon ink in water. *That doesn't sound fun*, the faces say, or *that* shouldn't *have been fun*. To which my only possible response is, I'm not telling you what was right or good. I'm telling you what went down and how it felt.

2

THE PULL

Title: *Senior Manager, Books & Media Merchandising*
Location: *Seattle, WA*
Date Posted: *January 6, 2006*

Do you want to change the world? Are you passionate about
helping customers shop online? Do you have the stamina of a
jacked-up mountain goat and boundaries fairly described as
"porous"? Amazon.com is seeking a North American leader
for its Books and Media Merchandising teams. In this role,
you will own the merchandising, editorial, and email content
for five Amazon storefronts, leading multiple editorial teams
in a 24/7/365 demand-generation process. You will drive
relentless, and we seriously fucking do mean *relentless*,
improvement in merchandising content on Amazon and directly
impact free cash flow. You will also build new internal content-
management tools with Band-Aids and Scotch tape by working
closely with understaffed technical leaders in a highly matrixed
environment (that is, one in which you have absolutely no
authority or leverage).

Amazon's culture is exciting, fast paced, and dynamic. Like,
highly dynamic. If you end up hating this job, no worries! It will

be unrecognizable in six months anyway. We offer competitive pay and a benefits package that is not the worst. Employee amenities include a desk and laptop, plus the option to request sandpaper for your desk (you'll see) and a coat hook from Facilities (please allow ten days for delivery).

Job Requirements:
- 5+ years experience leading content or editorial teams
- track record of delivering large, cross-functional, complex, customer-facing products under circumstances verging on psychotic
- intense fear of failure
- ability to be dropped into any situation with a blowgun, tourniquet, and Excel 97, and figure shit out fast
- thick hide/pelt

Also Highly Desired:
- superior physical stamina
- stay-at-home spouse
- acute impostor syndrome

EEOC Statement:
Amazon.com technically counts as an Equal Opportunity Employer.

3

HERMIONE IN BERLIN

I hate my clothes. Amazon's interview instructions said to dress "nicely but comfortably—a suit and tie won't impress anyone here." But translating that into women's wear is tricky, so I fall back on my superpower: overthinking. I've landed on the same skirt, wrap top, and low heels I probably would have chosen in the absence of guidance, but now it feels wrong; the skirt's kick pleat is too frivolous, the top too open, the pumps too matronly. I wish I *were* fastened into a gray carapace of a suit instead of this nexus between churchy and trampy.

But it's too late. I've already walked the five blocks from my hotel to Amazon's downtown Seattle offices. I have circled the mass of elevator banks, found the right one, hit the button for the eighteenth floor, waited in vain for the door to close, disembarked, recircled, passed a large sculpture I didn't notice before of headless people climbing a ladder, and sought help from security, who have to "badge me up" because it's Presidents' Day and the building is technically closed. I've made it to the eighteenth floor, past the lobby door I recognize as such only because a piece of eight-and-a-half-by-eleven-inch paper reading "Amazon" is taped to it. I've checked in with reception and am now waiting on a sagging, dormy couch among ten or twelve men in suits and ties.

The eighty-three homemade flash cards I've been prepping with are in my bag and I'd like to pull them out for one last cram session, but the men are mostly flipping through old copies of *Newsweek* or typing on those little devices I think must be BlackBerrys. I should follow their lead. So I pick up a *People* from last year and stare at it, reminding myself that this is just an experiment, a rehearsal for some future job hunt, a *lark*. I'm lying to myself, of course. If I were a woman of larks or whims,* I would never have made it through two phone screens and been flown here to sell myself in person. I'm a grinder, a hand raiser, a doer of extra-credit assignments. I'm the one who gets into the room with the men when there's only one space for a woman. And I've crammed so hard for this lark that if it ends in rejection, I'll be the one saying no. That's how I like it. That's how I need things to be.

I wonder how many of the men around me really want to work here. I'm far from sure I do, based on tech forum post headlines like MEAT GRINDER and RUINED MY MARRIAGE. All I really know is that I want out of the All Media Guide, the cozy but perpetually underachieving tech company where I've hit a ceiling—maybe glass, maybe just particleboard, at this point I don't even care—after seven years. And after twelve years in a Michigan college town, my husband, John, and I are both ready for milder weather and bluer state politics. Beyond that? I don't know. I applied for this job feeling underqualified, and Amazon called two hours later. I had a few phone conversations of increasing formality, and less than a week later I landed in Seattle, having told AMG I was out with a cold.

---

* Or gambols, frolics, and so forth.

At 8:00 a.m. sharp, a man in his mid-thirties in jeans and an untucked button-down enters the lobby and heads directly for me. "Hi, you must be Kristi," he says, Kristi being easy to spot because she's the only woman in the room. For one wild second I want to deny that I'm her. If I'm not Kristi, I won't have to spend the next seven hours being grilled. I won't have to risk failure, or even worse, success, which would require me to stop floating along and make a real decision about my life.

But I'm thirty-five and can't remember the last time I changed or learned in any big way. I'm bored with my job and my town, but also—especially—with myself.

Also, I'm not yet half the liar I'll become. "Yes, I'm Kristi," I say, heaving myself up from the saggy couch to shake his hand.

The man's name is Chuck, and he shows me to a windowless conference room with stained carpet, mismatched chairs, and a foot-sized hole in one wall. "I know it's not fancy," he says of the almost aggressively ugly space. "We prefer to put our money into things that make a difference to customers." We had already discussed the basics of the job during my phone screens. Now, after a brief recap, he dives right into the department I'd be running, Merchandising. "The work our merchandisers do is criminally manual, and their tool set is insanely outdated," he says, eyes squinting in his shiny-cheeked, slightly rubbery face. "They're clicking a button ten times when they should be clicking it once." Also, apparently it's hard to measure whether the content the merchandisers produce is leading customers to buy stuff. "So they're largely flying blind," he says. "It's very hard to know if their hard work is having any real impact on the business."

"In that case, how do their managers know if they're doing a good job?" I ask.

"Volume, frankly," Chuck says. "How much spaghetti they can throw at the wall."

"So their jobs are hard, tedious, and exhausting, and they don't have any meaningful way to know if they're succeeding or not."

"Exactly," Chuck says, his eyes lighting up as though I've just made his day by telling him how much it sucks to be a merchandiser. What's funny is that I think *my* eyes light up, too, at the prospect of real problems to solve. AMG makes its money by licensing entertainment metadata—like CD reviews and actor bios—to online retailers, Amazon included. I run the movies division, and while it's fun work that keeps me up to my eyeballs in Oscar screeners, my core job hasn't changed in years. I've been begging—he might say hassling—my boss for almost that long to give me something challenging or at least *new* to do, and he keeps saying, "I'm looking for something, be patient," and I believe him, but I also know he's never going to find it, which means I'm also never going to be at the table where AMG's all-male C-suite is making the big decisions. My ability to have an impact on either AMG's path or my own within the company is agonizingly limited. I try to tell myself it doesn't matter, that it's enough to make decent money doing fun work with people I mostly like. But it isn't. At AMG and in my liberal arts background, ambition is considered uncool and even a little embarrassing. I'm supposed to see work as a necessary evil. But I can't help it. I like to work, and I want my work to leave a wake.

And here, two thousand miles from home, is my chance.

"Your job would be to run the merch organization day

to day but also to overhaul the role. Beat the drum for better tools. Figure out which tasks grow the business and which don't, and kill the latter ones. Decide whether we even have the right people," Chuck says. "Your plate would be very full, but you would have a high level of executive support and visibility."

"That's great," I say. "Visibility matters to me." Still, when he asks what questions I have for him, I feel both compelled and emboldened by his own pleasant directness to address an elephant in the room, or on the web. "Reading about Amazon online, I get the impression it can be a somewhat intense place to work," I say. "Can you give me your perspective? Because if I come to work here, I don't want to sort of, you know, get divorced or become an alcoholic or what have you."

To his credit, Chuck looks only slightly taken aback. "Well, it can certainly be fast paced," he says. "But I have two little boys and I go home to them every evening." I'm so relieved to see him take the question in stride that I fail to notice he hasn't quite answered it.

An affable beanpole named Andy takes Chuck's place in the conference room at 9:00 a.m. and explains that he is the general manager for the DVD store. "Though what I'd actually like to talk about today is how you'd think through selling houseplants online," he says.

I spent hours of prep time scouring the Amazon media stores for examples of what I like about them and what I think should change. But I didn't anticipate being asked about selling a whole new thing. "Do you mean *how* to sell them online, or whether to do it at all?" I ask, to clarify but also to buy a beat of time.

"The latter," he says.

"Well, I know nothing at all about packing or shipping plants," I say. "But my first thought is that they're delicate and it's probably hard to protect them in transit, especially when you factor in different climate zones and delays where they might dry out or get too much sun exposure or whatnot."

"Absolutely, but let's assume that's all taken care of," he says. "What concerns or opportunities come to mind from a *shopping* perspective?"

"Customers can't smell or touch them," I say. "Of course you can help customers along with descriptors—'these leaves are soft and papery; these are robust and shiny.' I mean, Sephora's been selling perfume online that way for years, though maybe most people are just replenishing perfumes they already own. But plants are cheaper and less personal than fragrance, so maybe customers would be more willing to take a chance. Or, wow, this would probably be insanely hard and expensive, but what if you could order a *swatch*?"

Andy laughs. "Like a rug swatch, but a leaf?"

"Yeah, exactly," I say. "Who knows if that's even doable, but it would probably make customers more likely to be happy with whatever they eventually buy."

It turns out I could talk about selling plants all day. Maybe that shouldn't surprise me: My entire career has involved entering fields I don't know the first thing about, getting someone to hire me anyway, and learning on the job. In my master's program, they turned us loose to teach undergraduate creative writing with just two hours of training focused mostly on how to fill out the Scantron grade sheet. From there, I talked my way into a series of adjunct gigs at community and for-profit colleges teaching expository writing and public speaking, skills I possessed but had not the faintest clue how to explain to others. Next, in need of the living wage and health care that sixty hours a week of adjuncting didn't provide, I spent a couple of years as a research coordinator at a lab devoted to ending genetic diseases in purebred dogs, a job for which my main qualification was thinking all dogs should live forever. As for my AMG job, sure, I bring an above-average level of pop-culture fandom to it, but not nearly as much as the guys who work for me, and I lacked database experience entirely at the start. Here is how I got every single one of those jobs: I sat across a desk from a man old enough to be my father and I enveloped us both in a force field of earnest *competence*, the kind I'd been practicing since kindergarten with my hand permanently raised in class, the kind that says *I will die before I let you down*, and at some point in each of those interviews the man pronounced me "impressive" and gave me a job and the prophecy came true. I never let him down. I brought my inner Hillary Clinton to work and through sheer effort and practice learned to explain semicolons and to identify the specific golden retrievers whose DNA could help to solve genetic puzzles and to write SQL queries. So I can certainly be Impressive for Andy, talking his ear off about plant smells, textures, interactive garden planners, and return policies. I'm barely getting started when the next interviewer, a daddish man named George, arrives to take Andy's place.

"Hey, do you need a restroom break?" George asks before sitting down. I do, and I wait for him to give me directions. Instead, he walks me there himself. Gold records and movie posters hang on the walls, and the infamous "door desks" made of raw wood and two-by-fours are everywhere, including a few in the hallways. "Interns," George says, gesturing at one hallway occupant. "We're out of space."

"Can you give me directions back?" I ask when we arrive at the women's restroom. The floor seems to be laid out in some kind of triangle/spiral hybrid and I'm thoroughly disoriented.

"Oh, I'll wait here for you," he says. "We're not allowed to leave you alone." I was probably six years old the last time someone monitored me while I peed, but okay. Under the yellow sink lights, I already look a little shiny and frizzy, and with five hours left to go.

On our way back to the interview room, George tells me he manages the DVD Merchandising team. If I come to Amazon, I'll be his boss. So I'm not surprised that his area of focus seems to be my management style. Like a lot of people, I rose to management by excelling as an individual at tasks that have fuck all to do with running a team. For my first several years running AMG's movies division, "benevolent but chaotic" was the closest thing I had to a *style*, and I was lucky that my team was easy to manage, composed as it was of pop-culture geeks, mostly young men, who would have done their jobs for free. In their off-hours, they played in bands or made stop-motion animation or staged performance pieces. Not one of them wanted my job, which meant we weren't in competition. They were only too happy to have me be the boring one who did the weekly reporting and said things to them like "Stew, you *really do* have to take down your poster of the pope with devil eyes while the Barnes & Noble reps are here. Just hide it and you can put it back up when they leave." My boss, Jake, called us "Wendy and the Lost Boys," and maybe the woman-corralling-misfit-dudes element would have bothered me more if they hadn't been so much fun.

Jake let me fumble along managing them on instinct for a couple of years before sending me to a one-day course held in the banquet room of a local Holiday Inn. My classmates came from all over southeastern Michigan: offices, retail stores, a paint crew, an auto body shop. Two men dominated the room with questions about how to deal with employees who showed up drunk or started fistfights. So yeah, my sense of how to manage people is somewhat . . . intuitive. Is there a popular management-style vocabulary George expects me to know? Maybe I'm supposed to say "I'd call myself a Penguin manager, George," or "I tend to be a Panda." But rather than toss out random animal names, I opt to say I believe in *empowering* my people and playing to their *strengths* and whatever other no-duh basics I've managed to absorb over the years, and that seems good enough for him. "Really what we need is major change. How we get there is secondary," he says.

"What would be the most important change for you when this role is filled?" I ask.

"Well, there'd be someone to protect the team. Push back on some of the demands Marnie's team puts on us so we can get our heads above water." He keeps using names as if I'm just supposed to know who these people are, and I'm a little concerned that his first requirement in a boss is someone to say no to work. George manages his own team; shouldn't he already know how to negotiate and prioritize? But rather than argue or ask for clarification, I instinctively know to just keep him talking.

"It sounds like merchandising is a pretty tough job," I lob at him.

"It wasn't always," he says. "Before co-op became king, the site used to have a voice. We were able to talk directly to customers about DVDs we thought they should know about. Then co-op blinded everyone with dollar signs, and personalization on top of it, and that's all before the migration from Enumclaw to Urubu. They keep saying Urubu is going to solve all these problems, but frankly I don't see a direct benefit to merch, seems like we're being sold a bill of goods." George's rate of speech has been climbing steadily. He pauses for a breath. "We're in pods now and that's supposed to be good for efficiency, it's too soon to say, but once again, it's all about meeting co-op's needs, not the merchandisers'. So yeah, what we need is an advocate, someone who can push back hard and hold the line."

"Huh," I say, nodding. "Interesting." My notepad reads:

> Co-op king
> Migration
> Enumclaw
> Pod
> Angry
> Burnout
> Salvageable?

At last I meet a woman: Marnie, my lunch interview, who has bright green eyes and a hint of Texas in her voice. For the co-op leader who is ruining George's life, she seems nice enough. Once we're settled into our booth at the only restaurant in the building open on Presidents' Day, I grab the opportunity to find out just what the hell co-op *is*. "Have you seen the tables in the front of Barnes & Noble marked 'New and Notable'?" she asks. "That's co-op. Publishers pay for their books to get special placement in the store, so more customers will see them. It's the same for Amazon, only our front tables are digital." She's calm and unhurried, whereas my entire body is vibrating with George's nervous energy and my own confusion. *Don't let it show*, I remind myself. I try to take slow, deep breaths without calling attention to them.

"Does co-op influence how Amazon *talks* about products?" I ask. "Do the merchandisers have to write complimentary things they might not mean?"

"Never," she says. "We keep a bright line between co-op and editorial."

"Good to know," I say. "I'm a stickler for that kind of thing."

"I'm glad," Marnie says, squeezing lime into her iced tea. "My team's job is to sell placements and we'd like to be able to rely on the merchandisers to propose creative ways to execute them."

It isn't lost on me that she says the co-op team would *like* to be able to rely on the merchandisers, not that they *do*. But I file that as we move into the official part of the interview. "One of our Leadership Principles* is Vocally Self-Critical," she says. "We value admitting and learning from our mistakes and weaknesses. So, can you tell me about a time when you made a significant mistake that put an important deliverable at risk?"

I knew this question might be coming and have taken pains to choose an example where I really did fuck up, versus saying "I care too much" or some other self-serving "weak-

---

* The Leadership Principles are basically Amazon Commandments: a set of values and behaviors that show up everywhere from hiring loops to performance reviews to routine team meetings and, inevitably, employees' private lives. I have had nightmares about failing to Deliver Results. In the middle of the night I once told my dawdling puppy to show some Bias for Action and pee already so we could go back to bed.

ness." "Last year I was in charge of launching a whole new product, an audiobooks database," I say. "Barnes & Noble wanted to expand the listening stations in their CD departments so that customers could sample audiobooks, too, and they needed our data and sound clips to power it. I wrote up some basic software requirements and then walked through them with our lead developer. He seemed unenthused, but he's the kind of guy who's *always* unenthused, you know?"

"Oh, I know," Marnie says.

"But he didn't say he wouldn't do the work, so I left the meeting believing we were all set, which in hindsight was my first mistake. I checked in by email a few times and he never responded, but that was typical too, so I didn't worry too much." I stop for a sip of water. "And then of course I went to his office to check in a few days before the deadline and he told me he hadn't done the work, because he 'didn't see the value.'"

"That's nice," Marnie says. "So what did you do?"

"First I talked to my manager and let him know we were at risk of missing the deadline because the developer had unilaterally decided the project had no value," I say. "My boss was calm about it, but he also basically told me I should have known it would happen, because the developer was notorious for ignoring work he didn't feel personally invested in. My boss thought I should have tried harder to sell the developer on the project, or *charm* him into it. Which I didn't think was fair."

"In what way?"

"We had a signed contract from Barnes & Noble, a deadline, and requirements," I say. "I thought the dev's job was to say either 'yes, all looks good' or to tell me up front why something needed to change." It takes all I have not to add *like a goddamn grown-up instead of a spoiled man-child*. "I didn't see why I should have to charm him [*like a motherfucking courtesan*, I don't add] into performing the core functions of his role. So it felt like my boss was saying, 'This guy is allowed to be a prima donna and it's your job to manipulate him into doing the work anyway.' Which was infuriating." I don't mention that I literally screamed in my car on the way home that day. "But I guess in some ways he was right."

"Wait," Marnie says, "how so?"

"Well, I should have anticipated reality," I say. "I went by the way things *should* work. And I thought with a signed contract in hand, he'd have to take me seriously. But if I'd just admitted who I was dealing with and done the extra coddling he required, it might have saved my deadline." Marnie asks what happened next. "I fell on my sword with the client, and my boss and I met with the dev and his boss to work things out, and within a day or two the work was done. It took him less than an afternoon." After that meeting, my boss had chastised me for not doing more to conceal my anger.

"So what would you do differently next time?" Marnie asks, pen already poised to record my answer.

"I would operate from the world as it is, not the world I want," I say. I'm still angry. I just hope she can't see it.

By the time my final interview rolls around, I'm feeling over-stimulated but cheerful, all thoughts of the man-child developer gone. I don't have a great read on whether I'm going to get the job—and I'm still not sure I *want* the job—but I know

I haven't embarrassed myself. One more hour, and I get to reward myself with a trip to the Sub Pop Records store in Pike Place Market before my red-eye home.

And then Eldin arrives—fiftyish, with Billy Joel eyes. Eldin is general manager for the music store. Before Amazon, he tells me, he drove a cab in New York for a decade. It's hard to imagine the other people I've met today as anything but e-commerce workers, but I can totally see Eldin as a cabbie. I ask if he ever drove a favorite musician and he says yes, Lou Reed, who—true to his reputation—was crabby and a backseat driver and lousy tipper. "Oh no!" I say. "I'm so sorry."

"You know, I wouldn't change a thing," Eldin says. "It was the classic Lou Reed experience." There's something gentle and a little melancholy about Eldin that I find comforting, as though whatever trouble a day at the office brings, he's seen worse. I'm feeling alert but relaxed as we segue from small talk into the actual interview.

"Kristi," Eldin says, clasping his hands together on the table, "I was hoping you could talk me through an example of how you solve problems."

"Sure," I say, smiling breezily. I solve problems constantly on the Island of Misfit Toys. Just last month I had to ask an editor to stop having long, loud phone arguments with his girlfriend about their sex life.

"Great," Eldin says, smiling back. "So, if you would: tell me how you would determine the number of gas stations in America."

Well, fuck. I hadn't realized he meant a *math* problem. Thinking in numbers makes my head buzz with static. I got a D—my only D ever, at least so far—in trigonometry. By my calculations I'd really earned an F, but maybe the teacher was moved to mercy by my blend of total incompetence and wild-eyed effort.

Now, to buy time from Eldin, I borrow a spelling-bee tactic. "How would I go about determining the number of gas stations in the United States," I say in a measured, news-anchor cadence.

"Correct," Eldin says. "And take your time."

The other spelling-bee delay tactic—"could you please use that question in a sentence?"—won't fly here, and I doubt the answer is a nice round ONE MILLION. I tilt my head at an angle suggesting thought while unhelpful starting points pin-ball around inside my brain: the length of the average American commute, how many gallons of gas a sedan holds versus an SUV, how many times I have personally pumped gas in twenty years of driving. About twice a month, so 24 times a year, or 240 per decade, or 480 in my life to date. It kind of blows my mind to think I've pumped gas almost 500 times. My brain wants to dwell on how much time that adds up to, and what I've been thinking and feeling while I stand at the pump. But I reel it back to the problem at hand, or at least what I've settled on as the problem at hand, which is how many times I've pumped gas. I lop 10 percent off my previous total for times I was on vacation or home sick or otherwise not driving, then round up to 450. I'm so pleased and relieved to have solved *something* that I nearly blurt it as my answer: *There are 450 gas stations in America, Eldin!*

Fortunately, he speaks before I do. "Remember, Kristi," he says, "I'm more interested in your thought process than in you knowing the real answer."

Well, good, because I don't know the real answer. But honestly, that's the *least* of what I don't yet know. By tonight,

I'll know from the internet that this is a classic tech interview question. A few years into my Amazon career, I'll know that my brain is perfectly capable of working through complex analysis; it just needs a little space and quiet.

But I don't know any of that now. I've at least managed to stop myself from telling Eldin that American gas stations number in the low hundreds, but I also need to prove that I'm at least capable of asking smart questions.

"Does this include Alaska and Hawaii?" Yes. That's my smart question.

Eldin smiles gently, perhaps a bit sadly. "Let me open the kimono a bit," he says. "Amazon is a very data-driven company. We make decisions based on analysis, not intuition. So the purpose of a question like this, which might seem nonsensical, is just to observe how logically and methodically you're able to think through a complex problem."

He keeps talking, but I'm still back at the "kimono." Is that what he said? What does it *mean*? It sounds not only creepy but vaguely racist and sexist, though of course that's based purely on my intuition and not *complex analysis*. Also, I'm starting to feel a bit crabby about the hermetic situation I'm in. Surely Amazon employees are not expected to solve complex problems with no access to the internet, a calculator, or even an old set of the *World Book Encyclopedia*.

"That's helpful context," I say. "Let me just think for a moment." But mostly I'm thinking, *Well, at least I got to visit Seattle*, because I'm sure it's all over. Never mind how well the day has gone until now; I decide the entire process is built to catch me in a single mistake, and now the system will spit me out and the job will go to someone who can think fast about gas stations, someone with the *right* kind of intelligence, not my squishy, it-depends liberal arts brand. "The thing about Seattle is it's green all year round," my cabdriver remarked during the trip from SeaTac. Soon I'll be back in Michigan, where the odds are high that within a few days I'll step off a snowy curb into ankle-high garbage water. And that's fine, right? There's an aura of shoplifter interrogation room about my surroundings, and though the people are nice, they've all got dark circles under their eyes.

I do eventually walk Eldin through some sort of answer, based on a wild guess that 150 million Americans own a car and they need to fill up once a week and most gas stations have eight pumps and so on. My final response is probably closer to the number of otters in Belgium than gas stations in the United States, but he's kind about it. Something about his face says he's a man who is used to disappointment.

At Pike Place Market, I buy a coffee and wander down Post Alley. It's about fifty degrees and raining, but so lightly that the rain seems to just *exist* in the air rather than fall. Camellias are in bloom on a trellis outside a children's boutique displaying Mudhoney and Nirvana onesies. I go in and buy one of each, just in case anyone I know ever decides to have a baby. When I step back into the alley, a watery strip of light has broken through the mist, bringing all the colors a halftone up. It's like being in a hipster Diagon Alley. Which is sort of how I want to feel *all the time*, like if Hermione Granger ran away to Berlin. I want this pale light, these giant firs, this gentle urbanity. I plodded through thirty-five years of strip malls and office parks to get here, and if I hadn't fucked up today, it could have been mine. Well, at least for evenings and weekends, and other times I wasn't in an ugly room doing head math and solving problems for beleaguered people in thankless jobs.

One day in 1975, my kindergarten teacher waited with me at pickup to explain to my mother why I'd been crying for more than an hour—straight through pep talks from the teacher, her aide, and a Tigger puppet, straight through two miniature Krackels from the teacher's special stash. "I got an N," I said, sobbing as my mother approached in the new shag haircut I wasn't quite used to.

"She just got excited and did some extra coloring," the teacher said, handing over my phonics worksheet. We were supposed to color in the pictures with long-*a* sounds, like "baby" and "cake." But I'd recently leveled up to the Crayola forty-eight-pack and access to options like cornflower blue and carnation made me take leave of my senses. I colored in *all* of the pictures and earned my very first grade of N for Not Satisfactory.

"Well, that's not worth crying over," said my mother, as if she got to decide.

"It's pretty coloring!" said my teacher, a sweet young woman who was only trying to show me that I had not satisfactorily demonstrated my ability to identify long-*a* sounds. But I was only five. What else was I to do with my shame but keep crying?

My mom bought me a blue Slurpee on the drive home and I started to calm down. "I don't want to get any more Ns," I told her.

She glanced at me in the rearview mirror. "You don't have to, baby. Just try harder next time." She was trying to comfort me, not teach me that success and failure are all about effort. But I was a much weirder kid than she could have anticipated: hyper-verbal, already a newspaper reader, obsessed with proving my competence. "Five going on thirty-five," a professor colleague of my dad's said, and we all took it as a compliment.

"I will," I said, blue-tongued. "I'll try harder." And I did. I never got another N. I became Satisfactory, and except for goddamn trig I stayed that way. I'm not crying now, but as I walk back to the W to catch a cab, my little girl self is making herself heard anyway. She wants a do-over on those gas stations. *I'll make your dreams mine*, she says to Jeff Bezos. *And I will never, ever let you down.*

4

EVENTS IN THE HISTORY OF FEMALE EMPLOYMENT

1972: One month before my second birthday, and forty-eight years after its initial introduction, Congress passes the Equal Rights Amendment, and states are given seven years to ratify it. My parents and I live in Columbus, Georgia, where my father is getting his mathematics PhD. My mother supports the family by working as a hairdresser.

1973: With the Supreme Court's ruling on *Roe v. Wade*, abortion becomes legal across America. My father decides to pursue a second PhD in computer science. While my mother is working, I'm cared for by an older couple across the street.

1974: It becomes illegal for Visa and Mastercard to require women applicants to have male co-signers. My mother reads to me every night. Soon I am reading too, and making my first attempts at writing, and then I'm telling everyone I want to be a writer when I grow up. When my father gets a professor job in Florida and my parents tell me we're moving, my first and only question is, "Do they have bookstores there?"

1975: My dad gets tenure, which my mom says means they can't fire him. She stays home now with my little sister and me, but I already take it for granted that I'll grow up to have a job—or two, since my current plan is to be a circus clown in the daytime and a surgeon at night. I'm in first grade and have been designated "Gifted" and have been told I can be anything if I just put my mind to it. I love playing a board game called What Shall I Be? The Exciting Game of Career Girls, in which you draw cards qualifying or disqualifying you for six possible outcomes: model, actress, nurse, teacher, stewardess, and ballerina. ("You are overweight" is the worst card to draw, because it alone eliminates two-thirds of the options.)

1976: Sexual harassment is legally recognized for the first time as, like, a thing. I'm six. On TV, some people say "HAIR-as-ment" and some say "Har-ASS-ment," and I find the latter extremely humorous.

1978: It becomes illegal to fire a woman solely for being pregnant. Three states short of the thirty-eight needed for ratification, ERA organizers request and are granted an extension by Congress. In Gifted, I spend as much time as I can writing stories and poems and plays, and my parents read them all. "I just hope you don't expect me to support you when you can't earn a living," my dad jokes, which makes me bristle.

1979: The Susan B. Anthony coin comes out and everyone complains. It's too small, too oddly shaped, too much like a quarter. Some stores won't accept it as legal tender, which enrages me to a degree I can't explain. "They *have* to take it," I say. "It's the *law*." It occurs to me that maybe the coin people were mad about having to produce a woman coin and made it too much like a quarter on purpose, but I don't like thinking about that, so I stop.

1981: Sandra Day O'Connor is the first woman nominated to the Supreme Court. Her confirmation hearing is the first one ever televised, and most of the questions are about abortion. Grown-ups ask if I'm excited about her. "I guess," I say, because it had never occurred to me that having an all-male court was weird. The Republican Party removes ERA support from its platform.

1981: Sixth grade. A boy I've never seen before pushes me against the wall in a deserted stairwell and shoves his hand down my corduroys. I push him away and go to the principal's office to say what happened and the first question they ask in response is whether I have a hall pass. My mom gets a job at the front desk of a fitness center (called a "health spa" back then). She seems happier.

1982: The ERA extension passes without any additional states having ratified it, and with five states having *changed their fucking minds* and voted to rescind their earlier ratifications. At the public library, I stumble on the diaries of Sylvia Plath. Noting that she began entering writing contests as a teenager, I decide I should, too. The first is a Rotary Club essay contest for middle schoolers on the topic of brotherhood. My opening lines: "What is brotherhood? Webster's says . . ." I win first prize, twenty-five dollars. My dad complains that my mom's health-spa wages don't offset the tax loss, and she stops working.

1984: Geraldine Ferraro is the first female vice presidential nominee from a major party. Grown-ups ask if I'm excited.

"I guess," I say with a shrug, because she seems kind of boring and old, and also because I have a feeling people are going to be really mean to her and it's hard to be excited about that. I rack up a couple more twenty-five-dollar essay prizes and spend them on Simple Minds tapes. My dad still reminds me that he's not going to support me when I become an adult writer and I roll my eyes because clearly it's easy to earn money this way.

1985: On sabbatical from his university, my dad takes a research role at Sandia National Labs, so our family moves to Los Alamos, New Mexico, for the year. For an awkward, introverted teenager, there are many downsides to being uprooted like that. But the biggest is that Los Alamos is a forty-mile drive down winding, snowy mountain roads to the nearest bookstore, meaning I'm dependent on the crappy public library for reading material. At Los Alamos High School, the Western civ teacher with the bowl haircut says that if they didn't need the money, he wouldn't let his wife work. I mention it at dinner that night. "To hell with *him*," my mom says.

My father speaks for the first time since we sat down. "That's right," he says, deadpan but with an edge and a line-drive gaze at me. "All men are jerks." I'm not talking about *you*, I say, or men in general, just this one actual person with the bowl haircut. "No, you're right," he says, voice dripping now. "Men are jerks." I stop talking.

1986: Back in Florida, my history teacher asks us for examples of social or political organizations. The Red Cross, someone says. The March of Dimes, someone else says. The National Organization for Women, I say, and the class bursts out laughing.

1987: Junior year in high school. Every junior is required to take a semester of computer programming, but the teacher says almost every day that he doesn't think girls should be allowed to take his class. I rat him out at dinner. "Yep, all men are jerks," my dad says, as by now I know he will. Jesus, Dad, I'm talking about Mr. Shapiro, I say, not you. "You're man bashing," he says, and I want to say yes, I am bashing *one man*. But my heart isn't in it. I understand by now that my father believes in me enough to have big expectations for my future. I also understand that I have to pretend I live in his world, where things aren't different for me because of my body or my voice or the Bible. We are supposed to spend my life pretending I'm a man.

1988: Four of the five English professors at my college are men. Two of the four are fucking their female students; a third tries but it just never works out for him. In the female professor's class, I read Mary Daly and Andrea Dworkin and Carol Gilligan. I reread *Jane Eyre* and learn that the ex-wife in the attic is a madwoman—and a metaphor. It hits me that someone *wrote* the Bible, that history is a series of human decisions about what's worth remembering. I win a grant for young writers—three thousand dollars, the most money I've ever had—and spend it, against my parents' mild protests, on a month of writing workshops in Vermont, where I notice for the first time that there are other good writers my age, too. It makes me nervous. I don't like it when I might not be the best.

1990: A salesman at the insurance office where I'm summer temping as a receptionist asks me out five times in two weeks.

When I run out of friendly ways to say no, I tell my female supervisor and she talks to him, and he never says so much as "good morning" or "thank you" to me again. My mom gets a job at the Macy's Clinique counter. She seems happier.

1991: As I leave a thesis meeting with a new faculty member, he says "Mmm-mmm" to my back as though he were eating something delicious. At my law-office temp job, one client proclaims me "the most beautiful woman in this place." Another client says he'd like to win me in lieu of damages. A third, seeing me wrestle with a paper jam, says I must have broken the copier and deserve a spanking. I have developed a neutral, level gaze that I deploy over and over, silently. After many disappointing boyfriends I have finally found a keeper, a graduating senior named John who seems to instinctively grasp that women are real people to a degree I find both thrilling and strange. John and I talk about everything, but it rarely occurs to me to tell him about the things men say to me. I assume he already knows this is how it is out there. My mom has become the top-selling Clinique lady in Palm Beach County and is sent to underperforming counters to juice them up.

1991: For eight hours, Anita Hill tells a congressional panel that as her boss the Supreme Court nominee Clarence Thomas asked her out repeatedly and talked about her breasts and described porn he'd watched—rape porn, porn with animals— and pulled some prank with a Coke and a pubic hair that to this day I don't quite understand. The panel strongly implies that she is a loonball and Thomas gets his lifetime appointment.

1992: I vote for Bill Clinton, whose own presidential campaign has been dogged by rape and harassment allegations.

I get a skeevy vibe from him, but with four justices on the Supreme Court who believe that *Roe* was wrongly decided, who else am I going to vote for? I apply to six MFA programs for creative writing and am admitted to five of them but not Iowa. *Well,* no one *gets into Iowa,* I tell myself, except obviously *someone* does or else it wouldn't be a thing, and thirty years later I will still occasionally wonder what I did wrong.

1993: As far as I know, my male MFA professors aren't fucking any students, but I keep a polite distance anyway, just so I don't have to find out. I see the men in my cohort having beers with them, even going to their houses on weekends. They make it look so easy, but as far as I know, none of the women are following suit. Despite my self-imposed distance, I win two fellowships and a university prize and place two short stories in literary quarterlies. Clearly I will be famous pretty soon. My mom is over hoofing it around South Florida selling Black Honey lipstick and leaves Clinique. It's the last paying job she'll ever have.

1996: John and I are married. He's running a one-man software start-up, while I teach night-school English at a community college where four male students like to point at my legs and whisper and ask whom I'm dating and why I don't come party with them. I think about reporting them, but I'm an adjunct and don't even know my supervisor's name. Plus, I really need this job—I need all four of my adjunct teaching jobs, or I might have to ask my parents for money, which I absolutely will not do—and don't want to seem like someone who can't handle a tough room. So I experiment: first with steely rigor, which feels unnatural and puts the whole class on edge, then with eye-rolling sarcasm, which cows the guys a bit and even seems to win their respect. I run with the latter, but I never have a moment in that classroom when my body isn't the first thing on my mind.

I read about an internet bookstore called Amazon.com and check it out for myself next time I dial up on John's modem. I end up spending two hours there—reading reviews of new books, looking up old favorites, signing up to get an email when an author I like publishes something new. It feels almost compulsive, my need to find the edges of what Amazon can offer me. And the whole time, I'm thinking about that terrible year in Los Alamos with no bookstores and no driver's license, and how it might have been different if computers could have done this in 1985, if this Jeff Bezos person in Washington State could have just *mailed* me any book in the world I wanted to read.

1999: Tired of teaching and grading sixty hours a week for seventeen thousand dollars a year and aged out of my parents' health insurance, I apply at AMG. "What's the absolute least amount of money you can live on?" asks the CEO. I take a deep breath and tell him thirty thousand. "Then I'll pay you thirty-one," he says, and I feel like a master negotiator. Theoretically, I am still a writer at night and on weekends, except for the part where I actually do it. I place a story in a prestigious anthology. *This is it*, I think. Someone will come along and invite me to sign a book contract, and then I'll write my novel. When it doesn't happen, I find it easy to drift away.

2001: I'm promoted into upper management and invited to join the men in charge as leader of the movies division. An hour after my promotion is announced, my boss and an-

other VP summon me to a storage room crammed with por-
nographic tapes and DVDs. Not Cinemax soft core. The real
thing, the kind with money shots. Video distributors send us
one copy of everything they make, my boss explains, and since
we don't cover porn, it all gets stashed here in the absence of
a permanent solution. "It's your problem now," says the other
VP, grinning ear to ear. He's rumored to be dating a woman on
my staff, who is also rumored to be the first girl he ever kissed.*

I understand that this is a pop quiz. "Why don't we just
shelve it in the archive with everything else?" I ask my boss.

"It's sensitive material," he says. "The archive workers could
make hostile-environment claims."

"All on you to deal with," the other VP crows, and I look at
him just long enough for him to feel it when I stop.

"But data entry already catalogs porn, right?" I say to my
boss, grabbing a couple of titles at random and pointing to our
barcode sticker.

"Yeah," he says. "We give them the right to opt out of han-
dling adult material. There's a form."

"Okay, so unless I'm missing something, it seems like we
can just adapt that form for the archive staff." There are four
of us in the room now: the two of them, me, and my body.
Their chests are flat, but mine juts into the empty space between us, space that somehow still feels like theirs, as if my
breasts were trespassing on their air. I understand that an experiment is under way and I can't not participate. I have to
pretend this is normal.

Something seems to have dawned on my boss. "Wait, are
you uncomfortable?" he asks.

* I'm just saying what I heard.

"Porn's not a problem for me," I say coolly, which is true. What *is* a problem is that this is happening the very day I went from underling to executive. It feels as though they were reminding me that above all else, I'm a female body. And it's not because they're malevolent men. They just didn't think, because they don't have to think.

"How was your big promotion day?" John asks when I get home. The day I found out about it last week, he had flowers and Dom Pérignon waiting. "This is the beginning of a brilliant career," he'd said.

"Oh, it was nice," I tell him. It's all I can bear to say in the moment. He believes in my human potential so much. Why remind him that it's actually just woman potential I'm working with?

FIVE WORDS FOR FEAR

Thirty-six hours after my Amazon interview, John and I are in a fishing village on the southern coast of Jamaica. The resort was once owned by Ian Fleming, and our oceanfront cottage is called Octopussy. We take the Red Stripes they gave us on arrival into the outdoor shower to wash off the travel gunk. "Hey, this is pretty good beer," I say.

"Red Stripe? This confirms once and for all that you are really not a beer person," John says, finishing his all the same.

"I know I said I didn't want to talk about Amazon while we're here," I tell John. "But just so you know, I've decided not to take the job if they offer it. Which they won't." That last part is a lie. At some point during the red-eye home from Seattle, my how-many-gas-stations panic receded and I realized that based on the totality of my interview loop, I did pretty well. I'm often oddly receptive to reality in flight, and then I cradle both the reality and my disconnected state like a small jeweled egg until I land and have to deal with it.

"I'm good either way," John says. Like me, John started adult life as an artist—a painter, in his case—and then realized it would also be nice to earn a living. Over the last eight years, a freelance gig helping a photographer to catalog her slides in a database has grown into a successful software start-up. He works from home, has clients all over the world, and can make money anywhere a satellite connection exists.

"We have a great life in Michigan, right? My job is fine, you have your job, we have a house, we have Abby." Abby is our golden retriever, a rescue. We love her despite understanding very little about her, like why she barks at us for ten minutes every evening at exactly nine o'clock.

"Well, I mean, Abby would move to Seattle with us," he says. "We're not going to leave her in Ann Arbor with pizza money. And your job is not fine. You hate it."

"I have *issues* with it."

"You've been talking about leaving for three years. You're bored, you're stuck, there's no career path. And the local job market sucks."

"It's not ideal," I say, checking to make sure we can't be seen before I take off my towels and lay my body out on our warm deck, which juts out just feet over the ocean.

"And then there's the winter thing," John says. Ah, yes. It's true that in recent years I've begun to sag at the first snow, knowing it marks the onset of six months of freezing temperatures and muddy slush and dark skies. In November, I was driving home from the supermarket on a dry but frigid day and heard a folky, exuberant Josh Ritter song on the radio called "Snow Is Gone." "Hello blackbird / Hello starling / Winter's over / Be my darling," he sang with such joy that it made me physically ravenous for sun on my forehead and the nutty smell of spring grass. Seconds later, I was crying with a suddenness and force that shocked me, hard enough that I had to pull over and park. When I finally got home, I told John we *had* to plan a midwinter vacation or I didn't know how I'd make it through, and this trip to Jamaica was born. What I didn't tell him, because I thought it sounded crazy, was that I thought maybe it was time to leave the Midwest for good.

"I know," I say now. "I know all of that. But I just have a weird feeling about Amazon. Everyone was nice, but *so* stressed. Just because I'm bored at AMG doesn't mean I want to switch to constantly having a heart attack. And what if we hate Seattle?" I don't mention the darker questions in my mind, like Am I capable of doing the job? Is the job even doable by *anyone*? Why were things allowed to get so bad for Amazon's merchandisers, and does anyone really think one person can fix it? And what happens if I fail? I never fail, because I never take on anything I'm *truly* unsure I can handle; even when it looks as if I were stretching myself, I keep a secret 10 percent in reserve. So if I take this job and I blow it, will it mean I destroyed myself out of hubris, and deserve whatever misery comes my way?

"Why would we suddenly hate Seattle when we've always loved it?" John says, lying down next to me. I'm concerned about the tropical sun on his Irish American penis, but he's owned it for thirty-seven years, so I guess he knows what he's doing. John's brother and sister-in-law moved to Seattle in the mid-1990s, and once grandchildren came along, his parents followed. Our summer visits have been a wonderland of long sunny days, excellent coffee, and cozy, earnest West Coast hipsterism.

"We've never tried to live there," I say. "What if we can't find a house? What if we can't figure out how to get cable? What if we never rebuild the foundations of our lives? Et cetera." *What if I ruin your life?* I don't say. John followed me from Florida to Michigan before we were married, and that worked out fine. But am I really going to drag him across the country again?

"We would somehow figure out how to get cable," John says. "But for now, there's no decision to make, right? So we don't have to make it."

"True," I say. "But I've made it anyway. I'm not going."

"Okay," he says, taking my hand.

The next morning, we have cornmeal porridge on the hotel patio and then take a spectacularly bewildering yoga class, where the pose sequencing feels like fifty-two pickup and the teacher keeps sort of *barking* at us to lock our knees and look in specific directions. At home, my yoga teacher is constantly trying to get me to *stop* locking my knees, so I might have been jazzed to have a green light to do it if the instructor wasn't so militaristic. "LOCK YOUR KNEES," she says. "LOOK AT THE BEAUTIFUL SKY." My neck feels bad turned that way, so after a polite glance at the sky I turn it back to a neutral position. "BLUE MAT," she says. "LOOK AT THE BEAUTIFUL SKY." On the next mat, John's about to collapse trying not to laugh. I hope the teacher will notice and whack him with the broomstick she's carrying for mysterious reasons, but she's moved on to haranguing some poor guy who has clearly never done yoga before to bend deeper into a lunge he will never, ever get out of on his own.

At home, my normal, non-angry yoga teacher talks about the difference between pain and discomfort. A sharp twinge in your knee is pain, she says, a sign that something is wrong. But the muted burn of a muscle being worked or stretched? That's just discomfort, and not an emergency. "Can you subtly adjust your body to ease any discomfort you're feeling without coming out of the pose?" she asked once when we'd been in Warrior 2 for fucking ever. I shifted some weight to my straight left leg to relieve some of the demand on my bent right one, but the right quad still burned. "If not," the teacher went on, "can you just notice the discomfort and let it be?" Well, yes. It turned out I could do that, even though I was mad about it.

I'm thirty-six, which seems like a shockingly advanced age to a thirty-six-year-old. Can I really avoid change, failure, and risk for the rest of my life? Even if I try, they seem bound to track me down. Playing hide-and-seek as a kid, I hated hiding so much more than seeking; crouching in a small space just waiting to be found made me anxious. And I've never grown out of it, preferring to this day to spot my opponents from a distance, in an open field—to approach them in the stately manner of a duelist and take them down on purpose.

After yoga, I grab my notebook from the room and hide out in the cool of the resort library. An hour later, I have a list:

Pros
  Challenge
  End to boredom
  Smart people
  New city
  More money (?)
  Better weather (?)
  Company likely to grow

Cons
  Uprooting whole life
  Fear
  Anxiety

Vague sense of dread
Too much rain?
Might be stressful?

By the time I run out of synonyms for "fear," it's pretty clear it's the only real reason to say no and that if I do, I'll have no one to blame but myself for the sameness and stagnation that follow.

"What if I say yes and it turns out to be a mistake?" I ask John by the pool the next day.

"Then you'll move to plan B," he says.

"This is my plan B."

"Then you'll move to plan C."

"Hang on a minute," I say. "How many plans do I have to have?"

"It's a figure of speech," John says.

"I can't spend my entire life making backup infrastructures *just in case*."

"The bar is opening. Why don't you have a mojito?"

I think through the implications of having or not having the mojito. "Okay," I say. "I guess I could do that."

On our roof deck after dinner: "What if I'm such a disaster that I ruin both our lives and you leave me?"

"Why would I leave you?" John says.

"For getting fired and becoming unemployable."

"That's not going to happen, and the idea that I would leave you for getting fired is insane."

"Okay, but what if I also get *arrested*? For some sort of corporate embroilment?"

"I mean . . . don't get arrested," John says. "That should be manageable, right?"

"Yes," I say. "In theory, at least."

On our last full day, I walk to an ovoid, mud-brick building a quarter mile from the resort where a reedy woman in a Sade-tight bun greets me. This is Shirley, a massage therapist spoken of in semimystical tones by guests. She looks me up and down. "Okay," she says, and goes into another room, returning with two handfuls of herbs. "Here's what you need." She shows me to a wooden booth against the wall; okay, it's basically a box with a cauldron and low stool in it. I sit as Shirley stirs the herbs into the water. "This will feel pretty warm," she says, smiling. "But I'll be back for you in ten minutes." Then she closes the curtain and I'm alone in the near dark.

It *is* warm, and smells like lemongrass and ginger and something peppery. Other than sit, I don't know what I should be doing, so I just close my eyes and try to pay attention to my breath going in and out. It works for about forty seconds, and then I find myself telescoping outward as I sometimes do in strange places or circumstances. *I'm sitting on a stool in a box in a clay hut in a village on an island in the middle of the ocean between two continents on the planet Earth.* It sounds kind of unlikely, and yet here I am. I think of other places that sounded impossible to be until I was there, like the top of the Duomo in Florence or a bar on stilts off the Bahamian coast. Or the tiny French restaurant in the back of Pike Place Market where John and I ate *moules frites* and watched bald eagles acting all casual above Elliott Bay. In each of those places I'd had the momentary thrill of knowing my life had expanded a little more.

Shirley comes back for me as promised and works silently on my back for a while. "What's waiting for you at home?" she asks eventually.

"Oh, the usual," I say. "My job. A lot of snow." I feel nothing, I notice. I don't dread returning to my normal life, and I'm not looking forward to it either. I see myself stomping snow off my boots in the vestibule at AMG, walking the long hallway to my office, saying hi to my boss in his office next door, and asking "What's new?" even though nothing has been new in years. There will be no post-vacation scramble to catch up on work. Nobody will be waiting on me for anything that matters. At five I'll drive home, stomp snow off my boots on the front porch, pet my dog. "How was reentry?" John will ask. "Fine," I'll say, because that's all there is.

Shirley holds the sheet up so I can turn over onto my back. "I moved to New York on impulse once," she says when I'm settled, "just because I was tired of being here. I'd never even visited New York. It snowed six inches the day I arrived, my very first snow."

I open my eyes. "Did you regret it?"

"Oh, never. I'd had my fill in three years' time," she says with a small laugh. "Of snow and the city. So I came back home. But no regret."

"That's good," I say. I close my eyes and drift off.

Our first flight home lands in Orlando, and as we taxi to the gate, I dig my phone out of the bottom of my purse, where it's been sitting for a week. "Amazon knows I'm back in cell range today," I tell John.

He nods. "They're going to make an offer," he says. "You know that, right?"

"I do," I say. "And I think I'll probably accept it."

"Right on."

"And if everything goes haywire, we'll just fix it, right?"

"That's exactly right, baby."

I hold my phone as we walk up the jet bridge. I haven't turned it on yet. What if I just never turn it on? What if I alter my fate by refusing to press the power button?

Expand, I tell myself, and turn the phone on. Less than two minutes later, it rings with a call from Seattle. I show it to John, then lean against a wall between two vending machines and flip it open.

"Hello?" I say.

6

PEOPLE ARE LIKE MUSHROOMS HERE

"You have to make it stop," George says, squeezing his empty Diet Coke bottle. "You have to tell them we absolutely, categorically cannot do this for six more months. It will *literally* kill people."

"I hear you," I say, to buy time. It's my second day at Amazon, my fourth in Seattle. George and I are in Columbia Center's dim food court for our one-on-one; conference rooms are scarce resources that I'm told often book up days or even weeks in advance, and private offices are only for people above me in the food chain.

"We're *dying*," he says.

"I understand," I say, wriggling my blistered right ankle out of its shoe. I didn't sleep much last night. Until the moving van arrives, Amazon is putting me up in a corporate apartment near the waterfront with one of the worst beds I've ever encountered. Plus, between 2:00 and 4:00 a.m., a man paced the sidewalk five floors beneath me, screaming obscenities at the sky. But it's only five blocks from work; I'd be embarrassed to drive that distance even if my rental car, a bright-yellow PT Cruiser, weren't humiliating enough on its own. ("How can Hertz act like this is a normal sedan?" I said when John called from Montana on his road trip west with Abby.

"I feel like a *Dick Tracy* villain! This car should be *by request only*, and even then you should have to check a box affirming that you understand how dumb you're going to look.") So I channeled my nascent inner urbanite and walked, not realizing how steep the hills are in downtown Seattle. By midway my neck was sweating. By the time I got in line at Starbucks, my whole torso was damp and both feet were blistered. By the time George informs me that the whole team is at risk of imminent death, I've abandoned any suave-city-girl pretensions and decided just keeping it together counts as a victory.

George's regular job is to manage the DVD merchandisers, but he's also been the point person for all of Merchandising on a platform-migration project that affects all five teams under me, and that has literally doubled their workload.* It was supposed to be like this for just three crappy weeks, ending tomorrow. But this morning, the tech lead on the project side broke it to George that in order to gather more data, the plan is now to run the two platforms in parallel for six months. That's an *octupling* of the original time frame, which I know not because I've gotten any better at head math since my interview but because George has told me multiple times. George's emoting isn't helpful, but he's also not wrong about

---

* How is that even *possible*? I will explain the techy stuff in this book as simply and plainly as I once needed it explained to me, and beg your understanding if you're a techy person and it feels as if I were talking down. It means the entire website currently runs on one backend platform, and it's gradually being moved to a new one so that we can be sure the new one is fast and stable before we put all our customers on it and kill the old version. Unfortunately for the merchandisers, the two platforms are completely separate, with no way of sharing content between them. So instead of writing and coding one campaign advertising a two-for-one sale on horror DVDs, a merchandiser has to do it all twice. TLDR: their workload has literally doubled.

how fucked all this is. And in terms of the doubled workload, we're not talking about a one-minute task now taking two. On average, site campaigns take about half an hour to build, partly because the merchandisers not only write the words customers will see but also hand code the XML that makes the campaign appear on the site, versus just pasting their copy into a template. The other time-suck factor is that the home-grown content tool I was brought in to fix is even worse than I imagined. Yesterday I sat with a merchandiser for an hour as she wrote and coded a campaign, squinting to make sure she'd placed every bracket and backslash right. Then we stared at her screen as the scheduling page loaded at a pace best described as sullen. "Sometimes it times out and I have to start all over," she said. "Getting my job done involves a surprising amount of suspense." She sounds cheerfully mordant, though I don't know if it's from a genuinely stiff upper lip or if she's just hesitant to complain in front of her boss's boss.

"I assume you told the tech team the impact this has on us," I say to George.

"Of course I did," he says. "They suggested we 'find efficiencies.' Which is Amazon-speak for 'sorry your team is screwed, but it's not our problem.'" He's still using his Diet Coke bottle like a crackly stress ball and I've begun unrolling the lip of my Starbucks cup.

"Well, should we talk to the co-op team about dialing back for a bit?" I ask, to a harsh laugh in response.

"I mean, you can ask," George says. "But it's never going to happen. Co-op brings in too much money for that."

"How about I use my newness as an excuse to talk to the tech manager myself and ask all the dumb, basic questions you can't?" I say. "Maybe I can embarrass him into a more reasonable plan. In the meantime, could you put together a list of the work you'd recommend dropping so we can accommodate this, so I can make sure Chuck understands the trade-offs?"

George is shaking his head before I've finished talking. "No point. Nothing can be deprioritized. It'll be six months of nights and weekends for the whole team. That's how it goes at the bottom of the funnel."

"Let me just see what I can do," I say, partly to close out the conversation. I know George is telling me the truth as he sees it, but his burnout energy is so jangly and overwhelming that just a few minutes with him can rattle me. I also want this meeting to be over so I can go away and think quietly about how to solve the problem. It's already clear that to succeed at Amazon, I'll need to be able to solve problems in *front* of people and I hope to learn to do just that, but for now it's day two and I barely know where the restroom is. For now I need a few minutes alone—in said restroom, perhaps—to plan out my next steps. After all, I *have* to solve this problem, right? Amazon hired me to fix these people's jobs, and here's the first test of whether they made the right choice.

At first I assume my crash landing is unusual, that most new hires don't face a crisis on day two. But it seems like a luck-of-the-draw thing; if you happen to start your job in a calm moment, bully for you. Otherwise, well, better keep up. My new co-workers use phrases like "dumped into raging rapids" or "dropped by helicopter into the middle of a jungle" to describe their own first weeks at Amazon, as though it were a roiling ecosystem with the inevitability of the natural world. "Drinking from the fire hose" is the phrase I hear and relate to most, though. When you drink from a fire hose, you can't think much about the taste or temperature of the water barreling down your throat. And there's no time to consider whether you're drinking the right amount, or if the drops that end up on your face might actually be more important to swallow than the ones that made it in. You just try to keep your esophagus working and trust that clarity will come in time, and that in the meantime your whole face won't be blasted off.

My office mate, Arjun, pricing manager for Media, is slumped over his keyboard when I return to my desk. We share a cramped, windowless space that I've already realized I'm very lucky to have. Most people, especially at lower levels,* are in equally cramped cubicles, and sometimes just at desks shoved together with no physical boundaries at all. At AMG I had my own office, and just the extra steps required to have a private conversation at Amazon come as a bit of a shock.

"Hey," I say to Arjun, who came here from Mumbai by way of Stanford.

"Hello, hello," he says without turning his head.

I haven't yet figured out how to make my laptop, the first one I've ever used, hook up to the external monitor on my desk. I know it has something to do with this bar-shaped thing called a docking station, but for the second day in a row I turn the laptop this way and that, trying to fit various pro-

---

* Amazon is a level-obsessed environment. In Corporate, Level 4 is the bottom and Level 13 is the CEO. (For some reason there is no Level 12.) I'm an L7, one rung below the executive ranks. At AMG, I was a director, an L8 in Amazon terms, and the title downgrade rankles until I realize tons of new employees suffer title deflation, that it's a whole Thing, after which it rankles slightly less.

tuberances and slots together, without success. I'm staring at the slots wondering if I need to somehow attach the laptop *on end* when Arjun happens to spin around and see.

"Oh no, not like that. Let me show you," he says, and clicks the machine and dock together in a spectacularly obvious way.

"They didn't cover this in orientation," I say.

"Kristi, you may have noticed they cover almost nothing in orientation," Arjun says. It's true. In mine, there was a weirdly disproportionate amount of time spent promoting the company picnic and almost none on how this place actually works. "And that is because no one knows what is going on," he says, looking right into my eyes. "This is the most important thing to understand about Amazon. No one knows jack shit." He reaches back without looking for one of the five coffee mugs on his desk and drinks from it. "Take my job as an example. I'm supposed to be automating how we set prices."

"That's not automated now?" I say.

"No, Kristi, it's not, and you are right to look surprised because it's fucking insane that every price on this website is set manually by a buyer. So I'm hired to fix it, give buyers their time back to do something more productive. But guess what: every time I turn around I discover some new team of buyers asking, 'Who is this guy and why the fuck is he here?' I explain my charter and they freak because they didn't get to have input into the requirements, because I didn't know their team fucking existed and vice versa. So they escalate to their director, he throws a fit, and I'm back gathering requirements again while the engineers threaten to abandon the project if I keep making them wait. This is normal to *some* extent, Kristi. To *some* extent this is just what a product manager does. But it goes beyond normal at Amazon, because people are like mushrooms here."

I don't understand the mushroom comment, or most of the rest. But I find his voice and way of repeating my name kind of soothing.

"Oh, and that is the best-case scenario, Kristi," he goes on. "Half the buyers have flat out said they won't use the automated system because they don't *trust* a computer to set prices. Sure, buddy. I'm only building this at the directive of Jeff Fucking Wilke." Jeff Fucking Wilke is senior vice president of retail and, next to Jeff Bezos, the closest thing to a god at Amazon. "But sure. If you want to have your laptop open at your kid's soccer game, sitting in the bleachers setting prices all weekend because you think you're smarter than a computer, then be my guest, pal." He breaks into a sudden, radiant grin. "Speaking of kids, let me show you a picture of my son."

I make "aw" noises at the image on his flip phone and ask how old the baby is. "Four months," Arjun says. "And, Kristi, let me tell you something. I haven't slept through the night since he was born. My wife is taking him to India for a month next week and I can't wait. I love my wife and son and I also am excited for them to leave the country so I can fall into a coma. Please tell no one I said so."

He turns back to his monitor. "Catastrophe," I hear him murmur to himself a few minutes later.

About twenty merchandisers report up to me through their managers, but my job also involves working with engineering and product leaders in far-flung parts of the company. Amazon has no campus, just three buildings placed maybe a mile apart from each other near downtown Seattle, which means I spend much of my first month riding around in a rattling shuttle bus. The official headquarters is a decommissioned hospital on the edge of the International District with astounding mountain and water views from the upper floors. Another contingent is housed in rented space in the shadow of Safeco Field. And completing the triangle is Columbia Center, the seventy-six-story skyscraper I now call home. On the days I stay in Columbia Center, I can easily take fifteen elevator rides. John texts one afternoon to see how things are going. "I spend all day riding around in a series of tubes," I respond. TV screens in the elevators show ads and news updates via something called the Captivate Network, which is just a little too frank to be funny. "Maybe I shouldn't tell you that I'm messaging from a kayak in the middle of Lake Union," John replies. Already his life is different from mine. Working for himself, and with most of his clients back east, he can knock off by mid-afternoon most days and actually get to know the city.

"How are the people?" a friend from AMG asks on another day. "Friendly, smart, and panicked," I write back. In 2006 the book and media stores are considered "mature," meaning the trick isn't just selling books and CDs, but finding a way to do it profitably. The team is looking for bits of margin between the sofa cushions and in jeans pockets, clawing back money a tenth of a percentage point at a time. Progress is slow, incremental, and never sufficient. Resignation and shame permeate the air, as though everyone secretly thinks it's all their fault. The underlit, temporary-feeling environment adds to the sense that this whole house of cards could collapse—that we are in *Glengarry Glen Ross*, not *Wall Street*.

There's precarity in the way my new co-workers talk to me, too. "Now that you're here," I hear over and over. *Now that you're here, we can evaluate which email programs to grow and which to kill. Now that you're here, the merchandisers can develop innovative new features for the site. Now that you're here, we won't work Saturday nights anymore. Now that you're here, they'll see how hard this job is. Now that you're here, we will be loved.* It feels like being Jesus, if everyone had a task list for Jesus written in acronyms he didn't understand. I start an Excel sheet to track projects people think I should either sponsor myself or persuade an engineering team to adopt, and within a month it's sixty lines deep and there's no ranking system, sort order, or filter I can apply without letting someone down.

John and Abby arrive at the end of my first week, and the moving van a few days after that. Until our house in Michigan sells, we're renting a little Tudor house a few miles north of downtown in Ravenna, the kind of neighborhood where people drive Volvos and never miss *This American Life*. It doesn't have the kind of kitchen or yard we're accustomed to, and the street is too busy, but it's cute enough for now. I can already tell we're going to need some months to accept emotionally that a nice but normal house here costs almost four times what we paid back home for a hand-painted Dutch Colonial on a corner lot.

Just thinking about the cost of housing makes me queasy. My Amazon compensation is based on a salary just shy of six figures—no one in the company makes more than $127,000 in straight salary, including Jeff Bezos—plus enough stock grants to add up to a competitive package. Long term, I'll be making great money. The problem is that those stock grants won't start vesting for almost two years, so for now I'm living only on salary, meaning I'm actually *underpaid* for the tech industry and for Seattle. Of course, John also earns in the low six figures. We're hardly going to starve. But we'll be breathing easier once we aren't carrying a mortgage *and* a lease.

To celebrate his arrival, John and I have dinner at Pair, a wine bar in our neighborhood with the rustic-French aesthetic that I'll soon realize pervades Seattle restaurants. "So how is it going?" John asks. I've been giving him bits and pieces during his trip, but he wants my holistic evaluation now.

"I mean . . . I don't know," I say. "Okay? I guess? It's intense."

"Good intense or bad intense?"

I nod to the waiter that yes, I'd love another Viognier. "It's hard to say," I tell him. "I guess I'd say it's bad intense for now. I feel *really* stupid a lot of the time. But I keep reminding myself there's a difference between feeling stupid and actually being stupid. And I assume the intensity will modulate once I've found my groove."

"It totally will," John says.

"But just in case, I've been thinking we should stash my signing bonus in its own account so we don't spend it," I say. Amazon paid me ten thousand dollars on signing, and I get another ten thousand on my one-year anniversary. But if I leave within two years, I have to pay it all back.

"What, like failure escrow?" John asks, laughing. "I really don't think you need to worry about that, babe."

"Maybe," I say, which I realize means nothing. "It's just different from anywhere else I've worked." I don't have the words to show him exactly how, and I'm too tired to find them. For the first time in our relationship, the *feeling* of my work life is already fundamentally unknowable to John. I hope it won't always be this way. Or if it is, I hope he won't notice.

Every workday includes at least six hours of meetings, and that's not counting the *pre-meetings*. In 2006, Amazon has roughly fifteen different stores on the website, each run by a separate team. On Wednesdays, the top leaders of those teams meet for the Weekly Business Review, or WBR, where they review each store's performance. To prepare, each team's store-level leaders meet separately on Tuesday to walk through their store's data and decide which bits merit mention in the big meeting. So, the weekly store-level report has to be ready by Tuesday, which means everyone needs to complete the sections they own on Monday. But Mondays tend to be packed with weekend mishaps to investigate: maybe a famous musician died and there's a run on his biggest albums, or a bunch of customers reported that a new DVD won't play on their machines, or a marketing email went out with a broken hyperlink. Solving a problem at Amazon also requires a written summary of the root cause and the changes made to stop it from happening again, which can easily eat up a chunk of Monday. Also, Amazon's reporting systems weren't built to be used this heavily or by thousands of people; sometimes data queries for the pre-meeting take several hours to run, and sometimes they time out completely. So a lot of us have resorted to running our queries at, say, 11:00 p.m. on a Saturday just to stay out of the traffic jam.

For Media, all of this results in a twenty-page, double-sided document, mostly Excel grids with text callouts, on eight-and-a-half-by-fourteen-inch paper. Andy, Eldin, and Arjun are squinting at it when I arrive a few minutes early for my second-ever Tuesday pre-WBR. "Looking at the data," Eldin says to Andy, "my first question is whether you considered providing monocles for this meeting."

"I had a feeling we were screwed when Chuck asked me to add the S&OP data," Andy says, sliding a copy across the table to me. "It was either eight-point font or a paper size that does not exist."

"Madness," Arjun mutters while I flip through the pages in grim silence, looking for something, *anything*, familiar in those thousands of Excel cells.

"We promise that this deck will make sense at some point," Eldin tells me.

"But also, never *complete* sense," Andy adds.

"Well, no," says Eldin.

Chuck and Marnie arrive together with deli salads. "Sorry I'm late," Chuck says, sliding into a chair and grabbing a copy of the deck. "Jiminy Cricket. Am I going *blind*?" Phrases like "Jiminy Cricket" and "gosh-darn it" are part of Chuck's hyper-wholesome, hyper-cheerful brand, I've quickly realized. "Holy Moses," he says, "look at *High School Musical* go. We watched it three times at my house this weekend. Isn't it just *terrific*?" Everyone makes vague noises of agreement. This is something else I've noticed about Chuck: that he seems to expect us to be personal fans of whatever is selling well, even if that best-seller is aimed at teenagers and he's the only one with kids. It brings out the anti-authoritarian side of me that developed in my own teenage years. I'm a fan of customers easily finding and buying whatever makes them happy—isn't that enough? Why do I have to pretend to care about some square musical and shiny, plastic Zac Efron?*

* Yes, my teenage self sounded a lot like Holden Caulfield. Sorry.

But I smile along with everyone else. "So fun," I murmur.

At my first pre-WBR, I assumed we'd somehow walk through the entire deck in detail in a single hour. But even more remarkably, it turned out my co-workers knew *which* parts to talk about, and how. They can look at a page and find the one cell that represents good news or bad news or, more often, a riddle begging for further investigation. "I have no callouts on page 10," Andy says today. "Page 11, same. Same for page 12, actually." We reach page 13, focused on "Concessions," meaning returns and refunds. "Concessions saw a 6 percent spike last week due to a bunch of customer contacts on a Spielberg box set," he says. "It's labeled as 'All Regions' on the site, but customers in the U.S. can't play it on their DVD players, so either it's mislabeled or we're shipping the wrong version. The warehouse is going to check the actual product and update the trouble ticket by end of day."

I write down "trouble ticket" in my notebook so maybe I'll remember to look it up on the company-wide wiki. Everyone around me has mastered not only how to find the cells that matter but how to talk about them in concise but fully formed paragraphs: here's the metric, here's why it is what it is, and here's what we're doing to either change or sustain it, all expressed in neutral, non-defensive language. No data point is too small or buried to be exempt from scrutiny, and even someone as high up as Chuck is expected to be able to speak personally to all of it. I try to have faith that one day I'll be able to look at this deck myself and find something worth calling out. For now I float in a sea of undifferentiated information and pray no one asks me something I should know, but don't.

That's how I feel for weeks on end, actually, only I'm not floating on the water. I've been shot from a cannon to the bottom of the sea and have to make my way back to the surface, mostly unassisted, and weighted down by salt and seaweed, by figuring out which starfish and shells and old cannonballs I need and how they fit together. It's not that I'm being hazed. My co-workers are kind and helpful. But they're above the surface, so to reach one, I have to stretch my arm up blindly and hope I'm grabbing at the right person and that they have time to come hang with me under the sea. And even when they do, I can tell from their eyes that they don't *really* have time, that every minute spent orienting me is one where something else might be blowing up just out of sight. And Arjun's right: everyone here is operating on partial information. No one really knows what the fuck is going on.

On weekends, John and I explore the parks and cafés and shops in our new neighborhood, including his brother Sam's bookstore. Oh! Have I mentioned that my brother-in-law manages a beloved local bookstore chain, the kind that absolutely hates Amazon for single-handedly destroying Main Street and threatening the existence of bookstore cats? And that he is on the board of the American Booksellers Association, an organization devoted to protecting small bookstores and full of people who hate Jeff Bezos, Amazon, and by extension probably me with the passion of the blue center of eight thousand flames? In college, Sam worked part-time at Miami's legendary Books & Books, and when he moved to Seattle after graduation, he parlayed that experience into a full-time job as a bookstore clerk. Fifteen years later, he oversees three really excellent stores. My working at the Death Star is less awkward than you might think; we've tacitly agreed to talk about other stuff, and it probably doesn't hurt that I buy most of my books from his shops. (And not to keep the peace, either. I just prefer to buy books in person.) But it does mean that from the very beginning I'm attuned to the fact that a lot of people see my employer as, you know, pure evil.

My own views are complicated. It's clear that by undercutting bookstores on price and offering fast delivery, Amazon is an existential threat to the kinds of shops I've loved since toddlerhood. But then, I've spent most of my life in cities that *have* good bookstores. When I think back to that miserable teenage year in small-town New Mexico, I can only see it as a net good that people in rural areas or exurbs with only a big-box store can now have nearly any book in the world delivered to their doorstep. As for price wars, the big book chains have been competing on discounts since before Amazon existed.

Working at AMG during the rise of MP3 technology has also made an impression on me. The music industry in the early years of the twenty-first century is famously run by Men Who Don't Get It, guys who are clinging to their shiny suits and gold coke spoons and old distribution models no matter what it costs them. For years I've watched the big record labels mostly fold their arms and say, "Nope." Just nope. They didn't seem to understand that change was coming no matter what. They didn't understand they had a golden opportunity to help shape that change, to wrangle emerging technology into something that could make them money. And most of all, they didn't seem to care that consumers *wanted* MP3s, that they were sick of schlepping to the record store to see if maybe what they wanted was in stock, and then bringing home a disc in splintery plastic packaging. It was agonizing to watch, and though the book business isn't an exact parallel, some commentary I've read in the media makes me worry that bookstores might also be so busy saying "nope" that they're overlooking ways to serve customers that an impersonal machine like Amazon can never hope to.* Sam's warm, beautifully curated shop doesn't make that mistake, and shopping there makes Seattle feel like home even as Amazon continues to feel like an austere alien land.

Except for George, my direct reports are all women, and while they're nearly as panicked as he is, instead of expressing it with hostility and sarcasm, they spend a lot of time *apologizing* to me for things that don't demand it (a small typo in an email, not knowing a minor fact off the bat, the need for sleep) or matters beyond their control. One routinely breaks out in stress hives. Another is pleasant but dead behind the eyes, as though conserving her energy for a siege. The third has all but given up on acting as a manager and is personally building co-op content all day alongside her team just to try to get on top of demand.

It horrifies me that they blame themselves for not being able to bend the laws of physics and biology. At first I think, *Well, at least I'm here now to set their minds at ease!* But they don't seem to hear my attempts to reassure. Sometimes I think I'm actually making things worse, that now they're worried they have a dummy for a boss who can't see their essential

---

* Before everyone sends me hate mail, keep in mind that 2006 is *really different* from today. In 2006, independent bookstores by and large have no online stores and haven't figured out how to ship efficiently and at scale. There is no Bookshop.org providing fulfillment services to small shops. When the pandemic forces stores to close to browsers for many months, they'll survive in large part by turning to online fulfillment and curbside pickup. But in 2006 that's all a long way off. Mea culpa?

wrongness and thus can't help to repair or hide it from the powers that be. In some ways, telling George he isn't doing enough is easier and less emotionally taxing than trying to convince these high-achieving women they're not about to be fired. When one of the women comes to me with a problem, just by agreeing that yes, this is something in need of fixing, I run the risk that she'll decide *everything* she does is in need of fixing. I empathize, because inside I feel the same way, and I used to be just as bad at hiding it. Now, as I struggle to communicate transparently without destroying their self-critical souls, I sometimes imagine my old AMG boss nodding and saying, "See? *See* what it's like to manage someone who's already decided she's a failure?" By comparison, George is a rhino. I can say anything and he won't take it personally.*

I may be bewildered by my directs, but it quickly becomes clear why the merchandising role they oversee is considered such a clusterfuck. For one thing, the people in it were mostly hired in Amazon's early days, when the job called for merchandisers to write reviews and use their taste and expertise to help customers discover the best books and movies and albums. Then two things happened. First, co-op, the pay-for-exposure system I mentioned earlier. As vendors paid up to have potentially *millions* of eyeballs on their products, the merchandisers' curatorial skills became less relevant, and their writing skills were redirected away from thoughtful, persuasive reviews on books, music, movies, and video games they love and toward neutral descriptive copy about products they likely hadn't read/listened to/watched/played. Gradually, the skills they'd been hired for came to be viewed as quaint, and

---

* Even when he should.

their taste considered a potential liability, as though a devotee of freak folk or opera couldn't write competently about Maroon 5, too.

Second, Amazon discovered that letting an algorithm make recommendations for customers resulted in many, many more sales than an editorial recommendation. Which makes sense: an editor's pick is aimed at what you "should" like, while an algorithmic recommendation is based on what you've actually bought.* Plus, if Amazon shows a Regency romance novel to millions of customers, maybe a handful of them will click or buy it. But if it shows the same book to just a few thousand people who've bought multiple other Regency romances, maybe *half* of them will click or buy, making the latter strategy a much smarter use of digital shelf space. On top of that, algorithmic recs don't need custom-written copy, just a template headline like "Recommended for You" or "Customers Who Bought This Also Bought." After the algorithm is done serving up the "perfect" recommendations, all that's left for the people who used to be Amazon's prized critics and tastemakers to do is to make the automated widgets and vendor-purchased placements show up in the right places on the site. When their tools are working, that is.

For all of that, the merchandisers are a welcoming and fairly congenial bunch. They show me the Book Room, where publisher galleys are free for the taking. They tease each other affectionately and host polls on their whiteboards in their aisles, like the long-running one about the long-delayed sixth

---

* Which can also be a problem if you bought it for someone else, or bought it and hated it, or if it's embarrassing and you don't want a reminder that Amazon knows you bought it.

Guns n' Roses album: "Which will come first: (a) *Chinese Democracy* or (b) actual Chinese democracy?"

Still, there's an unmissable undercurrent of passive resignation. Many of them bring their laptops to meetings and work right through them, with no pretense of paying attention. The Books leader tells me it's learned helplessness, that they've been ignored or condescended to by co-op managers for so long that they've made themselves invisible. But my eyes are fresher than hers, and while it's true that a couple of co-op managers are vacuous bean counters who treat the merchandisers like servant monkeys, I see others looking to them for creative ideas and getting a polite shrug in response, as though they've taken themselves off-line.

That shrug shows up on the site, too, which I spend thirty minutes a day faux shopping. One morning, the top slot on the Movies home page says, "30% Off on DVDs from Sony," which strikes me as almost meaningless from a customer perspective. I take my laptop to George's office and show him. "Do we have to use Sony's name in the campaign?" I ask. "Like, contractually?"

"Nope," George says, typing away. "But there are two hundred DVDs in the sale and Sony is the one thing they all have in common."

"Do they all have to be shown together, though?" I say. "Or could we do one campaign for horror, and one for rom-coms, and so on? Just so customers know what they're clicking?"

George stops typing and looks at me for the first time. "Well, sure," he says, turning his palms up flat. "But let's say we do five separate genre campaigns. That's five times the writing, coding, and scheduling. We don't have that kind of bandwidth."

He's right, of course. And yet I can't quite live with the idea that because building content takes time, our customers should give a fuck that Some Conglomerate's DVDs are 30 percent off. "So, this is pure brainstorming," I say, feeling as if George were *my* boss and I were at risk of pushing him too far. "But other studios are probably running sales too, right? What if we combined different studios into one genre campaign? You know, like horror films from Sony, Paramount, and MGM? Customers would get a better experience, and we'd be fulfilling multiple co-op obligations in one campaign."

George shakes his head. "We've tried it. But Shelley's assigned to Sony and Hugo's assigned to MGM and Craig works on Paramount and so on. They're moving too fast to stop and coordinate." He rolls his Diet Coke bottle between his hands. "The ugly truth is, co-op is king and there's really no time for doing things optimally."

He's crackling that bottle again, a sign that I am probably not going to be able to reach him. I shift my weight to my right foot, the foot that will pivot me back into the aisle. But then I don't move. "There has to be *something* we can do to present a more coherent experience," I say.

"There is," George says. "Get the co-op managers to lower their projections for the year and then we'll be able to think about customer experience again. Well, in five months, once we've stopped doing double work on every campaign."

Oh yes. How could I forget, when I'm the one who failed to save the team from that double work? As I promised George that day in the food court, I've been riding the tubes and shuttles all over Amazon, pleading our case to the tech leaders who decided to stretch out the platform migration. To a man (and I mean that literally) they heard me out, made sympathetic utterings, and then told me that unfortunately there was no other option. I don't yet understand the words they used—latency, weblab, significance, orthogonal meatspace GUI—enough to fight back. What I should do is admit it and say, *Talk to me like I'm a really smart kindergartner. Teach me your language.* But I'm too worried about looking as stupid as I feel, and too self-conscious about being the slow newbie asking them to jog alongside me when they need to sprint, and too afraid of making the merchandisers seem like weaklings who can't *handle* a doubled workload. They can't, of course. Who could? But already I understand that at Amazon normal human limits are an embarrassing affliction like IBS or erectile dysfunction, not to be discussed in public.

At all my other jobs, within a few weeks I've found some solid ground to stand on. At Amazon, every time I take a steady step forward, something knocks me a step and a half back, and my days feel no closer to taking on reliable patterns than they did when I arrived. As I see it, the only way out is to make myself competent fast, which calls not just for learning new skills but for becoming *inherently* less stupid, for somehow upgrading my brain's ability to reason and analyze. Until I figure out how to do that, I just nod thoughtfully and pretend to understand why there is absolutely no hope for us.

And though George doesn't know it, I *have* met with the co-op director above Marnie to see if anything at all could be done on her end to lessen the load, and as George predicted, she suggested I "find efficiencies." I'd hoped we might find them together, but I'm starting to grasp that "together" is not in the Amazon vocabulary. In the end, I had nothing to take back to George but a sincere "I tried."

"I know," I say now, and maybe I sound as sad as I feel because George softens a little.

"It takes a while to figure this place out," he says, and I laugh because uh, *yeah*.

"It's just interesting," I say. "Because I took the job with the mandate to solve editorial problems, and then I got here and realized they were actually operational problems. And *now* I'm starting to think, no, they're *cultural* problems."

George's tight, angry smile is back. "Welcome to Amazon," he says.

7

DEBRIS IS FLYING

6:30 a.m.: I wake suddenly on my fifteenth Tuesday at Amazon as though coming out of anesthesia. It feels like this every morning: I was nowhere, and now there's light and noise and the memory of worry just before going under. In his office downstairs, John is already on a work call with the Ohio state government. I pour coffee, kiss Abby hello, and stare at the oddly comforting *Today* show for exactly twenty-five minutes. In 2006, Matt Lauer is still seen as a decent guy, and his programmed amiability reminds me of Amazon men, so watching him feels like wading into the day. By seven thirty, I'm dressed in boot-cut jeans I brought from Michigan, jeans that make me feel like a ranch hand every day among the skinny-jeaned women of Amazon. I was *aware* of skinny jeans back in Michigan—hello, I do read magazines—but I didn't understand people actually buy them and just wear them around in normal life. The time is coming for me to switch sides, to admit I'm not just touring this new landscape but would like to join it. But I'm just not there yet. The jeans, the mountains, the shipyards, the clouds of lavender and rosemary in every garden, all seem impossibly exotic.

———

7:30 a.m.: The beginning of the process of backing the Jetta out of the driveway. The house is on a busy street and it's as if all the other drivers took a blood oath that I can go fuck myself. When I finally do seize a gap, I drive the five miles to work via side streets. I-5 would be faster, but I need the extra minutes and the enforced pauses at traffic lights to gear up for the maelstrom. It's a sign of progress that I no longer get trapped in the box of one-way streets around the Space Needle. Just a month ago I pulled into the parking lot of the sketchiest McDonald's in history to call John in tears. "I keep making turns and it's *still there*! I can't get away from it. I can't get away from the Space Needle."

"Breathe," John said. "We will get you away from the Space Needle."

"Not if it's sentient," I said.

8:00 a.m.: Meetings at 8:00 a.m. are just *mean*, so of course we have them all the time. Chuck called this one to talk about CRAP, the new acronym for Cannot Realize Any Profit, focused on items where the accumulated costs of Amazon buying and storing them outweigh any money to be made by selling them. A week ago, I'd never heard of CRAP, and now the need to get rid of CRAP is everywhere; I hear people talking about it in the elevators and in line at Starbucks. This is what happens when Jeff B. has a new idea, Andy explained. It propagates in hard-to-trace ways. All retail teams are now obsessed with getting the CRAP out, and as Chuck's team discusses the mix of promotions and returns and renegotiations required to deal with ours, I realize that it's kind of depressing to hear the word "crap" over and over so early in the day. The line between plainspoken and ugly is so fine, and Amazon seems to like crossing it just because it can.

9:30 a.m.: Every single conference room is booked, so I meet Naomi, the leader of my music team, at the fortieth-floor Starbucks for our one-on-one. We share this building with other companies, but nearly everyone I see is wearing an Amazon badge and trying to have a private conversation. It's a clear day and I can see Mount Baker, Mount Rainier, and Lake Washington all at once. When John's parents first moved here, his dad used to send nature photos with captions like "This is God's country!" and John and I would kind of snicker, like, is everywhere else Satan's playground? But I'm starting to get it.

"Jack just gave notice," Naomi says as soon as I sit down. Jack is the most senior editor on her team, the kind of dyed-in-the-wool music guy who was born for what this job used to be. He's been loudly unhappy for more than a year about the way things have changed; Naomi says he stabilized for a bit when I first got here, but recently he started spinning out again, maybe when it became apparent that I couldn't wave a magic wand and fix everything. "This place is *tearing me apart*," he said just last week in a meeting we called to talk about how he had kind of stopped doing his job and really needed to pick it up again.

"Well, I'm not really surprised," I say now. "And it's probably for the best."

"I know," Naomi says. "I just feel bad that I tried so hard to make him happy and I failed."

"You did everything you could reasonably do," I say. "The

job just isn't right for him. This isn't how he wants to spend his time anymore."

"I know."

"His mood has been stressing your whole team out and now it won't."

"I know."

"And now you get to bring in someone new. This is actually a happy outcome, Naomi."

"I know." But she doesn't believe any of this, of course. She's still thinking about how she failed. Why can't I make her see that she's doing a good job? Why can't I ease her stress? Am *I* failing? I'm probably failing her. I bet she thinks I am, and she probably also knows I know it, and because she's a nice person, that causes her even *more* stress, to know that I know that she knows that I'm a bad manager.

10:30 a.m.: I ride three elevators down to the *other* Starbucks, still thinking about Jack and George and how stubbornly both have insisted on playing to their natural strengths even when it was clear their natural strengths were no longer particularly relevant. Is it a man thing, to keep doing what you're best at even when no one wants it anymore? I mean, I'm not sure this job plays to *my* natural strengths, either. Almost everything I'm called to do here is something I've never done or even contemplated before, like estimate how much money a new email template could be earning Amazon three years from now, or market a newly deceased musician's records without seeming ghoulish. Nothing in my career has prepared me for this stuff. But of *course* I'm going to adapt, shape-shift while no one is looking. Of course Naomi is going to twist herself into knots

trying to make Jack happy even when Jack is no longer doing his job. That's the only story of work women like us know:
cramming, speed learning, passing. I kind of admire the men's
insistence that Amazon use them as they wish to be used, even
though it's currently making my life harder.

The elevator fills up as it moves toward my floor, and I
wedge myself into the corner to accommodate.

11:00 a.m.: Eldin of the Gas Stations is waiting for me at the
first-floor Starbucks, where the views are of a tire shop and
sometimes a man puking on the sidewalk. Chuck assigned Eldin to be my department mentor, officially tasked with helping me learn the ropes. Eldin is a sweetheart. He just seems so
sad most of the time, and of course I can't help but wonder if
it's related to me, if he thinks Amazon has made a fatal mistake in hiring me. "How's your week going so far?"

"Not bad!" I say, because I'm obsessed with seeming brisk,
sharp—Amazonian—in front of him. "What about yours?"

"Eh. My mother's having foot surgery tomorrow, so that's
on my mind." Eldin's parents live in Queens and he has mixed
feelings about being so far away from them. "And this get-out-
the-CRAP project . . . I understand the need for it, don't get
me wrong. But between us, it's one thing too many right now."
He straightens up a bit. "Anyway, what's on your mind today,
Kristi? You're doing very well, you know. I can tell you're going
to be successful here." He tells me this every time we meet and
I can never bring myself to ask why.

I've never had a mentor before and I'm not really sure
what's supposed to happen at these meetings, so I've taken
to using Eldin as a factual resource. I open my notebook to a

page labeled "Assimilation Notes." "Can you tell me the difference between GMS and OPS?" I say. "I know they're not interchangeable, but I don't know why not."

"Okay, so GMS stands for 'Gross Merchandise Sales,'" Eldin says. I nod and make a *mm-hmm* sound to claim credit for knowing this part. "Which refers to all the revenue from website sales. Whereas OPS means 'Ordered Product Sales,' and that's GMS minus the cost of shipping and gift wrap."

"Got it," I say, assuming it'll sink in later. "Let's see . . . oh. When someone says revenue has been 'peanut-butter spread.' What is that all about?" Eldin doesn't seem to mind serving as my encyclopedia. Maybe these meetings are a chance for him to feel like a genius, or at least act as if he knows more than he usually feels that he does.

11:55 a.m.: I pick up the Cobb salad I preordered online, swanning right past the ten people in line to order and the other ten waiting for their number to be called. At least from a salad standpoint, I am nailing urban life. Marnie and I share an elevator back to our floor. "Can you just tell me what kind of jeans to buy?" I ask her, and write down "Citizens," "Seven," "Earl" in my Assimilation Notes.

12:00 p.m.: The co-op team has started letting vendors pay for dedicated head count, a.k.a. junior merchandisers straight out of college who work on just one vendor's behalf, ensuring their product pages are flawless and that even their deepest catalog gets featured on the site. We meet with Jeff Fucking Wilke to brief him on the program and bring the juniors along to give them some exposure to executive leadership. Wilke likes the idea. "But the minute it stops being profitable for us, those heads are *gone*," he says. This would be a perfectly logical and fine statement to make in a leadership-only meeting. But it never occurred to me that he—anyone—would say something like that *in front of* the actual barely post-teenage heads, who look a bit stunned to hear it. Welcome to Amazon, kids, where the provisionality of your existence is right out in the open.

1:00 p.m.: "Sorry to kill trees," the scrum leader says as he passes out Excel packets. "The projectors were booked." Amazon doesn't have any kind of AV system, just four portable projectors managed by the receptionists. Like meeting rooms, they are reserved with difficulty.

I only associate the word "scrum" with rugby, and even then I don't know what it means. But the purpose of this bimonthly meeting is for everyone who needs software built to get together with the engineering team and hash out whose projects should come first. There are 122 lines in the Excel handout, each one a separate project, and my name is next to 36 of them. I've practiced describing each one out loud and why it matters. Some are huge and critical. "It takes each of my five teams a full day to download, manually calculate, and format weekly performance metrics," I say when we get to line 19. "I'm requesting dashboards that can return the same reports in a few keystrokes, freeing up over two thousand man-hours a year for other work." I used to say "person-hours" but everyone else says "man-hours" and I don't want to stand out for the wrong reasons.

"This absolutely needs to get done," says a stocky guy in a Google hoodie who seems to carry much of the room's gravitas and who tends to sit back and let others talk unless the group is at an impasse. My heart leaps, not just because it's nice to have someone validate the problem, but because I think that means it *will* get done, because I am wildly naive.

Some of my other asks are tiny: "There's a bug on the content calendar page where the merchandisers have to click the final Schedule button twice for no reason. It's a small matter, but honestly, it's driving people out of their minds."

"Death by a thousand cuts," says the guy next to me. I'm one of just three women in a room of twenty people. It took me a couple of months to notice something *lumpy* about Amazon's demographics. When I'm in a room with people beneath me in level, like the merchandisers, a solid third of them are women. But when I'm with my peers or senior leaders, men usually outnumber women at least three to one. And if it's a meeting of developers and other tech employees, it's a brofest at *all* levels. Both my ceiling and my floor are made of glass.

It turns out none of my projects is the right size to actually get done. The double-click issue has to wait for the next bug-bash session, when tiny but annoying stuff gets fixed, and there's no time for a bug bash this quarter. As for the data dashboard, *everyone* agrees it needs to happen. "But just high-level scoping the work will take two weeks," says the guy on the dev team in charge of knowing such things, and even then the work itself will be in line behind other projects like, oh, making sure the site doesn't crash during holiday peak. Everyone already knows the merchandisers can stay miserable and inefficient and Amazon will survive.

The Google-hoodie guy approaches me as the meeting ends. "The work you're proposing is years overdue," he says. "But what you need is dedicated head count. Nothing's going to get done in bits and pieces, especially if you're competing with other teams."

"Okay," I say. "So how do I get dedicated head count?" Maybe he'll say, *Well, I just dedicate it right here and now!*

"Just put it into your OP1," he says. "I'd start by asking for three developers and half a manager, and we can get more precise later on."

I understand only the broad outlines of what he's saying. What's an OP1? *Which* half of a manager? But it's enough for me to make it to the next square on the board.

4:00 p.m.: I see my office for the first time today. Arjun is there, shaking his head slowly at his monitor. "You are alive," he says without looking away. "I was beginning to worry."

"I'm fried," I say, tearing open a Clif bar wrapper with my teeth. A long beep sounds over the PA, followed by a recorded announcement. "This is a routinely scheduled earthquake drill. Take shelter under the nearest stable structure, such as a table or desk." The announcer has an Australian accent. Arjun and I look at each other and then shrug and push our chairs toward the center of the room and sit cross-legged under our desks. "The building is swaying. The floor is shaking," the Aussie continues.

"This is weird," I say.

"Somewhat," Arjun agrees.

"Why is he Australian?"

"Kristi, we will never know," he says.

"Debris is flying," says the Aussie.

"So much debris," says Arjun, which makes me laugh.

"While I've got you here under this table," I say, "could you tell me what OP1 is?"

"Only your worst nightmare come to life."

"That's kind of what I figured."

"Around you, glass is shattering," the Aussie says.

"It's kind of nice here, under the desk," I tell Arjun.

5:30 p.m.: I guess we've survived the earthquake. I slip out of the office casually, as though maybe I were going to pee, and drive like absolute fuck to yoga, four miles north of downtown. "Jesus, move your *ass*," I mutter to the woman whose parking spot I'm waiting for as she applies makeup in the rearview mirror. I make it onto the mat with an elevated heart rate and two minutes to spare. I lie on my back and stare at the ceiling and try to believe the earth is holding me.

7:30 p.m.: I meet John down the block from yoga at the place with small plates and large wine pours. Like me, John's been working all day, but because he works from home, I'm the only person he's actually laid eyes on today. I'm worried he's getting lonely and that I'm not doing enough to prevent it, but the worry comes in sharp flashes that vanish in the next onrush of Amazon. He *seems* happy enough, and at least he's getting out and exploring the city instead of spending eight hours, sweaty and disoriented, in windowless conference rooms. Lately, John's been thinking about turning his company's custom calendaring software from a service into a product, and today he spent all morning talking to a local tech incubator about raising a round of funding. "How about you?" he asks. "What did you do today?"

"I don't know," I say. "I genuinely don't." I'm worried about Naomi's hives and Eldin's sadness. I don't know how to hire half a person. I knew earthquakes were an issue here—the last big one knocked a crater into one of my brother-in-law's bookstores—but I'd never thought about being in a high-rise when one hit. I have 170 unread emails from this afternoon alone.

"I just keep feeling like they're bound to fire me," I say.

"You've felt like that at every job you've ever had," he says.

"I know," I say, nodding to the waiter for another glass of wine. "But maybe I finally made it come true. Maybe I've been working toward this failure all my life."

He just laughs. "Dream big, baby."

The second glass tastes even better than the first, like confirmation that I've switched off the day. John tells me that when his calls wrapped up around two, he walked to a neighborhood pub to watch the World Cup. "It's great," he says. "I can just take my laptop and answer a few emails while I drink beer and watch soccer."

I should be purely happy and relieved for him, but something must change on my face because he asks what I'm thinking about. "I'm thinking about how I have to do all of this again tomorrow, and the next day, and the next," I say. "It feels so *heavy*."

"That's just because it's new. It'll get lighter," he says. I married him for his optimism. I wouldn't want to live without it. Still, *what the fuck would* he *know about it?* I think, and smile tightly to hide the spark of anger he has no idea he just lit.

ASSIMILATION NOTES

There are so many men here, men from Sloan and the University of Michigan and McKinsey and Deloitte. They're transitioning to barefoot running. They bought Vibrams last month, and a sous vide machine. They like Big Hairy Audacious Goals, and in college they once saw Modest Mouse five times in a year. They have three kids and a wife with an expired law license because it just made more *sense* for her to be the stay-at-home parent. They work standing up. They've slowly come around on Belgian ales, and Tim Ferriss's book really made them think. They wish they had more time to read. They like their steak rare and their hot sauce vicious. When they interrupt you at your desk, they're *sorry for the drive-by.* When something goes wrong, they're *working on a path to green.* They don't just agree; they *violently agree.* They're blocking and tackling and focused on the inputs and not getting distracted by orthogonal matters. Going paleo has been huge for them, and tequila is allowed. Can they just play devil's advocate for a second? Can they just pressure test your idea? Can they just push back on that a little? These last three are them saying *you are wrong.* Sometimes they say it in an Amazon way and sometimes in a man way, though already the difference is getting pretty hard to discern.

THE LIFEBOAT

Contrary to John's prediction, even eight months in, work just doesn't feel any lighter. In addition to overseeing the projects my teams are working on, I have eight of my own, and with six or more hours of meetings a day I can only work on them after hours. Judging by their gallows humor and emails time-stamped 3:00 a.m., I'm getting off easy compared with Chuck's other direct reports. "Do you ever just step back and find it fascinating that we're expected to live like this?" Marnie says pleasantly to Andy and me one day in the elevator on the way to my fifth half-hour meeting in a row.

"So this isn't just normal?" I ask hopefully. Andy and Marnie have worked here for more than five years. If *they're* losing it, maybe life with Chuck is, in tech-speak, an edge case, and I shouldn't judge all of Amazon by it. Maybe there are places in the company where my breath can reach my lungs again instead of stopping at my throat. Where I won't get so many canker sores, or depend on wine to tell my body the day is over.

"It's bad everywhere," Andy says. "But Chuck is a little bit extra."

"Not to mention you never know which Chuck you're going to get," says Marnie. "Nice Dad or Mean Dad."

I haven't met Mean Dad yet. With me, Chuck is cheerful and encouraging in a sitcom-dad way that I respond to like heroin. But I've heard stories. Once at a team happy hour, Eldin teased him about being the only one in the group over forty. Chuck just laughed along in the moment, but the next day Eldin came to my office looking flattened. "Do you have a second? I need to vent," he said, and shut the door. "Chuck just *tore me apart* for teasing him about being over forty."

"What?" I said. "That's ridiculous. We were all being silly."

"He said it 'profoundly shook his trust in me.' *Profoundly.* He's worried I'm not capable of representing Amazon in vendor meetings without insulting someone." Eldin got more ashen as we debriefed. "I apologized. But he's taking it all the way to eleven." I was gratified for the *Spinal Tap* reference. We speak so much Amazon language in this building that it's easy to forget we have things in common outside it.

"It'll be fine," I said, though I didn't actually know.

"I mean, I'll be forty next month, Kristi," Eldin said. "Andy's right behind me. And Chuck's only forty-two! It's a trivial age difference. I would never have said anything if he were *really* older."

I had read Chuck as closer to fifty, based not on his appearance but on his *Truman Show* barbecue-dad manner. It was shocking to learn he was only six years my senior. But I kept that to myself. "He'll forget it ever happened by the end of the week," I promised, making a note to continue avoiding meeting Mean Dad.

By early fall, stress levels are so high that Chuck invites Jeff Fucking Wilke to the weekly staff meeting to give us a pep talk. JFW in a small group is much warmer than the guy I witnessed threatening to ax a bunch of adolescents, plus he's a movie geek who wants to hear about our favorites.* For forty-five minutes, Amazon feels loose and human. "Look, this place is intense," JFW says toward the end. "It's important to find a sustainable balance. Maybe that means a few times a year you leave at five thirty on a Friday to hang out with your family. That's great! You absolutely should take those opportunities." We all smile and nod, but the energy in the room collapses, and from Chuck's face I can tell that "leave at five thirty on a Friday a few times a year" isn't quite the pep talk he wanted for us (or needed to hear himself, maybe).

Next Chuck schedules a "fun social event" for his directs, which depressingly takes place after hours. We try to pry the plan out of him—laser tag? Paintball? Just drinking?—but he just keeps telling us to wait and see. When the night comes, the five of us and Chuck go to happy hour at Chuck's athletic club down the street, the kind of place you can't join without a personal sponsor and a five-figure initiation fee. (It's dowdier than I expect, more like an airport lounge than the E. M. Forster gentlemen's club I was hoping for.) Then we return to the office, where a woman in a sheath dress is waiting in the conference room.

Chuck introduces her as a wellness coach he met because their kids go to the same school. "I have heard you all loud and clear that your plates are so full they might crack," he says. "So I asked Tammy to come in and give us all some tips on attaining healthy work-life balance."

I find his gesture touching, and also I'm relieved not to be

---

* Our *real* favorites, not whatever Chuck has decided we all love because it's selling.

playing paintball. And yet, as Tammy goes through her presentation, it becomes clear that nothing she has to offer can actually save us. She talks about the importance of maintaining a consistent sleep schedule. Demonstrates how certain breathing techniques can calm the nervous system. Encourages us to drink a glass of hot water with lemon first thing in the morning. Eldin and Andy take notes. But as yogafied, *Oprah*-reading women, Marnie and I are already saturated in petty life hacks like making breakfast the night before, or finding and eliminating "hidden carbs" to make our bodies acceptably small. We've heard all of this before, and sorry, but ginseng tea and an "energizing cold plunge" are not going to mitigate the effects of working in a wind tunnel full of projectiles.

I keep a straight face while Tammy tells us to spray lavender on our pillows and watch for the 3:00 p.m. sugar crash. "Almonds are great to keep around as a snack for steady energy," she says. "Just make them raw almonds, because the roasted ones are carcinogenic."

Turns out being told I need to worry about getting cancer from *nuts* is a step too far for me. Marnie is in my line of sight, and I give her the tiniest eye roll in the world. Tammy's back is turned, so she can't see, and the guys aren't looking. Except for Chuck. Chuck catches my gaze, and from the slight narrowing of his eyes, I can tell I've just made a very big mistake, that I will soon meet Mean Dad for the first time.

He calls me into his office just after eight the next morning. "The way you behaved last night was deeply hurtful to me," he says. "I want to make sure you know what a significant negative impact you made."

Even though I knew what was coming, I'm still at a loss, and a little hungover from the three glasses of wine I had at home last night. "A negative impact," I repeat, just to convey that I'm listening.

"I spent my own money to bring that wellness coach in to speak to the team," he says, "and to see you *roll your eyes* was profoundly disrespectful of my efforts."

"I rolled my eyes," I say in a musing way as I pull out one of his visitor chairs. "Oh. I think you must be talking about the almonds."

"Yes," Chuck says. "Do you have any idea how hurt that made me feel, when I was only trying to help this team?"

He's really angry at me, not acting. My instinctual reaction when anger is coming at me—especially from a man—is to cry, which I know I absolutely cannot do now, even though trying not to cry in front of your boss is like trying not to laugh in church, or roll your eyes over killer nuts. "Chuck," I say, "I didn't mean to have that effect at *all*."

"Then can you help me understand why you did it?" "Help me understand" is Amazon-speak for "you are an absolute fucking moron."

"Well, it was late, and I was really tired," I say, hoping he won't think I'm griping about the wellness session taking place after hours. "The idea that almonds or lavender could erase all my stress just hit me wrong. I'm truly, truly sorry that I hurt your feelings and made you feel like your efforts weren't appreciated." He's just looking at me, so I keep talking. "I know you care a lot about our stress and how to alleviate it, and if I have given you reason to doubt that, I really can't apologize enough. I feel absolutely terrible about this."

I'm lying. I mean, of course I wasn't *trying* to hurt anyone's feelings, but my thinking mind is finally catching up to my primitive one and realizing Chuck's reaction is out of proportion. Still, I have to respond in kind. "I feel very lucky to be on your team," I add.

"Well, I'm glad to hear you say that, because I really do try to make this team a fun and rewarding experience," he says, more beseechingly now.

"And it *shows*!" I say. "Again, I'm *so* sorry if I seemed unappreciative. That was not at *all* my intent."

"I appreciate your apology, Kristi, and I'm glad we could clear this up. You know, you have so much potential here that I just didn't want this to fester and get in the way." And just like that, he's beaming at me again.

"Please tell me honestly: Should I be looking for a new role?" I ask Marnie an hour later. We're on the sparsely traveled second level of the food court, kind of crammed behind a potted tree so hopefully no one we know will see how hard I've been crying.

"*No*," she says. "I really do not."

"You should have seen his face, though," I say. "This was a *big* fucking deal."

"I know," Marnie says. "But he's done it to everyone. Last year at CES, he took us out to Delmonico's, and I asked the waiter for a vegetable plate because I just wasn't in the mood for a steak. After dinner Chuck accused me of 'sending a signal' that he wasn't inclusive of vegetarians. But then it was done, and he's never mentioned it again."

"I don't get it," I say, pulling out a compact and dabbing concealer under my eyes before realizing that just makes the rest of my face look even redder. Should I conceal the entire thing? "I mean yes, I was in the wrong, but . . ."

"Don't even start," Marnie says. "What you did was *nothing*. I'm surprised he even noticed. Anyway, if you leave me to be the only woman in his directs, I'll never forgive you."

We've noticed Chuck is generally easier on us than he is on the guys, but not in a condescending way. He seems more comfortable with us, more willing to give us the benefit of the doubt or to have us question his strategy or his interpretation of a piece of data. It's as if knowing he can't measure his dick against ours sets him free.

"That almond thing is actually true, by the way," Marnie says as we head back upstairs. "I saw it on *Oprah* and switched to raw."

"Yuck," I say. "Aren't they just *gummy*?"

"You can get used to anything," she says with a shrug, which I take as a yes.

Marnie's right: what felt like a huge event to me is just another day in Chuck's life. A week later, I tell him in our one-on-one that I know that the new email program I'm in charge of launching is progressing too slowly: the email template has to be modified first, but we're dependent on borrowed design resources, plus the engineers keep getting derailed by fire drills and emergency fixes. In other words, the timing is largely beyond my control, but I'm afraid there's *something* I could be doing that I'm not thinking of, and that Chuck might be waiting impatiently for me to figure it out and on the verge of blowing up again. But he just smiles and shakes his head. "Look, there are people on this team who really do need to step on the gas," he says. "But they don't realize it. You *don't* need to push any harder and you think you do. If anything, I'd tell you to relax a little. You're doing a fantastic job." Oh, the dopamine. I feel so safe for the rest of the week that I take a real lunch hour one day and walk to the mystery bookshop on Cherry Street, a steep brick block near Pioneer Square. It's easy to forget there's a city outside Columbia Center, but when I do leave, when I'm waiting at a crosswalk with bike messengers and street people and lawyers pulling file cases, I realize I'm starting to feel as if I belong.

By the time the midyear performance review cycle kicks off two months later, I feel firmly in Chuck's approval halo in all ways but one: how I'm managing my own team. Or rather, which members I've kept around for too long. "You've had time to make an assessment and put a good-faith effort into turning some folks around," he says in our one-on-one. "My advice is that now it's time to bite the bullet and make some changes."

"I completely agree," I say, and I really do. It's clear to me by now that at least a third of the merchandisers are *never* going to thrive and that's dragging down their co-workers and maybe the business, too. Making fun of almonds won't kill my Amazon career. But keeping poor performers around might, and it would be my own fault.

I tell Chuck that Naomi and my other female directs are already having frank conversations with their problem people about where they're headed if things don't turn around. "Then there's George," I say with a sigh. "I suspect at least half his team needs to go, too. But with him as their manager, I can't say for sure, because he's coddled them into helplessness and irrelevance. Also, I've met with his closest colleagues, and they dread working with him because every little thing is an exhausting fight. I don't think I can salvage him. He's too angry and he's burned too many bridges." It's scary for me to say all this, because deep inside I think I should have been able to erase the years of burnout that brought George to this point. Being this transparent with Chuck is a conscious risk, and from the sympathetic look on his face I think I made the right call.

"But you think some of his people might be salvageable under a better manager?" he asks—as a real question, not in disbelief.

"I mean, I'd like to give them that chance, and reevaluate in sixty days," I say. "But they *love* him. They're going to see me as a villain for taking him away."

Chuck is nodding down at his desk. "I hear you," he says. "But does that matter?"

"No," I say. "It really doesn't."

"It takes courage to make an unpopular decision," Chuck says. "I'm proud of you.* Why don't you use next week's Lifeboat Exercise to lay the groundwork?"

"Sure," I say. "But what's a Lifeboat Exercise?"

It is as grotesque as it sounds: a meeting where management ranks all the employees in order of whom we'd keep on the aforementioned lifeboat in a dire, business-threatening situation and whom we'd throw overboard first.† When the day comes, the twenty-odd managers in Chuck's org gather in a conference room that reeks of onions from some pizza a previous group left behind. It's windowless except for a panel by

---

* DOPAMINE.

† In response to a 2021 news story about Amazon performance management, a company spokesperson will deny that Amazon has *ever* used this kind of stack-ranking system. All I can say is I participated in at least four Lifeboat Exercises, and I did not hallucinate them.

the door that HR has covered with blank paper. Handwritten signs reading DO NOT ENTER!!!!!! ORGANIZATIONAL PERFORMANCE REVIEW IN PROGRESS are posted on both doors. By 6:00 p.m., we're an hour over the scheduled end time and are only halfway through the alphabet. The doughnuts Chuck's assistant brought have been sitting untouched in the middle of the table—doughnuts don't really sync with onion fumes—but now people are starting to pick at them, sensing dinner could be a long way off. I wish someone would at least call for a ten-minute break, but it's not going to be me. If I've learned anything this year, it's that the kinds of people who openly admit to needing food or pee breaks are also the kinds of people who get hurled off lifeboats around here.

"Okay, moving on to Grant," says our HR rep after we have agreed that the co-op manager Lena can stay on the lifeboat until at least half of everyone else has been fed to the sharks.

"Grant is solid, but a bit of a dark horse," says his manager, consulting a stack of note cards. (At Amazon it's always "solid, *but*," as if it were not enough to be stable, sturdy.) "Honestly, it's largely on me for not giving him the right opportunities to step up. Next quarter I'm planning on handing the S&OP reporting over to him to give him a chance to show leadership."

"Agree," says someone else. "Solid, but needs to show some growth."

"In a junior role we can't have anyone maxing out at just solid," Chuck adds. "If it's the same conversation six months from now, we'll need to look at putting someone in his role who has higher growth potential." In the meantime, Grant gets to perch at the top of the bottom third of the Lifeboat list.

I walked in here expecting to feel queasy about, you know,

stack ranking the human beings I see and talk to every day. What I didn't expect was how insidiously *comforting* it would feel in some ways. In an environment where my entire day's plan can be wiped out on a moment's notice, Grant being the thirty-sixth most valuable member of the organization feels simple and solid. *Careful*, I tell myself. *This maybe isn't the kind of thing you want to be too good at.*

"On to Max," HR says, and it's back to queasiness as I glance across the table at George. We've ranked ten merchandisers so far. As their managers and I expected, the two obvious stars are near the top, and the rest are scattered through the bottom half, for largely similar reasons: they're too passive, they do only what's asked of them, they don't generate ideas. Before the meeting, I made a little speech to my team about how it was better to present ourselves as actively engaged in housecleaning rather than gloss over our dust bunnies, and the women have followed my lead. But Max is the first of George's people to come up, and I have no real control over whether he sticks to the plan.

My own view of Max is that he's a nice guy who performs his daily tasks adequately and without complaint. I also have no clue why he's working at Amazon versus a hundred other companies, or if he even likes movies more than your average joe. At our get-acquainted coffee, when I asked where he'd like to be in a couple of years, his response was, "Leading small tour groups around Europe." I give George a tiny wink as he starts to speak. "Max has had a great year," he starts. "He was the merchandiser for both Sony and Lionsgate, and a good teammate to the vendor managers for those accounts." He glances at one of those vendor managers, who gives a tight nod. "Because of the *extremely* prolonged platform migration, Max also managed a double campaign workload for half the year without ever falling seriously behind." This is fine; I told all my direct reports I had no issue with reminding people of the insane operational challenges the merchandisers faced all year. George's tone is about five clicks bitchier than I'd like, but there's nothing I can do about it now.

"Where I see Max needing to step up is as a curator and writer," George continues. "For next year, I'm asking him to propose four new curatorial features per quarter and to write at least two movie reviews per month. I want to see him develop confidence as a tastemaker for our customers."

What? No, no, no. This is not okay and George knows it's not okay because we talked yesterday about how his people need goals demonstrably tied to things Amazon actually cares about, like *growing the goddamn business*. Whether Max has taste is irrelevant. What's relevant is Max's ability to take a data dump of three hundred direct-to-DVD movies and turn it into a customer experience better than *hey, here's some random shit, cheap*. George's one job in this meeting was to reinforce that he's on board with that, and even in front of Chuck he can't pull it off. I don't think George is *trying* to fuck me over, at least not consciously. I think he's just so unshakably sure he's right that he's talked himself into some kind of Lone Rebel stance.

As a general rule, I don't jump in when my directs have the floor in a Chuck meeting unless they actually look to me for help. They need practice holding their own, and I don't want them feeling second-guessed on small matters we can always discuss later. But if I stay silent now, at best I look weak. And if I look weak, I'm fucked. People will stop seeing me as someone who can make change happen. They won't seek out my input on tough problems. I'll fade into the background as the nice woman who supervises the least effective people in the organization. And next time around, they will pitch me straight into dark waters and never look back.

I tore up my life to be there, and John's life. Abby's, even. I left a job I could have had forever, and a decade's worth of friends and neighbors. We're still paying for two houses. And I've still got fire-hose water sloshing from my pockets and shoes. Also, I'm a Taurus, the astrological symbol of maniacal obstinance. I'm not sure I want to stay at Amazon, but I'll be goddamned if I'm getting thrown out of the fucking boat.

"George, I'm all in for Max generating creative new features," I say. "The site could use personality. But he needs to do so in ways that support our co-op goals. Pure editorial work has not been central to our jobs for several years."

"He'll consider co-op," George says, which means fuck all.

"I'd like him to explicitly design these features to support co-op," I say. "To be crystal clear, I'm in no way suggesting Max present random co-op titles as his personal picks. We don't lie to customers." This is for the benefit of the vendor managers, a couple of whom would be only too happy for merchandisers to lie to customers. But in my vision of a future where the site has a point of view again, it only works if customers trust that when Max says he likes something, he means it.

"I hear you," George says, which also means fuck all, but I let it go. I've signaled my side to everyone in the room, and now I just need to finish the job.

We finally break at 7:30 and I text John that I'm on my way home. "Pizza and Manhattans await," he replies, and I'm relieved because it means I don't have to think of what to eat *or* feel guilty that he cooked with no clear sense of when I'd be home. John has been on the hook this year for mundane domestic tasks like letting the Comcast guy in or taking Abby for vet checkups or buying midweek groceries. I technically *could* take time off for those things, but doing so will set off a cascade of canceled and rescheduled meetings that will snarl my calendar for weeks. He insists he doesn't mind, but I worry a little more each month that my job is forcing him into a housewife role that no human should have to play.

"So I stopped by an open house in Montlake today," he says, mixing our second Manhattans at the kitchen counter. Ostensibly, he's getting a feel for the Seattle housing market, but the truth is, he just loves open houses and will make any excuse to go. "Mid-century modern ranch, almost freakishly pristine. Very *Atomic Ranch*. You would hate it. Anyway, I ended up talking to the realtor for almost an hour, and she thinks she can help us sell our house." The Michigan real estate market is in free fall, and despite cutting the price to less than the $140,000 we paid for our house, we still haven't gotten a single offer. The selling agent has pretty much ghosted us by now. But John says Betsy, the woman he met today, thinks a couple of changes could do it. "She thinks we should replace the living room carpet with hardwood," he says, "and also consider having it staged."

"Staged?" I ask. "What is that?"

"Basically someone comes in and styles your house with rented furniture and art," John says. "So buyers aren't just looking at empty rooms."

"Like set dressing," I say. "That's kind of wild."

"I think it makes sense," John says. "It's a beautiful house. We just need to help people see it as a home."

"How would we even find someone to do it?" I ask. "Staging isn't really a thing there."

"Betsy says she can help us find someone for that and the hardwoods," John says. "In all, it'll cost about twenty thousand. And she'll project-manage the whole thing herself for free."

"For *free*?"

"What can I say, I am delightful to talk to," John says with a shrug. "And also I imagine she'd like to sell us a house here once we've unloaded the old one."

I shrug. "I mean, what do we have to lose except even more money?" We've become numbly resigned to the ongoing mortgage payment, but the house is a psychic drag on us both. John worries it could be broken into and turned into a drug squat like a couple of others in the area. He's begun to talk about flying back and boarding it up before winter, which might save it from occupation but would also be a sure sign of giving up on selling it. "Do you think it's an omen?" I ask him. "Is the house inevitably going to suck us back to our old life?"

"Do you want it to?" John asks, sliding a Manhattan across the counter to me.

"No!" I'm surprised by how quickly and surely the answer comes. I work twice as hard here as I ever did back there. I'm anxious all day every day that the very best I can do won't be enough. Money feels tenuous, especially because the people around me have so much of it. And yet I want to be here in this permagreen and vibrant city, at this maniacal company where I've finally been trusted with a really big job. My old life was comfortable and charming, but the new one means *possibility*. I can change here; in fact, I know I'll have to if I'm going to make it. I will have to let Amazon turn me into someone new.

"Me either," John says.

"For real? Because I know it's hard to make friends without an office to go to, and I'm half-crazed and whatnot."

"That'll all come in time," he says. "I'm on board. My family's here, and the city is a dream."

So I've heard, I think ruefully. But I walk around the island and kiss him with real relief. He's okay. We're okay. And I'll be okay, once I deal with a few loose ends.

A smaller group convenes in the still-oniony room at ten the next morning to rank the junior managers who were here with us yesterday. I imagine my directs at their desks wondering what we're saying about them right now, how much we want them on the boat. We trudge through the list, and when we get to George, I take a three-part breath as Chuck's wellness coach taught us and say, "George is a longtime Amazonian, a caring manager, and a gold mine of institutional knowledge. He unfailingly does what he thinks is right for his team. But in my time working with him, it's become clear that his instincts are out of sync with the realities of our business, and despite frequent feedback he shows no signs of growth. As I know many of you would agree, it's become a stumbling block for the entire organization. And so I will be making a change."

"You haven't even given me a chance to improve," George says a week later.

"This *is* your chance," I say, tapping my copy of his performance improvement plan, or PIP. He's had *months* of chances, and I said so at the outset of the meeting, but I'm not going to repeat it. There's no point getting lured into an argument over a decision I don't intend to change.

"My chance?" he says, tapping his own copy. "No, this is just prewarning of being fired."

"Not if you complete it successfully, and everything I'm asking for should be doable for a manager at your level." I've asked him for a data-driven evaluation of Movie's email programs and recommendations for optimizing how the home page is used. I've also noted that at the end of sixty days I'll be asking the co-op leaders if they've seen changes in George's willingness to work with them. "It's just a matter of whether you're willing to do them or not. I would genuinely like to see you come through this, George. But it's in your hands."

He rolls his eyes. "Fine. I'll see what I can do." From the way he says it, I suspect he'll resign within a few weeks. And honestly, that would be fine too. Either way, my problem is solved.

Word spreads fast, and I see it in how people treat me. "You did a tough thing. Hang in there," a vendor manager says at the restroom sink. "It probably feels like shit to have to do what you did, but you made the right decision," Andy tells me when we're the first two to arrive at a meeting.

Before, I felt like a respected-enough newbie; now I'm in the fold. Probably some people wish I'd done it sooner, but no one brings that up. Walking the hallways, I feel my muscles grip my bones in a new way, because they made change happen.

George has an offer from Microsoft within ten days. His team throws a going-away party to which I am not invited, which saves me from having to make an excuse to bow out. No one wants the executioner hanging around with her plastic cup of New Zealand white. He doesn't say goodbye on his last day, and because I've decided to leave that choice up to him, neither do I. Anyway, making nice would feel like tempting fate. The mood in the lifeboat room was respectful, even elegiac, but there was nothing nice about it. George did well here for many years, and then the tide turned and we culled him. I'm doing well now, but when the tide turns—and the tide always turns—I have absolutely no doubt they'll cull me too.

10

PROFESSIONAL HELP

By day I learn Amazon, and at night I seek out articles and listicles and TED Talks on femaling in the business world, just in case there are tips or hacks or something that could help me do it better. This is how I know I should lean forward in my chair far enough to show warmth but not cleavage. But also sit with my shoulder blades against the chair back and my feet on the floor. That I should stand with my hands on my hips but never cross my arms. Make eye contact for at least two seconds but never more than five. Look at a man's forehead and eyes—a.k.a. the business triangle—but never his nose or mouth, the social triangle. Listen with attentive interest but without nodding or tilting my head. Speak naturally, but never end on an upswing. Speak assertively, but don't interrupt. When interrupted by a man, insist on finishing my thought, but charmingly, so he won't feel as though he did anything wrong. Don't volunteer to take meeting notes, because it will seem secretarial. But do volunteer to take meeting notes because it's the only way to make sure my contributions will be captured. Do negotiate for more money, but don't let on that money motivates me. Be an advocate for women at work plural, but not myself as a woman at work singular. Always take credit for my accomplishments, but also let my accomplishments speak for themselves. Raise my hand for new assignments to be *helpful*, not eager. Dress to embrace my femininity but also to de-emphasize my boobs, shoulders, waist, hips, legs, lips, and hair. And smile. But not too much. Less. Less. Yes, like that. Now hold.

11

THE RED PHONE

As if to cement my sense of finally *actually working at Amazon*, not long after George leaves, I have my first Jeff Meeting.*
My parents are visiting and I'm checking email in the living room when the invitation arrives. There's no body text, just "Discuss Plogs" in the subject line, and as it sinks in, my stomach invents an entirely new gymnastics move called the Panic Tripleback DoubleLutz. The *idea* of meeting Jeff Bezos is exciting; I just don't want to actually *do* it, or at least not for several more years.

My mother is excited. "You'd better impress him," she says.
Thanks, that's helpful, I think. "Mom," I say.
"What are you going to wear?"
"*Mom.*"
"Jeff Bezos is a very smart guy," my dad chimes in. Lately, the media has been scoffing at Amazon's new Web Services† arm as too disconnected from its core retail business to suc-

---

* There are multiple prominent Jeffs at Amazon, but the others are referred to by their surnames or nicknames. You don't say Jeff unless you mean *the* Jeff.
† Basically providing back-end internet services for other companies. In about a decade I'll write a case study on the origins of AWS, which is now worth well over a hundred billion dollars.

ceed. But my dad's bullish on it, and since he's an actual computer scientist, I figure he might be right.

"Yes, I have gathered as much," I say.

My mother again: "Well, he doesn't know smart until he's met *Kristi*."

Behind them I can see John in the kitchen, silently dying laughing. When I make an excuse to "check on" the coffee he's making in there, he asks what the meeting is about. "Something called a 'plog,'" I say.

"You mean a blog?"

"Oh my God, John, I know what a blog is. This is about *plogs*."

"And a plog is what exactly?" he asks.

"How would I know?"

"Does Jeff Bezos want you to write a blog?" my mother calls from the living room.

"I deeply doubt it, Mom," I call back.

"Well, he'll be begging when he finds out what a beautiful writer you are."

"Would you do me a huge favor?" I whisper to John. "Would you murder me?" I pour two mugs of decaf and bring them out to my parents. "I don't really need or want Jeff Bezos to beg me to write a blog," I say.

"He might even be one of the smartest people in America," says my dad.

When I arrive at the meeting the next day,* merchandisers have already filled most of the chairs at the conference table

---

* Having prepped secretly and desperately and learned from Naomi that "plog" stands for "personalized blog," where an algorithm decides which entries each customer should see.

(eight door desks pushed together). There are three seats left: one at the far end, and two in the middle right across from each other. Much as I play the shoe-gazing teenager to my parents, I'm actually not one, and I take the seat I guess correctly will be in Jeff Bezos's direct line of sight.

What I fail to anticipate is how *weird* it's going to feel being across a table from Jeff Bezos, making actual eye contact with the man I know runs the company but who I also saw on the cover of *Time* magazine, notable because it was a fixture in our house growing up. "If you guys consistently post short, interesting stuff on the plogs, it will help to make Amazon a daily habit* for customers," he says, and I just think, *Magazine-cover guy.* "You don't need to labor over the entries," he says, and I imagine rows of his face on a newsstand. "The best blogs—or plogs," he says, laughing his already-famous laugh—"curate for their readers, and curation doesn't take a lot of heavy lifting." I really am trying to focus on Jeff's actual words, but by now I'm mostly thinking about myself watching him, how I'm unable to see him as a standard-issue person, and I'm wondering whether everyone in the room is watching him the same way, and if he knows it—he would have to know it, right?—and what it's like to live as someone nobody can *really* see.

I get pretty far out there, stoner-like, but luckily I've drifted back to the table by the time he has a question for us and every goddamn head at the table turns to me as if they were part of a single organism. This is a whole thing with my team, wanting

---

* Jeff only has to mention a new idea in a few meetings for it to spread through the whole company. Within a few weeks, *everyone* is talking about making Amazon a daily habit, at least until the next idea trickles down and drowns it out.

me to speak for them even though I'm by far the newest one to Amazon. In my third week, the English musician Robyn Hitchcock was on site with his label reps and played a mini concert for about fifteen of us in a conference room. For me, a fan for twenty years, sitting five feet from Robyn Hitchcock and having him *take my request* was possibly even more surreal than meeting Jeff Bezos. Afterward, he told the group some new editions of his 1980s records were about to come out, but he'd also noticed that old versions were available on Amazon through third-party sellers. Could anyone explain how to make sure the new versions would be visible to customers?

Huh, good question, I thought. *How* does *that work?* before noticing that everyone had turned to look at me, the least likely to know. But that was the way of the team, whether out of prematurely granted respect or diffidence: wanting the boss to be the one to talk. And my way, as the girl who always muddled through no matter what, was to never say "no" or "I don't know." Which is how I ended up giving one of my musical idols earnest, detailed, almost certainly incorrect advice—advice he *wrote down*—based on a very limited understanding of Amazon's third-party business, catalog systems, product IDs, and I don't even know what else.*

Fortunately, Jeff's just looking for confirmation that we're on board. "Absolutely," I say, and he nods. I already know that outside this room, blogging falls into the category of merchandising activities the store leaders and vendor managers call "fluff," because they can't be immediately monetized. But here, in this room, with Jeff looking at me to speak for

---

* Yes, I still feel kind of bad about this. Sorry, Robyn.

a roomful of people, what other choice do I have? When Jeff says to do something, you do it. Even if there's no time, even if it's not monetizable, even if it goes against everything else you've learned at Amazon.

"What was he like?" my mother asks that night. We're drinking wine in the living room while John cooks dinner.

"He was fine," I say, and I'm not trying to be withholding. He *was* fine. He was a confident, enthusiastic person leading a meeting. He was nice. He seemed like the kind of man you could ask for directions.

"I bet you impressed the hell out of him," she says.

"If sitting at a table with fifteen other people is impressive, then sure," I say. John silently emerges from the kitchen to refill my glass.

"Well, just wait," she says. "You'll knock his socks off."

It would be cruel for me to tell my mother how strangled I feel when she talks like this, how much I don't want the immediate pressure to dazzle Jeff Bezos. Can't it be enough for now that I didn't accidentally spill something on him or freeze up? I know she's trying to be supportive, but in the moment it's just one thing too many, like when I started exceeding a 4.0 grade point average and suddenly that became the new standard I was expected to meet. My chest and throat feel tight with the knowledge that it isn't fair.

"I've hired many people at Amazon, and Kristi is one of the best. In my opinion, she is a rock star." Speaking of overpraise, that's the last line of my first Amazon performance review. "No way. Seriously?" I say to Chuck. I was prepared to call it a win if he just didn't mention the almonds. "Absolutely," he says, beaming as I imagine a dad might beam when his daughter gets a home run in T-ball (my most notable T-ball achievement was losing a thumbnail, so my father didn't really have a chance to be proud). "You have had a world-class first year. You've taken on some really hard problems and moved the ball down the field on every one of them."

I also had no idea Chuck thought my job was hard, which I realize now made me wonder all year if it actually *was* hard, or if I was just soft. I want to lean forward and say, *Oh my God, it is* so *hard!* "It's been challenging at times for sure, but I try to just stay focused on the road map," I say instead.

We trade a few more niceties back and forth, and then I move us along to my areas for improvement; it's important to me that I be the first one to acknowledge them. "I will absolutely work on Have Backbone,"* I say. Peer feedback suggested that I'm very likable but they want to hear me dissent more often, because they value my perspective. I knew this would happen, partly because for the first six months or so I was too drenched in water—fire-hose water, lifeboat water—to feel confident I actually *knew* anything.

But also, I don't really know *how* to disagree. My family had two settings: Everything Is Fine, and Screaming Fights with Lasting Damage. There was no tradition of lively debate around the dinner table. So when I see two Amazonians

---

* Have Backbone; Disagree and Commit Leadership Principle: "Leaders are obligated to respectfully challenge decisions when they disagree, even when doing so is uncomfortable or exhausting. Leaders have conviction and are tenacious. They do not compromise for the sake of social cohesion. Once a decision is determined, they commit wholly." In theory, this leads to healthy conflict and better ideas. In practice, it tends to be used as cover by loud, rude men who talk before they think and weaponized against anyone enculturated *not* to act like a loud, rude man.

bluntly countering each other's ideas in a meeting, it's like watching an exotic martial art that I don't yet have the muscle to practice, even if I had the guts. Also, when a bunch of men are arguing, or even just talking, it's hard to break in. My habit at AMG was to wait for a pause, but there are so few pauses here; conversations are more of a *round*, like "Michael, Row the Boat Ashore," the men's voices overlapping and echoing until I'm no longer sure my point is relevant or what it was in the first place. And things move so fast that sometimes I change my mind before I have a chance to open my mouth, and it feels silly to speak up just to register that: *Hi, I'd like to take credit for having an opposing view two minutes ago, before Andy mentioned the marginal costs and I decided I agree with him after all.* But maybe that's what it's going to take to show that I know how to disagree: arguing awkwardly and off the beat.

"You'll get there," Chuck says. "I know from the way you handled the George situation that you can be tough. Just don't be afraid to show that side of yourself in meetings." Then he slides my compensation summary across his desk and everything else goes blurry.

"I mean, *what*?" John says a few hours later at the bar underneath his brother's bookstore. The walls and all the furniture are roughly carved from old-growth pine, so it's like drinking as a hobbit. He waves the comp summary at me. "Basically they said, 'Hey, good job! Here's an extra hundred thousand dollars.' What the *fuck*?"

"Not extra," I remind him. "Stock is part of my normal comp. It just seemed a lot more *theoretical* until now." The shares won't start vesting for another six months, and I'd almost forgotten they were going to keep adding to the initial grant I received on my start date. I tap the line showing my projected comp for the next year. "If the stock doesn't crash, my pay could double," I say. "I could make almost two hundred thousand dollars. Keeping up with rent *and* a mortgage won't be so stressful anymore, just for starters."

"I just want you to think back to where you were a year ago," John says. "Bored, stifled, making 50K."

"Yeah," I say. "It wasn't *so* bad, though." Everything John just said is true. But a year ago I was also less threadbare. I rarely worried about work at night, and almost never had to bring it home with me. I worked with reasonably happy people whom I never had to contemplate hurling off a lifeboat. It didn't feel as if any small wrong move might bring down the whole company and ruin my life.

"Of course it wasn't *so* bad," John says. "My point is that you wanted a big change, and you made it happen. All of this"—he gestures around the hobbit hole, but I think he means Seattle in general—"is because you took a leap. We did. But it started with you."

The wine seems to wave in my stomach for a moment. "Oh my God, in retrospect the size of the leap is horrifying," I say, putting my head in my hands.

"Okay now, stay in the room," John says.

"And I have to *keep doing it.*"

"C'mon back."

I resurface. "Let's talk about something else."

"We can talk about the new phone I got today," John says. "My calls finished at two, so I took the kayak out to practice my rolls, and I lost my phone in the drink. So I picked up this one at T-Mobile." He flashes a metallic-red flip phone.

"It's very jaunty," I say, awash in stale cortisol but trying to play along.

"Yes, and it's actually my lucky phone," he says. "Our lucky phone."

"Why?"

"Because it's the phone that brought us an offer on the house. Full price, no contingencies."

"From *humans*? With *money*?" I take a large gulp of Viognier.

"They love the new hardwoods in the living room," John says.

"I was secretly prepared to own that house forever," I say.

"Yeah, and I was secretly fantasizing about burning it to the ground for the insurance," he says. "But we're going to be free."

We clink glasses and he waves to Miller, the vegan* bartender, for another round.

"I think we really live here now," I say. "We've landed."

The next morning, I'm hungover for the third time in a week but buoyant with Amazonian approval, the imminent arrival of serious money, and our lucky phone. (If only we had bought it sooner!) The badass internal transfer I hired to replace George grins and waves as I pass her cube, and I practically salute her in return. "Good *morning*!" I chirp at Arjun's back, dropping my bag on the floor and hanging up my jacket.

Arjun wheels around. "You are here," he says, and slides our door shut. "Kristi, I have bad, bad news. It's very bad."

His eyes look bloodshot. "Is your family okay?" I ask.

---

* We only know this because he works it into nearly every interaction.

"My family? Yes, they are fine, of course," he says. "It's about the reorg."

"What reorg?"*

"Exactly," Arjun says. "Kristi, this is the exact question to be asking. The answer is, the one we are now becoming aware of. You will have a meeting with Chuck today. I just had mine."

"And?" I say.

"And basically we're fucked."

* Reorgs happen so frequently at Amazon that in retrospect it's hard to believe I've made it this long without one. It basically means Amazon shuffles who runs what, who reports to whom, and so on, sometimes for perfectly logical reasons and sometimes to accommodate Jeff's flights of fancy. At a lot of companies, reorgs come with layoffs. At Amazon, that wasn't common, and so I began to think of a reorg as Amazon Boggle: clattery and dizzying, but you *will* land in a slot again, just not the one in which you started.

PART II

BOGGLED

2008–2010

12

THE LAND OF BIGGER THINGS

My stomach falls a few floors. "Define 'fucked,'" I say.

"I mean your job is going away," Arjun says. "Mine, too. They're turning every Media product line into a separate organization. Books all alone, movies all alone, et cetera. Those of us who work across all of them don't have jobs anymore."

"We're getting *fired*?" I feel floaty, as if someone cut my tethers. How will I find a new job in the wilds of Seattle, especially with such a short stint at Amazon? Will we have to call off the house sale and go back to Michigan? What if I can't find a job there either? I see myself in line at a dusty gray unemployment office, dirty snow water pooling around my salt-stained boots.

"What? No," Arjun says. "Why would we get fired?"

"Well, laid off," I say. God, I don't want to tell John I dragged him across the country to this unaffordable-without-Amazon city for nothing.

"Kristi, no. It's just a reorg."

Finally it occurs to me to sit down. "Arjun, let me explain. I'm from the upper Midwest. When I hear the word 'reorg,' it generally means an entire plant's worth of people are losing their jobs. Plus, you did just say I was fucked."

"Kristi, this is not a car factory. You'll have a job. But you're losing *this* one. That's why you're fucked." I notice that the internal job board is open on his monitor.

"How will I have a job if this one's gone? And why are you looking on the job board?"

"They have a plan for us," he says, pronouncing it with a capital *P*. "And it sucks. So I'm looking for something else. You should too. They'll give you thirty days to find something that sucks less." Immediately I remember my gas-station fail. It feels as if I've only gotten dumber since then—how could I possibly survive another round of interviews?

My laptop pings with a 10:00 a.m. invitation from Chuck titled "Quick Check-In." It's 9:56 now. "Fuck, this must be it," I say.

"Be strong, my friend," he says.

Chuck takes one look at my face and says, "Arjun talked, didn't he? I asked him to let you hear it from me."

"There are rumors," I say, to avoid either lying or implicating Arjun. Calista, a woman around my age who used to manage Amazon's graphic design team and was promoted weeks ago into a job overseeing the entire retail customer experience, is also in the room, which makes no sense to me. I've met her only a few times and find her both really cool and unfathomably terrifying. Her cropped hair and sleek, rich punk wardrobe stand out in this city where "style" is a fleece vest or hiking pants that zip off into shorts. At work, pleated Dockers and a billowy Brooks Brothers button-down* are as fancy as it gets for men, and I'm pretty sure some of the younger guys

---

* A few of them eventually discovered the slim fit, thank God.

wear literal pajama bottoms as pants. The women make more effort,* but the overall Amazon/Seattle aesthetic still lands somewhere between granola and utilitarian. Calista carries serious designer bags like someone who knows she can always acquire another one and thus treats them like actual functional objects, not like me, terrified of getting a pen mark on my sole deep-discount Prada satchel. She's physically tiny, but I have no doubt she could hold her own in a bar fight, maybe using a lit Camel as a weapon. And unlike me, she's not afraid to Have Backbone, as I learned a few months back when she wrote me a courteous but no-uncertain-terms email about the continual chaos my merchandisers were inflicting on her designers with their last-minute requests for custom co-op graphics. She's been nothing but warm and encouraging during our occasional in-person encounters, and she laughs easily and loudly. But she's rumored to fly off the handle under pressure. And I've heard she once took off her shoe and winged it across a conference room during a meeting—not *at* anyone, but still, a four-inch Louboutin spike flung at high speed could probably lobotomize someone. I desperately want Calista to like me and I'm just as desperately afraid of what could happen if she doesn't. "Oh, hey, Calista," I say with a jaunty nod.

"Well, then as you may have heard, we're dividing the five media lines into separate organizations. That obviously impacts people like you who currently work across all of them. The five teams you manage will each exist within its own org now." He takes a moment to let me absorb the fact that everyone I've spent the year with is going away. "But, Kristi, we don't want to lose the excellent work you've been doing

* Shocker, I know.

on behalf of those teams, and in fact we'd like to give you a broader scope of influence."

He pauses again. "Oh. Okay," I say.

"Speaking of which, you're probably wondering what I'm doing here," Calista says with a smile. "So, *my* newish job covers all the parts of customer experience that aren't specific to one kind of product. Like wish lists, or the gift registry, or holiday shopping. We were thinking you could come work for me, and keep doing what you're doing, but expand it to include *all* merchandisers worldwide. That's about two hundred people."

That's ten times the number of merchandisers I currently represent. "Wow," I say. "Would all those people report to me?"

"No," she says. "That would be the biggest change. They would have a dotted line* to you but report to different managers. But you would have the executive sponsorship needed to be very influential. So what do you think? I'd personally be thrilled to have you join my team."

I don't see how I have much of a choice, but it's still sweet that they're trying to make it sound as if I do. "It sounds like this is actually a bigger job than the one I have now," I say, wondering how this squares with Arjun's warning that I'm fucked.

"Substantially," Chuck says.

"And there will be head count for you to build your own team," Calista adds.

Chuck's admin knocks on the door frame. "Oh, heck,"

---

* A dotted line means influence without authority—that the person on the other end of the dots is supposed to give your opinion a boss-like weight, but you can't actually tell them what to do. It is a complete myth. The dotted line is vapor.

he says. "I have to run and catch a plane." He stuffs his laptop and VPN* into a backpack and stands up. "But let's grab more time to talk when I'm back on Monday, okay?" Except for "hello" in an elevator three years later, this is the last time we will ever speak.

I watch him go and then turn to Calista, who is smiling. "Okay," I say, smiling back.

"I don't *feel* fucked," I tell Arjun a few minutes later. "Freaked, yes, but not fucked."

"You're a media person," he says. "Now they want you to sell vacuum cleaners and towels and vitamins and other shit you don't care about."

"I don't mind," I say. My role is already far removed from the actual books and movies we sell. Plus, as soon as Arjun mentions it, I realize I *am* curious about what makes people buy vacuum cleaners and towels and vitamins and other shit.

"You're losing your team," he says. "You will lack direct authority."

"Yeah, but I get to build a new team. And it's a bigger job. It's like . . . planetary." As soon as I say it, the prospect of responsibility spanning six countries makes me want to curl up under my desk à la the earthquake drill. Other than my knack for Figuring Shit Out on the fly, there is nothing, absolutely nothing in my background to indicate I'm ready for that kind of scope. I've never even *been* to that many other countries. But I instinctively know not to voice my fear to Arjun, lest

---

* Yes, young people, in 2008 these were still physical devices a little bigger than a pack of playing cards that Velcroed onto our laptops. I was too embarrassed to ask what mine did, so John had to clue me in at home.

he magnify it. "Anyway, do I actually have a choice?" I say instead.

He taps his screen. "Say yes for now while you quietly look for another role. But move fast, because otherwise it'll be eighteen months before you can apply for another transfer."

"How would I even get another role? This is the only one I know how to do."

"Kristi, please try hard not to be an idiot," Arjun says. "You know how to manage people, yes? You know how to write a solid document and think critically. You understand how Amazon uses data. You can persuade people on other teams to do things. This is 90 percent of most jobs at Amazon. The other 10 percent is just shit to learn, which you can also do."

He shrugs as though all this were blindingly obvious, not knowing he's just fundamentally altered how I'll approach the next decade of my Amazon career. *I* don't know that yet either. But it starts to land that if I know how to merchandise books and DVDs in America, I can figure out how to merchandise kitchen gadgets in America, or CDs in France, or sweaters in Japan. *I just have to scale up what I do now*, I think. *How hard can that be?** "You can plan and go for another role, like I am," Arjun says. But I already know I'm not going to do that. I left AMG because I wanted a career with chances to expand my horizons. Here it is.

John has champagne waiting at home, the good stuff. "It's a promotion!" he says.

---

* *Unbelievably fucking hard.* In a few years, "just scaling what I do now" will bring me to my knees. But I don't yet know that either, thank God.

"It's not a promotion," I say, dialing my parents. "I'm still an L7. It's just a bigger job. Amazon doesn't tie promotions to job changes. And anyway, it takes most L7s at least a few years to get to L8. I've got time."

"Kristi got promoted," my mother calls to my dad.

"It's not a promotion," I say. "Just a bigger job."

"Well, why haven't they promoted you yet?" she asks.

"So you got promoted," my father says on the extension.

"They didn't promote her," my mother says. "They want her to do more work for the same money."

"Well, Jeff Bezos didn't get where he is without knowing how to work people hard," my father says.

"You guys, Amazon isn't cheating me out of money," I say, making save-me eyes at John. "The promotion thing is complicated here. The point is, it's a bigger job. It means they like me."

"So they're *going* to promote you," my mother says.

I sigh. "Yes," I say. "Eventually they are."

I move nine floors lower in Columbia Center, this time to an office with a window overlooking the old stone church on Cherry Street. My new office mate is Louie, a UX design manager who wears dark glasses and a hoodie all the time, which would seem Unabomberish if he weren't such a gentle bear of a guy. Todd, the graphic design manager next door to us, is covered in tattoos and leather. Goths and part-time EDM musicians are also on the scene, and all the overhead lights are kept off to help designers see colors more truly on their monitors. (Or that's the explanation I get, anyway; I'd also believe they just like it dark.) *So this is where they stash the weirdos*, I think, unclenching a little inside. These are my people.

Calista continues to enthrall and panic me, sometimes simultaneously. "Something to know about me is that I'm the only daughter from a big Greek family," she tells me on an early lunch date. "I grew up with four brothers. Yelling and being dramatic is how we show we love each other."

"See, and I'm from a small Waspy family that doesn't talk about love, and when we yell, it's because someone has finally, truly lost it in a scary way," I reply, and out comes that big laugh.

"Well, we can meet in the middle," she says. I haven't worked for a woman since a college job as a deeply inept barista.* I find myself watching everything Calista does: the way she sets up a discussion in our staff meeting, how she delivers bad news, how her body language sometimes telegraphs her mood. She'd probably be alarmed by how closely I'm observing her. Even *I'm* a little alarmed. But I'm trying to figure out how to *be* at Amazon—be successful, be a woman, be heard—and here she is, doing it. I had no real hope of mapping myself onto Chuck, with his weekend Little League coaching, polo shirts, and Janus-like personality flips. But if I can be even 20 percent like Calista, maybe I'll stop being terrified all day every day.

Also, Calista has the guts to openly maintain that no, hard data can't tell us *everything*. She even says so via the William Bruce Cameron quote in her email signature: "Not everything that counts can be counted, and not everything that can be counted counts." As part of my expanded role, I'm continuing with the dreaded content-tool overhaul I started in my first

---

* I know I've presented myself as someone who can learn just about anything, but that excludes frothing milk.

job, but am now adding on bigger projects like . . . you know, they all seem small now. Do you really want to know about the hundreds of A/B tests we ran to measure the effectiveness of campaigns? Do you really care about special holiday stores or the gift registry or whether underwear can be advertised on the home page? Let's just say I was busy with things that at the time, and for a brief time, were considered "important." But from the start, Calista also wants to talk about the site's personality, or lack of it. "Amazon used to have a *voice*," she says, showing me a well-buried internal website with a list of brand voice traits I'm sure are long forgotten. "Can you help us get it back?"

I could almost cry when she asks me to do something I'm naturally good at. I've proven to myself by now that I have a decent head for data, and it fascinates me; there's nothing like having an audience of tens of millions of people to test ideas on. But it's the squishy, nonmeasurable places where I really excel, and with Calista I no longer have to pretend those places don't matter. "We probably couldn't prove with data that a typo hurts the business," she says, "but they're still wrong, because they make the brand look dumb, and dumb isn't trustworthy." (Ironically, with her sponsorship I'll later make a pitch for Amazon to have more than three proofreaders worldwide, and our senior VP will shoot it down because no, I can't actually quantify the effect of typos and snarled syntax on free cash flow.)

I'm also really *in it* now to a degree that makes my former Amazon life feel cloistered. It's half because Calista's org is such a miscellany of anything shopping related, and half because of my aforementioned talent for squishy stuff, and then the third half* is because as someone who isn't tied to any one product category, I can be dispassionate in a way the categories can't. I've barely set my coffee down one morning when the design manager Todd appears in my office doorway, practically hopping up and down. "Oh my God, are you ready for this?" he asks.

Last time he asked me this, he ended up ripping his shirt off to display the puffy, weeping new segment of his whole-entire-back tattoo. "Possibly?" I say now.

"Jeff got an automated email about lube and he shut down marketing emails for the entire company!"

"*What*?" I say.

"I KNOW!"

"*Jeff* did? And *the* lube? Lube-lube?"

"I mean, I haven't *seen* it, but that's what people are saying," he says, beaming like it's Christmas morning and grabbing a seat on the windowsill. "He said, 'We can be a hundred-billion-dollar company without sending a single marketing email,' and shut it *all* down."

"Forever?" I ask. I can't imagine Amazon without marketing emails; the merchandisers spend nearly half their time building them, experimenting with subject lines and targeting, measuring performance down to hundredths of a percent. "And wait, where did you even hear this?"

"Glamazon," he says, as though it should be obvious. And he has a point. Glamazon@, the listserv for Amazon's LGBTQ affinity group, is a better source of company news than any official Amazon channel.

Louie shuffles in. "Please, please, pretty please let me be

* By now we've established that head math is not my strong suit.

the one to tell him," I say to Todd. "Louie, Jeff got an automated email about lube and he shut the whole channel down."

Louie sits and docks his laptop before reacting. "Lube-
lube?" he asks, and we nod. He takes that in for a moment.
"Dude," he says.

I hop on Glamazon@, where details trickle in all morning.
From what we can piece together, shortly after Jeff got The
Lube Email, he forwarded it to the VP of Marketing with a
single question mark. Question Mark emails are sent when
something is so wrong or strange or seemingly inexplicable
that words and sentences are a waste of time and Jeff wants a
full accounting of what happened, exactly why it happened,
and what is changing to ensure it doesn't happen again. The
universal reaction to receiving one is *fuuuuuuuuuuck*, because
responding can easily consume several days and nights of your
life and because the response has to satisfy one of the most
terrifyingly powerful people on earth, who knows your name
and is already not happy about something connected to you.
Everyone sympathizes with the recipient of a ? email, but
there's also a tendency to avoid direct eye contact lest you be
sucked into the response vortex. Eldin answered one on my
old team, and even the minor supporting data he needed from
me took hours to vet and re-vet and re-re-vet until the numbers looked like an alien code and I had a sweaty nightmare
that I'd gotten them wrong.

In this instance, word is that Jeff also called a meeting
of the S-team* and relevant VPs to announce the mail shut-

---

* Amazon's name for the senior vice presidents who report directly to Jeff,
his inner circle.

down. As owner of the email channel, the Marketing VP got the brunt of it, and I hear that afterward Jeff Fucking Wilke came over to offer a shoulder pat. This is the detail that chills me, because while the Marketing VP is a really good guy who deserves the support, JFW is not a cuddler. If he's patting shoulders, it means shit has become profoundly destabilized.

Within a day or so, Lubegate has landed on my desk. Amazon sells much racier products—dildos, bondage gear, crotchless panties—but customers have to go looking for them. Even if someone buys six whips and nine ball gags, we won't advertise other sex toys on his home page or in email. But now we need to expand that fairly small group of do-not-market products to cover not just X-rated stuff but *anything* that could embarrass a customer if their spouse or kid or boss happened to see it over their shoulder. And we need humans making the call, not algorithms. From a Marketing product manager, I receive a massive .csv file of health and personal care products and assign a chunk to each of the editors and product managers on my team, who slog through line by line. We meet after a day to calibrate our judgment, which leads to conversations I did not anticipate having in my career. "*Are* Crest Whitestrips inherently embarrassing?" I ask Petra, the team's senior editor, who has marked them for walling off.

"They are," she says. "Because once someone knows you use them, they're going to be scrutinizing your teeth to see if it's working."

"It's like Rogaine," says Tobin. "Whitestrips and Rogaine both say you're trying to fix a flaw that people might not even notice otherwise." He points at his shiny shaved head. "Someone who meets me probably just thinks *bald guy*. But if they saw that I was using Rogaine, they'd think *sad bald guy*. I don't want that for myself."

"None of us want that for you, Tobin," Petra says to general agreement.

"Okay, I'm sold," I say. "But what about whitening toothpaste? Is that embarrassing?" Petra thinks for a moment and says no. "Why not?" I press, like Plato before me.

"Because it's just a side benefit," she says. "The main purpose is for toothbrushing, which everyone does." We decide whitening toothpaste is fair game. But over the next few days, we kick a *lot* of products off the safe list, enough that I assume the Health & Personal Care team will probably be unhappy with me, someone with no responsibility for their bottom line.

But when we send our recommendations to the S-team,* the feedback is that we haven't been tough *enough*. They kill the whitening toothpaste along with a bunch of other products we left alone, including all hair dye and most skin care. "What do they have against *retinol*?" I ask Calista, directing my question to her office floor, because she has thrown her back out and is lying on an absolutely spectacular life-sized Barry Manilow body pillow. "Retinol is a proven and cost-effective anti-aging product, and I would be happy to discuss my use of it with literally any human on earth, just to be helpful."

"Same," she says. "I don't care if people know I color my

---

* Dive Deep Leadership Principle: "Leaders operate at all levels, stay connected to the details, audit frequently, and are skeptical when metrics and anecdote differ. No task is beneath them." This means Amazon executives are expected to understand the business's broadest strategic issues *and* what's on the Lube List.

hair, either. But consider the source. It's all men. Their egos are fragile."

"Maybe they'd feel more confident if they availed themselves of some retinol and hair color," I say. I'm tempted to suggest we push back. It's conventional retail wisdom that women make most household purchasing decisions, so why should a group of men be the final arbiters on what will embarrass them? But Calista, who never hesitates to argue an important point, doesn't seem inclined to this time, and the idea of urging my boss to fight isn't yet fathomable. "I guess it's not the hill to die on," I say.

"I wouldn't," she says, shifting a little and wincing.

For the first time, Amazon starts to seem like a place where I might thrive. Yes, Calista can be a bit intense, but she's also a lot of fun, and she treats me like an entire person, not just a set of responsibilities. Without direct authority, I sometimes hesitate to weigh in as strongly as I should on an editorial issue, and one day I CC her on an email to a merchandiser saying something like "Per the home page guidelines, I strongly recommend you reconsider the campaign featuring the scantily clad woman" instead of just "Please take down the naked-woman campaign." As soon as I hit Send, I think, *She's not gonna like how I handled this*. And I'm right: she thinks I was mealymouthed and unclear (because I was). But per her early promise about meeting in the middle, when we talk about it, she doesn't just tell me to be more like her. Instead, she says, "Being tough isn't the same thing as being mean, you know. I think you need to internalize that." A decade later, I'll still hear those words anytime I find myself dreading a hard conversation, and I'll repeat them to some of my directs. And by fits and starts, I start to grow into the influence the role has handed me.

In this role, I also now have the kind of visibility and space for ambition that I longed for at AMG and that could have taken years to gain at Amazon. I send a monthly update on my team's activities to twenty of Amazon's top executives around the globe, and some of them seem to actually read it. Maybe it should worry me that writing that update takes a full afternoon, so broad is my team's scope. Maybe it should freak me out that my job is so amorphous, and largely unmeasurable, and that as the only person with this exact job I have no peers to learn from or be compared with at promotion time. But I'm too busy grabbing at more, more, more to think about it, my current career strategy being to hit people over the head with the sheer volume and diversity of work I can manage, like a well-spoken, harried octopus.

Even better, I start to be pulled into weird, unwieldy projects, the kind of shoot-the-moon stuff AMG didn't have the cash or the patience* to invest in. And to my surprise, that's the work that lights a fire inside my cautious, competent heart. There's a saying in tech that some people are builders and some are operators. From birth all the way through my job on Chuck's team, I would have called myself an operator, someone who takes something already built and makes it run smoothly, refines it, improves it incrementally. But working under Calista is where I start to realize that what I really want to do is build, and more specifically that I want to build things that sound kind of nuts at first. Crazy is the high I'll chase for the rest of my Amazon career, even as it starts to ruin me.

---

* Which, to be fair, also comes easier with cash.

It's 2:00 p.m. on a Wednesday a few months after the lube thing, and I'm talking through a project plan with my team's lead copywriter when Calista calls. "So, Jeff's assistant just asked to move our meeting from four o'clock to *right now*," she says. I can tell from the background fuzz that she's on her BlackBerry, maybe sneaking a cigarette in the courtyard. "Can you meet me in the lobby ASAP?"

"So we're, like, technically already late to this meeting," I say to Calista on the drive to the building Jeff works in. By Amazon standards, we're both dressed up for the occasion, meaning I'm wearing a blazer with my jeans and Calista's wearing four-inch pointy-toed Manolos instead of her usual three-inchers. Now that my stock has started vesting, I guess I could afford a pair of Manolos too, but I feel as though grievous injury would be inevitable.

"Well, hopefully he understands we're bound by the limits of physics," Calista says. We're both speaking breezily, but I'm anxious, and from the set of her jaw I know she is too. Calista may have natural swagger, but this is her first year in Amazon's executive ranks, and she's a decade younger than most of her male counterparts, and her job seems to grow every month. When she cuts off one of her directs for giving a rambling answer, or starts rapid-fire demanding details about a project she's worried about, it feels scary and aggressive to me. But when I step back, I see her fear, too. She's not immune to the sense that any wrong move around here could be your last.

Our Jeff meeting is to review the launch materials for something called Frustration-Free Packaging. I first heard about it just ten days ago, when the original product manager abruptly resigned. I don't know who came up with the idea, but FFP is just packaging that's minimal and easy to deal with—no plastic clamshells that have to be attacked with scissors, no children's play sets where every tiny piece is wire tied to a piece of cardboard. Holiday shopping starts soon and the Packaging team has been working all year with manufacturers like Mattel to make FFP versions of toys like an eighty-seven-piece pirate ship, betting that parents will appreciate saving an hour (or more) of setup on Christmas Eve. And with the product manager's departure, introducing FFP to the world has landed in Calista's world, and subsequently in mine.

Even late, we arrive in Jeff's eighth-floor conference room before he does. Samita from Packaging is already there, setting up the aforementioned eighty-seven-piece pirate ship as a display. "I was thinking of getting one of these for my son, but I might be too sick of looking at it," she says, placing a little parrot on the mast. As always, any reminder that some women who work here have kids takes me aback. Most of my female colleagues are childless, and I sometimes wonder whether Amazon attracts women who are inherently uninterested in motherhood or if it just chokes the interest out of us once we're here. Unlike most of the big tech companies, Amazon doesn't offer paternity leave or any assistance with day care. I didn't witness it myself, but company lore says a brave employee once asked about day care during Q&A at a company all-hands meeting, and the sole female member of Jeff's S-team stood up and said, "I have kids. And if *I* can make it work without company day care, anyone can." Maybe it put a tiny damper on things for other Amazon moms to be chastised by someone with many millions of dollars to spend on household help, because, though day care still arises as a topic on the women@

email alias now and then, it fades quickly and with agreement that things are unlikely to change. My own interest in motherhood has never been more than casual and passing, but since I've been here, I've begun thinking of kids as a literal impossibility, as though Amazon has altered my anatomy.

"Hey, guys," Jeff says when he arrives half an hour later.

"Hey, Jeff," we all say in semi-unison, though if my thoughts were sounds, he'd hear me saying, *That's Jeff Bezos right there. Jeff Bezos. There he is.* I can't help it, even now that he knows my name. I doubt it will ever stop.

He grabs a document from the stack I've placed on the table. "Should we read?" he asks. The six-page document—six pages *max* no matter how sprawling the topic*—is the cornerstone of Amazon communication. You can bluff and hand wave your way through a PowerPoint presentation, but a six-pager forces you to present a coherent argument and commit to your facts. I've written one so far and it took eight drafts before Calista pronounced it ready for prime time. "Being a good writer is actually hurting you," she said around draft five. "These graceful segues and lovely sentences will read like fluff or obfuscation to those guys," meaning the VPs who were my eventual audience. She also crossed out my three uses of the phrase "we believe" and replaced them with "we think." "We don't 'believe' or 'feel' things at Amazon," she said. "Not officially, anyway. We only *think* them, based on data."

Calista and Samita wrote most of today's six-pager. My part is the Jeff Letter, Amazon-speak for the "Dear customers" letter from Jeff that runs on the home page for only very big announcements. The senior editor on my team has been writing

---

* With an appendix as big as your heart desires.

Jeff Letters for years, but she's on maternity leave and so this one fell to me. We've already done three rounds of edits by email, and yes, having Jeff Bezos edit the copy you wrote *as* him is a deeply weird and unsettling experience, but it also means there will hopefully be no surprises today. I actually like writing as Jeff, because unlike with six-pagers, grace and color matter. It's nice to sound like a human, albeit a different human.

The other six-pager custom is that the first twenty minutes of the meeting are devoted to reading it in silence. That way, no one can say "I didn't have time to read the document, but" before spouting off about whatever, and it also ensures that everyone in the room is operating with the same set of facts. But when *your* document is the one being read, it's twenty minutes of pure torture. Why is that one guy writing so much in the margins? Why did that other guy finish so fast—does it mean he loves the proposal and has no questions, or that it's not even worth his time? Why did Jeff Fucking Wilke just circle an entire paragraph, and is it a happy circle or an angry one? I've been in six-pager reviews full of challenging but friendly debate, and others where a VP's first comment was, "There's a typo a third of the way down on page 4," delivered with the same gravity as if the author had used the wrong financial model.*

And those VPs are *mortals*. This is my first six-pager review with Jeff, and watching him read is a whole different game of "What is about to happen to me?" I read the Jeff Letter four

---

* Insist on the Highest Standards Leadership Principle: "Leaders have relentlessly high standards—many people may think these standards are unreasonably high. Leaders are continually raising the bar and drive their teams to deliver high-quality products, services, and processes. Leaders ensure that defects do not get sent down the line and that problems are fixed so

times, including backward, suddenly worried I inserted a typo since the last draft. Next to me, Samita is making notes on her own sections, presumably trying to anticipate Jeff's questions and pre-answer them. Across the table, Calista looks chill enough, but the unusual stillness of her body tells me she's hyper-attuned, too. When Jeff puts the document down and looks up, Calista says the customary opening line: "Looks like we're ready to discuss. Does anyone have comments on the overall doc?"

"I think we should be careful when we talk about this program to always focus on the customer experience," Jeff says. "Frustration-Free Packaging is easier to open and means less packing material for customers to deal with. We can talk about waste, but waste shouldn't be the focus." I know Samita hates hearing this. There *are* environmental goals for the project, and it's a chance to say publicly that Amazon is trying to reduce its footprint. But it would only lead to questions about things we *aren't* doing. Also, I know by now that when Jeff says "I think" or "we should," it means "This Is How It Shall Be." Despite the Leadership Principles, if he were inviting disagreement, he'd say so.

"Great," Calista says. "Shall we go page by page, then?" Going page by page is also customary, but you're still expected to say it.

Page 1. "I don't think we should call out the exact amount of colored ink we're doing away with unless we can also tell customers the industry average," he tells Samita.

"We tried to come up with an apples-to-apples estimate,

---

they stay fixed." Like "tireless" and "hard," "relentless" is a popular word at Amazon, and in fact was nearly the name of the entire company. (Type www.relentless.com into a browser and see where it redirects.)

but I don't feel superconfident about it," Samita says. "Let me go back one more time and see if there's an approach we've overlooked that seems intellectually honest."

"Cool," Jeff says. "Otherwise, let's cut it."

"Page 2?" Calista says. Nothing. We fucking nailed page 2. We continue on and finally hit the Jeff Letter on page 4. I knew it had to happen, but it still sends a little chill down my spine. *Even keel*, I think, and pick up my pen.

"I have the same feedback that I had on the colored ink," Jeff says. So many of his sentences follow the same deliberate cadence. He wouldn't say, "Same feedback as on the colored ink." All the pronouns and articles are there and in their places. "We should make absolutely sure that these counts are correct," he continues, referring to the 36 inches of wire ties and the 175 square inches of PVC blisters the Jeff Letter claims we've eliminated from the pirate-ship packaging.

"We've confirmed the count twice with Mattel, but we'll do a third just to be safe," I say. When I speak to Jeff, I feel like Philippe Petit, the high-wire artist who walked between the spires of Notre-Dame. It doesn't matter how anodyne the topic; all might be fine now, but his questions could go in any direction, and if I have to improvise, I might slip and hit the ground as liquid and gore.

"Great," Jeff says. "Samita, I think we should also do our own count if we haven't already." He looks back down at the page. "Also, we shouldn't say we *know* customers are going to love Frustration-Free Packaging. We should say we *hope* they love it."

"I thought this might be a place to express a little pride in the innovation," I say, also nodding to indicate I'm explaining, not arguing.

"We want to take credit, but we also want to always sound humble," Jeff says, big round eyes unbothered. "So we shouldn't pretend we know what customers will like before they've told us."

"Got it," I say, making a note. It makes a lot of sense to me, not that my agreement really matters; it's his name at the bottom of the letter, I'm just the channel.

"Just change those two words," Jeff says. "From 'we know' to 'we hope.'"

"I'll update the master copy right after our meeting," I say. That's the final line in the letter. Are we done? Have I lived through my first presentation to this pleasant, frightening man? Calista, who has mostly stayed quiet so far so that Samita and I get the Jeff practice, shoots me a tiny smile.

Then he turns to Calista. "Also, I think we should say that within ten years every product Amazon sells will be available in Frustration-Free Packaging."

Calista takes a beat. "*Every* product?" I've heard her sound alarmed in private settings, but never in a meeting like this.

"Sure," Jeff says. "Ten years is a long time. We should set a big goal and hold ourselves accountable to it." I don't dare look at Samita, whose team spent more than a year getting vendors to make FFP packaging for just our nineteen launch products.

"Is it a long time for millions of items of all shapes and sizes and materials, though?" Calista asks. "Until we know more about what it will take to get there, we might want to set a less specific benchmark for the press to track." This is the real high-wire act: conveying that of *course* we'll eventually ship every table lamp, chess set, and light bulb in minimalist packaging while also hinting that it might be insane to promise it'll happen by 2018. She risks Jeff deciding she's not Thinking Big* enough, or that she doesn't know how to Invent and Simplify.†

But her angle works. "How about this?" Jeff says. "'It will take many years, but our vision is to offer our entire catalog of products in Frustration-Free Packaging.'‡ I like that. It's bold but not overly specific."

Samita sighs with relief. "Thank you," she says, which makes Jeff laugh. I type the new copy in the live mock-up right then and there, as though that can stop him from changing his mind.

"Exhale," Calista says on the drive back to our building, though I'm not sure if she's talking to me or herself.

"I appreciate the exposure I'm getting to him," I say. She didn't *have* to include me in the meeting; some of my friends' bosses don't, to their frustration. I want Calista to know I know what she's doing for me by putting me in that room and letting me talk.

"You did well, my love." She hangs a right onto Fourth Avenue. "I could actually do with a little *less* Jeff time next year. Ever since I stepped into this role, it feels like all I do is prep for Jeff meetings." I think about the weeks we spent on this document alone—the drafts, the multiple reviews with other

---

* Think Big Leadership Principle: "Thinking small is a self-fulfilling prophecy. Leaders create and communicate a bold direction that inspires results. They think differently and look around corners for ways to serve customers."
† Invent and Simplify Leadership Principle: "Leaders expect and require innovation and invention from their teams and always find ways to simplify. They are externally aware, look for new ideas from everywhere, and are not limited by 'not invented here.' As we do new things, we accept that we may be misunderstood for long periods of time."
‡ As of 2022, more than 750,000 products will be in FFP.

stakeholders, even the layout of the Jeff Letter on the page—
and I get where she's coming from. But I'm not there yet. I
want more. After all, exposure leads to comfort, right? Maybe
with enough direct exposure to Jeff Bezos's power, he won't
be scary anymore. Maybe bits of it will even seep into me, and
then nothing about Amazon will scare me ever again.

At home that night, John mentions that a casual friend's
start-up just folded. "But *why*?" I ask. "They were onto something good. Why not let it play out a bit longer, until the public catches up?"

"Well, I didn't ask, but I assume it's because they ran out of
money?" he says, scrambling eggs on the new Wolf range, the
stove of our dreams.*

"Oh, right," I say, but I still can't quite wrap my head
around it. "But they couldn't just get a new round of capital?
New investors?"

John laughs. "Not everyone has Jeff Bezos writing infinite
big checks for crazy ideas." It's not the first time he's had to remind me. I've long since forgotten that money isn't just an endlessly renewable resource, Jeff's faith turned into cash.

"But were they burning money in dumb ways?" I ask. "Free
on-site pedicures and whatnot?" Frugality† is so deeply em-

---

* What? Some people have dream stoves.
† Frugality Leadership Principle: "Accomplish more with less. Constraints
breed resourcefulness, self-sufficiency, and invention. There are no extra
points for growing headcount, budget size, or fixed expense." You know,
there's a fine line between Frugality and Frupidity, or refusing to spend
money even when it makes long-term sense. Amazon replacing employee
laptops only every three years: frugal. Amazon refusing to make an excep-
tion for my two-year-eight-month laptop that shut down randomly multiple
times a day and took a full ten minutes to reboot each time: frupid.

bedded at Amazon—in the sweater-snagging desks, the travel policies that encourage red-eyes and Saturday stay-overs if it means saving a few bucks, the almost total absence of perks other big tech companies provide—that I've taken to talking about struggling companies the way boomers talk about younger people who would be financially *set* if only they'd give up that reckless daily latte.

"No, they were not offering free pedicures or dog grooming or Segways," John says. "They just ran out." He slides a plate of eggs and toast across the counter to me. "Every single time I use this stove is an absolute fucking joy," he says, and I agree.

By eleven thirty on the night before Frustration-Free Packaging launches, everything has been locked and loaded for two days. Tobin has built the store and the announcement email and Jeff is happy with the home-page letter and pirate-ship video and Design has laid both out gracefully on the home page and PR is ready for the press release to hit the wires and we have plenty of pirate ships and other FFP products in stock. All that's left is to set it all live at midnight, and to freak out in the interim. At home, I read the final Jeff Letter backward one more time, and then I make John read it twice, too. On the conference line, Tobin and Calista and the PR rep are talking about *Mad Men*, and Calista, who normally goes to bed at nine and wakes around four, is apologizing for yawning. Samita's work is done for now but she's here too, just because.

At five to midnight, Tobin gets ready to make the store publicly visible. It's 3:00 a.m. on the East Coast; odds are slim that a lot of customers are up fucking around on Amazon right now. If something goes wrong, we have time to fix

it. But it *feels* as if this were our one shot, and I'm haunted by
the possibility that Jeff is at home, staring at his laptop waiting to send a "?" if a line breaks weird in the letter layout or a
product image is subpar. For now, there's nothing for me to
do but pace around our third-floor den clutching my phone
on speaker. With so many trees bare by now, from the side
window I can just glimpse the lit-up Space Needle a few miles
south of our house.

"Shit," Tobin says under his breath.

"What's up?" I say with as little inflection as possible so I
don't rattle him further.

"The tool is hanging." Slowly, that goddamn broken content tool I was hired to replace is getting better. But it's still
unstable and slow, and that won't change until the final stages
of the project, a year from now.

"Shit," says Calista, also clearly working to contain her
tone.

"Take a breath, everyone," Tobin murmurs. "We have three
minutes. I'm going to refresh and try again." We sit silent as
he types. I find myself breathing shallowly to reduce stress on
both Tobin and, somehow, the tool. "Argh," he says. "It's fine.
I just switched two numbers in the campaign ID because I'm
nervous."

"You're doing great," I say.

"Thanks, boss. Okay, here we go again." Twenty seconds of quiet. "And we're live," he says. "It's a bouncing baby
Frustration-Free Packaging launch." I refresh the site a couple
of times on my laptop and yep, there it is.

"It looks beautiful," Calista says. "Good work, everyone."
We say our good nights, but I'm too keyed up to sleep. I can't
stop thinking about how my words are up there for scores of

millions of people to read, and how FFP will be all over the tech media tomorrow, and how much that reduced waste we don't want to talk about yet could add up to over time. What we're doing is so small in some ways, at least for now, but we're *doing* it. We took a thing that had been one way for decades and changed it, just because we thought it should change.

I lie in bed thinking of all the times at AMG when I craved bigger things and there were none for me to do. Sometimes I wondered if I was just imagining that the grass was greener in the land of bigger things, that perhaps small would turn out to be my scale after all. But now I know. Big is a rush. It's addictive. I want more. I'll know when enough is enough. Right?

13

PEOPLE LEAVE

People leave, of course, though we don't say "leave"; we say they "promoted themselves to customer." Lashanna leaves to have children. Jacie comes back after her first kid but leaves before her second. Matt leaves to become an Anglican minister. Todd leaves to breed irises. Liza leaves to sail around the world. Kelly leaves for an NGO. Eino, thirty-six, says in his goodbye email that he's leaving to regain his health. Holly leaves to get some sleep. Amy leaves for Microsoft. Dennis leaves for Microsoft. Hiroshi leaves for Microsoft. Google, LinkedIn, eBay, Airbnb, Facebook, Twitter, Expedia, Tableau. Tim wins big on *Jeopardy!* and leaves to open a bookstore. Victor leaves for more reading time. Nina goes on medical leave for stress and never returns. Lance leaves to sober up. Noah goes home to Denmark. Anna leaves and starts a firm that helps vendors understand Amazon. Jack leaves and starts one that helps people interview at Amazon. Pat leaves to work on Zune and a year later he boomerangs back. That's what we call the people who return: boomerangs. Brent leaves for Apple and better work-life balance and boomerangs back when Apple's work-life balance turns out to be even worse. Anton boomerangs from start-up land. Ira boomerangs from retirement in the South of France. Nathan and Prakash and Eric all boomerang back from Nordstrom corporate, which they call "retirement," better dressed than we remember them. Pete spends one day at a new company and boomerangs back. *I never thought I'd come back*, the boomerangs say, grinning and wild-eyed, and when we ask what brought them back, they always say, "The people. I missed the people," and I know what they mean; I missed some of them even if we hadn't worked together in ages, missed their camaraderie, their under-eye circles, their gallows jokes, the way they kept showing up for me and I kept showing up for them because no one of us could make it alone, though it's arguable whether we could make it together, either. As for me, I keep staying, past the point where I'd owe back my signing bonus, past my first seven door desks and four bosses and five reorgs, three U.S. presidents, two unfounded rumors of stock splits, the nonupling of the employee population. Sometimes I take it year by year, sometimes stock vest by stock vest. At one point my staying is a week-to-week thing. I keep a go bag under my desk for the few possessions I can't see leaving behind. But I don't use the bag. I stay.

14

ITINERARY

Goals

Bon voyage! In line with your role's global scope, the main purpose of your trip is to train merchandisers around the globe to write in the Amazon brand voice: humble yet proud, friendly but not too friendly, enthusiastic but not carnival barker. Yes, most of the merchandisers write and speak other languages. Yes, it's hard enough to teach this stuff to English speakers. But you will figure it out! Somehow. We know you will, because it is required.

The secondary purpose of your trip is to reinforce that Amazon is a global brand that presents one face to the world. You may be told international teams "need" custom, specific widgets and graphics and site features in order to grow their business in their countries. Resist this! Reassure them that Seattle loves them and understands their needs better than they do. Reassure them their needs are already being met and that in time they will agree.

Safe travels! Keep in mind that taxis, hotel laundries, Wi-Fi surcharges, and room service are discouraged in the name of Frugality.

England

Welcome to London! Well, sort of. From your hotel with the dodgy electricity, walk a block each morning to Paddington Station (thinking, *Oh my God, I'm at PADDINGTON STATION in LONDON*) and hop a commuter train to Slough, best known in America as the setting of the original BBC *Office* series and in the U.K. as a punch line. Seattle co-workers accustomed to gleam and new money have overplayed Slough's blight. Hum "you ain't a beauty but hey, you're alright" as you walk from Slough station past the Tesco and the *Office* theme bar to Amazon's offices in a 1980s mid-rise. The open-plan office is harshly lit and cramped, with conversations conducted in near whispers and a sense of resignation hanging over all. Still, people are "well chuffed" to meet you. You have a desk. You are invited out for lunch, and to the basement canteen for coffee, and the merchandisers show up to your training and ask questions and even laugh at your jokes. In the evenings, take the train back to London to go record shopping in Ladbroke Grove and buy ties for John at Paul Smith and take walks along the Serpentine, suffused with a strange warmth you think might be the feeling of success.

Germany

Go straight from the Munich airport to Amazon's offices in an old Mercedes factory. "Werner would like to speak with you first thing," the receptionist says, Werner being the Head of Country. Think, *Oh my God, an hour in Germany and I've somehow already fucked up*, as you beam and say, "Wonderful!" On the top floor, Werner's assistant offers you a cappuccino and a seat on the roof deck, which is really just an umbrella table on the roof itself, but by Amazon standards feels luxe. Sit alone on a German roof thinking, *Oh my God, I'm in GERMANY, on a ROOF*, and wondering what Werner is mad about until he's there, greeting you like his favorite human on earth and promising his unqualified support for whatever you need to fix Merchandising. *Act normal.* Do not let on how bewildering you find his joyful, supportive energy or the way it trickles down to the German merchandisers, who have the same sucky jobs as their global counterparts but are downright peppy about it. Your hotel is on a generic ring road, inconvenient for evening sightseeing; still, wander to a nearby gas station one night, gaze upon a whole wall of Haribo candies, and reflect that Munich really is a land of miracles and wonders.

France

Take the Metro to Charles de Gaulle–Étoile, walk down streets of freakish architectural unity and beauty, and find the one building that looks like your dad's first PC tower in 1985. Bienvenue à Amazon France, and prepare to be barely tolerated! Find yourself a desk space at the kitchen counter. Try to build rapport by asking the Books merchandisers if they've read anything good lately, and play it cool when one of them replies "We're not big readers" without looking up from her laptop. Also don't react when they openly whisper and giggle to each other and roll their eyes during your voice training. Not even when two of the women *point* at something about you—your jeans, your bag, your ass?—and giggle. Keep smiling when the Head of Country is so visibly bored during your meeting that he reminds you of a lizard sleeping with its eyes open. In the evenings, tell yourself, *Okay but at least I'm in PARIS*. Keep this in mind when the bank, having finally noticed your credit card is being used in Europe, locks it, and you can't call them because the landline in your shitty hotel doesn't work and you didn't think to get an international cell plan and so you go hungry for a night. And when a strange man gropes you on a side street, and when your clothes reek so badly of cigarette smoke that you break down and use the hotel laundry service even though Amazon policy is that you're supposed to hunt down a coin laundry. *What am I* doing *here?* you ask yourself one night, eating a stupid salad at a stupid café on a street lined with stupid cobblestones, somehow understanding that "here" means not just Paris but Amazon, and that if the merchandisers learned nothing this week, it's your fault.

Japan
Have a safe and pleasant flight in the very back row, between a lavatory with a door that won't stay shut and a toddler who would rather press your touch screen than his own. (All in keeping with Frugality, though you are welcome to spend six thousand dollars of your own money on an upgrade.) Fourteen hours later, arrive with a headache and an eyelid twitch at the Cerulean Tower in Shibuya, an *actual business hotel* with good beds and hot showers and room service (remember not to expense the delivery fee). Almost cry from gratitude/exhaustion. In the mornings, walk to work via a route composed solely of overpasses, doglegs, switchbacks, and alleys. Realize that due to jet lag, you will be a little bit dumb all week, exacerbated by the way your brain says *Oh my God, I got in a metal tube and now I'm in TOKYO* every five minutes. You can jack yourself up on caffeine to try to mitigate the dumbness, but the flabbergasted wonder cannot be helped.

The merchandisers show you their competitors' websites, teeming with color and animations and pop-ups. "They want access to elements like this," the manager acting as translator explains. Here is your test! They are asking to *deviate from the global brand*.

Nod sympathetically and deliver the party line: "I understand. But Amazon prefers simple pages that load fast and keep focus on the products we sell. Amazon wants us to think only about customers, not about what competitors are doing."

The merchandisers and translator discuss this among themselves. Eventually the translator turns back to you. "It's about customer trust," she says.

"Trust?" you repeat back.

"Yes. Next to our competitors, the Amazon site looks poor. Poor in money," she clarifies. "Like we might not be a stable business." Seeing your confusion, she stops translating and just talks. "Rakuten was here before there was an Amazon.jp. So it sets the standard for how a respectable store should look, and we are failing to live up to it."

You have never thought of it like that before. Say "I've never thought of it like that before" to the translator, who looks relieved.

"It's not just that we like flashy colors and sparkles," she says. "I know Seattle thinks so. But we only want to look legitimate in Japan." Realize she is right. In the next instant, realize that you are not going to be the one to fight that battle back home. Word from On High is that the U.S. brand is *the* brand. It would be Amazonian of you to Disagree on Japan's behalf. It would also be Amazonian to Commit to the current standard, even if you question it. Take the easy way out. You will only feel guilty about it for a year or so.

Tell the translator she's given you a lot to think about, which is just vague enough to be true.

After work, cut through Shibuya Station and emerge at the largest intersection you have ever seen, where you wait with scores of other people for the walk signal. *"Lost in Translation,"* says the woman next to you to her companion in a French accent. Of course. This is where Bill Murray whispers something secret to Scarlett Johansson. Imagine his arms around you now. "Expansion," he whispers. "It's what you always wanted."

"Expansion," you whisper back into his neck.

15

THE FLOW STATE

6:00 a.m.: I wake up afraid of the day, just because it's there and I can't stop it from happening. "The only way out is through," people say, but they're talking about heartache or grief, not Tuesday. As always, I half expect to see Abby on the downstairs landing with her stuffed otter, though Abby died four months ago.

6:30 a.m.: I dump coconut water, kale, frozen mango, and flaxseed into the Vitamix to cancel out the calming bottle of wine I drank last night. Just looking at the Vitamix makes me feel as if everything were going to work out okay. I recently learned the word "superfood," and every week or so I add a new one to the rotation: maca root, goji berries, camu powder. "I'm optimizing breakfast," I tell John, and when he asks why, I say, "Well, why *not*?" And I mean it. Why would I not optimize anything optimizable? I drink the smoothie standing up, fast enough for a shard of headache.

8:00 a.m.: I wave bye as I pass John's office off the dining room. The house we finally bought is beautiful, maybe 20 percent nicer than our Michigan house for 400 percent of the cost. We included a heartfelt letter to the sellers with our bid, because on the West Coast sellers have so many options that you have to charm them into accepting your money. John's on the phone but flashes a thumbs-up at my new black McQueen pencil skirt. I-5 is slow, affording time for a full unit of the Mandarin lessons I'm taking in preparation for a work trip to Beijing next month. "Wǒ de zhōngwén bù hǎo," I repeat on cue: "My Chinese is poor." I am clearly going to be totally fucked language-wise in China, but at least this gives me some illusion of control.

Mitch, the SVP of my org, is in the parking garage lobby. "Morning!" he says, his pointy eyebrows giving him a look of perpetual skepticism to go with his actual perpetual skepticism. Mitch oversees all of Amazon retail outside the United States, which is to say he runs the world.

"Morning!" I parrot back. Calista and I have a meeting with Mitch at four to present my proposal for ripping up the merchandiser role and starting over. It took two months to get this meeting, long enough for me to successfully sell it to Jeff Fucking Wilke and the North American VPs. Mitch's approval is all I'll need to leverage global* change, at least for my corner of the Amazon globe. I don't mention any of this now; Mitch's not a small talker—to say the least—and it would only be embarrassing to watch him struggle to remember who I am.

8:30 a.m.: I go straight to the printer room to make copies for the 4:00 p.m. meeting, not just to get it done early, but because printing now will discourage me from the kinds of frantic last-minute edits that tend to make a document worse.

---

* "Global" being the Amazon buzzword du jour. It's not enough to make change; it must be planetary in scope.

The copier is out of order, so I go up a floor to find one copier out of order and the other in use. Both copiers on the floor above *that* are free, but of course the one I choose jams in seconds. I try the lid, the door, the lever, before grabbing the originals back and sliding on over to the other machine, which is weirdly operational. "Shoot," mutters the man who arrives just afterward, staring at the jammed machine. "Not working?" I ask sympathetically, glancing at him over my shoulder.

9:00 a.m.: I'm Bar Raising for a junior role in Finance. Being a Bar Raiser means I'm a trained and trusted interviewer who sits in on meetings to evaluate candidates across the company for "culture fit." After the interviews, I run the meeting where all five or six people on the loop discuss whether we should make an offer. Technically I have veto power over any hire, though I've never had to use it. The intranet hiring site says this is my 237th Amazon interview, which seems insane only because I don't realize it will one day be more than 800.* The thought of spending one more intense hour with a total stranger pre-exhausts me sometimes, especially this early in the day. But most of the time I end up enjoying myself. I try not to think about the fact that even the hires I'm proudest of are statistically unlikely to stay at Amazon more than a year or two.

I don't know a single thing about Finance, and I certainly couldn't do that job myself. I'm here to assess whether he's a fit for Amazon overall. The candidate is just a few years out of college, coming from a midsized start-up that sounds as though it might be circling the drain. He's earnest, smart, co-

---

* And 800 is just where the counter breaks; the real number is probably closer to 1,000.

herent without being too packaged. My Leadership Principle
focus is his ability to be Vocally Self-Critical,* so after a few
warm-up questions I dig in.

"Can you tell me about a time you made a significant
mistake at work?" I ask. "Something with nontrivial conse-
quences?" Panic crosses his eyes, as it does at least half the time
I ask this question. "We really value it here when people can
own and learn from mistakes and failure," I explain to try to
set him at ease. "My boss once told me that people who don't
make any mistakes probably aren't making enough decisions."

That relaxes him a bit. "The first time I was in charge of
pulling together the financials for an investor presentation, I
based one of my calculations on the wrong assumption," he
says. "My boss discovered my error about thirty minutes be-
forehand and it was a wild scramble to get everything fixed
and reprinted in time and he was *not* happy with me. It all
worked out okay from the investor perspective, but it damaged my boss's trust." From the look on the kid's face, he's
slightly reliving it all now.

"How did you land on the wrong assumption?" I ask.

"Well, *technically* I didn't," the kid says. "Our projected
growth rate had changed, but whoever owned the template
hadn't updated it. Which I didn't know. But something *felt*
kind of wrong. I knew enough about how the outlook was
changing to think, *Huh, these numbers are surprising.* So my
mistake was not asking questions about the template."

---

* Vocally Self-Critical Leadership Principle: "Leaders do not believe their or
their team's body odor smells of perfume. Leaders come forward with problems or information, even when doing so is awkward or embarrassing. Leaders benchmark themselves and their teams against the best." Pretty good
principle, but God do I hate that body-odor line.

I nod. "Or listening to your own Spidey sense." I tell him that Jeff has said that data can obscure the one anecdote you have that tells you something weird might be going on. It can hide the iceberg.

"But you can't look at *every* anecdote, right?" the kid says. "How do you know which ones matter?"

I smile. "That's the part I haven't figured out yet."

10:30 a.m.: I head up to the fortieth-floor Starbucks for a one-on-one with Maeve, the PM on my team in charge of replacing the merch content tools. Maeve used to run big operational projects for Delta, and I knew I wanted to hire her when she told me how *exciting* she found it to spend hours at airports watching people navigate baggage claim. Today, her shoulders are up at her ears. "The Platform team is threatening to pull dev resources from our project *again*," she says.

"Well, it *has* been a whole three months since last time," I say. As the director in the Google hoodie told me in my first year, dedicated head count is the key to getting anything built. It took months of documents and meetings to secure those five heads, and for a year now they've been engaged in the long, carefully staged process of replacing Amazon's content-management tools with one system that actually works. Except it turns out that "dedicated" really only means they're dedicated in the *exact moment* that word is used, and you'll need to fight in every moment that follows to stop them from being defunded or redirected. At least this time the dev team *told* us about potentially losing resources; last time, they kept quiet for months, assuming they'd make up the lost time in some imaginary land of wonderment, because when has that ever happened, and then of course they ended up missing a major deadline, and I looked like a fucking idiot when I had to explain to Calista that Maeve and I had trusted them to level with us if things started going sideways instead of smiling and lying.

"You know I hate escalating this to you," Maeve says now. "You know I consider escalation a sign of failure." I'm crazy about Maeve, a triathlete with a poker face and a fighting spirit. Even when she's proclaiming herself a failure in that way so many Amazon women do, there's a solidity underneath that tells me I don't have to worry about her, that she knows her value.

"Yes, I know," I say. "And you know I do *not* believe escalation to be a sign of failure. It just means you're at an impasse. What reason are they giving this time?" It's more accurate to say I don't think *other* people are failures when they escalate; the few times I've had to do it myself filled me with shame.

"They need the heads for something to do with the checkout pipeline in China."

"Oh, fuck the checkout pipeline in China," I say. I look out the side window to Mount Baker for help, to no avail. "Who do I need to talk to?" I ask, and when she says his name, I sigh.

"I know," Maeve says. "I'm so sorry. He's the worst."

"It's totally fine. Just tell me what I need to say."

11:30 a.m.: I see my desk for the first time today. Louie is looking at chicken-wire designs for the new gift registry on his desktop monitor. "Rachel was looking for you," he says of the woman on my team who runs the big shopping events like Mother's Day and Halloween. "She seemed nervous. Like, more than usual."

Just then Rachel reappears. "Hey, I really need to talk to

you," she says, and pulls up close to me in the visitor chair. "Kristi, I'm worried that Holiday is going to go *catastrophically* wrong this year."

"Oh my God, why?" I ask. "What happened?" Holiday going catastrophically wrong would be the kind of fuckup I'd have to explain directly to Jeff and I really, really don't want that.

"Oh, nothing happened," Rachel says. "It's just a fear I have."

I exhale.

"Like a vibe," she says. "There are like a hundred moving pieces and I have to control *all* of them."

"Which you've done with great success for several years in a row now," I say.

Rachel lowers her voice. "Yes, but don't you think that means my luck is due to run out?"

"I really, really do not," I say, staring directly into her eyes. "I think it means you have a ton of skill and experience that will continue to serve you well and the problem-solving ability to manage any issues that arise." I actually think any number of things could make Holiday a disaster—accidentally sending customers a blank email template, all the prominently merchandised toys going out of stock, the death of Santa. It's my second year owning Holiday shopping, and if anything I'm more scared than I was last year. But none of my nightmare scenarios are about Rachel per se, and if I share them, she'll spin out even further. The only option is to project absolute confidence and hope she catches a little of it by osmosis.

"Maybe," Rachel says.

Louie waits until she's well out of earshot before asking, "How's your polyvagal nervous system today?"

"Oh, it's *active*," I say. "Thank you for asking."

12:00 p.m.: A merchandiser from Kitchen pulls me aside after a meeting. "Can we find some time to talk this week?" she asks. "Even fifteen minutes." She's obviously been crying. Of course, I say. I've talked to a lot of crying merchandisers by now, usually women. The talk usually takes some form of "I can't anymore": the weekend work, the midnight emails, the Sunday night stomachaches, the sense that none of it adds up to much in the company's eyes. I tell them they need to make peace with the fact that they'll never *really* feel finished when they stop working for the day. That they're all doing the jobs of at least two people and it's normal to live underwater.

As with the women on my own team, I don't tell them that I feel just as crushed as they do, that I spend every Sunday feeling the first tugs of the tsunami. And yet it has never occurred to me that I'm lying to everyone. I want to help, and somewhere in my subconscious I think the way to help is to be a beacon of calm and encouragement, and I become that without stopping to question why, or if I might be making things worse by pretending any of this is sustainable.

And even though I live underwater too, my timelines are weeks or even months long, and I have a team of eight. "You're not a *monkey* like we are," a merchandiser once said, in response to my "make peace with it" spiel. That's what they call themselves, monkeys, and I hate it but I get it. My job is to turn the monkeys back into people, and for all the movement in the right direction, so far I've only managed to give them an incrementally better monkey life. At least until 4:00 p.m. today, when I can finally make real change happen. Globally.

1:00 p.m.: A twenty-minute coffee walk with Marnie, who is still slogging it out on Chuck's team. "I'm starting to think Andy might *like* me," she says as we wait in line at Starbucks.

"Oh, you think? I told you this a *year* ago," I say, and ask if she might like him back.

"I think so. Except am I *allowed* to?" she says. "He's been collating his WBR printouts ten feet away from me for five years. We might legally be siblings by now."

"You were both on my hiring loop," I say. "So if you fall in love and get married, does that make you, like, my Amazon parents?"

"Ew, creepy."

"I didn't say it wasn't," I say.

1:20 p.m.: From the shuttle, I see a man on Jackson Street grab his crotch at a passing woman and wonder for the hundredth time how it is that not one of the crying merchandisers has ever talked to me about sexual harassment. Surely it's happening *somewhere* in a company this size, right? Journalists have begun reporting on Silicon Valley's libertine culture, with the coed hot tubs and parties with paid models in attendance. By comparison, Amazon is like a meeting of the Presbyterian budgeting committee. "I had two office affairs at Expedia just because I was bored and had free time," an Amazon friend once said, trying to explain our weirdly asexual culture. "Here I literally forget that men have parts, and they must pick up on that vibe."

"It's probably harder to harass women when you're in meetings nine hours every day," speculated another.

Marnie put it simplest and best: "I think the constant fear makes them forget sex exists."

1:30 p.m.: I'm at PacMed, our decommissioned-hospital headquarters, to lead the interview debrief for a merchandising role. Everyone agrees we should make an offer except for Mike, the hiring manager's boss. "I don't want any more merchandisers with writing and marketing backgrounds," he says, and turns to the recruiter. "We need to be hiring people with degrees in the hard sciences. Physics, geology."

"To sell housewares?" I ask. "Why?"

"Because this job isn't about housewares. It's about hard data."

"Point taken, but it's going to be hard to sell physicists and geologists on this role," says the recruiter.

"You explain it as a stepping-stone to better jobs at Amazon," Mike says. "Merchandising should always be a stepping-stone, not a career role." The hiring manager, an eight-year merchandiser, looks down at the table.

"This person also needs to be able to write," I note.

"Any college graduate can write," he says.

"Not marketing copy. Not for tens of millions of people to read."

"That can at least be taught," Mike says. "Unlike an analytical mindset."

"Data analysis can absolutely be taught," I say, and we go back and forth like that until Mike asks the hiring manager if she feels strongly enough about the candidate to fight for her.

"Come on," he says. "Push back on me. Convince me she's the right fit."

The hiring manager sighs. "She doesn't have the quant background you're looking for. I think she's a very strong candidate, but I can't make her into the person you have in mind."

"I'm not trying to steamroll you," Mike says. "If you feel passionately that she's a great hire, you should fight me over this."

"I know that," she says. "But I'm choosing not to."

Afterward Mike finds me in the cafeteria, eating yogurt with a fork.* "I think I came on too strong back there," he says.

Oh, you think? I want to reply. Instead I say, "It's just that you're looking for the Purple Panda. Everyone is. You want great creatives who also have MBAs and world-class quantitative skills, and you want to hire them to do mostly low-level grunt work. These people do not exist."

"I mean, that's fair," he says. "But it doesn't change the need."

"I know," I say. "I get it. I have a plan. We're reviewing it with Mitch later today."

Honestly, my big fancy plan boils down to *stop looking for the Purple Panda*. Hire quants to make the business decisions, and creatives to sell those decisions to customers. Share head count across teams if you don't want to pay for a writer all by yourself. Use contractors. Just de-Frankenstein the role. I've done time studies, analyzed masses of campaign data, and pored over performance scores and attrition stats to try to make the job work as is, to no avail. Even then, Calista had

---

* I fantasize about an Amazon multi-tool: emergency utensils, electric tape for frayed power cords, under-eye concealer, acronym cheat sheet, styptic for torn cuticles, and a small vial for whatever pills get you through the day.

to read me the riot act over my fifth lousy draft before I could bring myself to lay it out plainly.

"Kristi, just *say* it," she said. "You know what needs to happen. You don't need math. Take a commonsense stand."

I was too embarrassed to tell her, but that was the first time in my Amazon career that anyone had ever told me to just trust my common sense. I hadn't quite known it was allowed.

2:30 p.m.: On the shuttle back to Columbia Center, I read an email from our decorator about light fixtures. Marnie suggested the decorator when I confessed that John and I had been deadlocked on a coffee table for six months and couldn't even begin to face replacing the mid-1990s chandelier over our dining-room table. It kind of feels as if I've hired someone to be an old-school housewife for me, part of a combo pack with the wardrobe stylist and trainer and house cleaner I've also acquired in the past year. Maybe outsourcing all this stuff isn't so different from breaking up the merch job. Maybe expecting myself to work here and look presentable *and* light my own home is just too much, and it takes professional sister-wives to make the center hold.

3:30 p.m.: T minus thirty minutes to Mitch. In the sixth-floor kitchen, I see a VP and senior manager from the Books team looking at color printouts of something. Actually, they *used* to be on the Books team; I heard they're working on something mysterious and Books adjacent now. "Well, hey, let's ask Kristi," says the VP, an affable man named Ron who came to Amazon right out of school. "Blue or red?"

Lorna, the senior manager, turns the printouts so I can see

them across the counter. They're covers for what looks like an Arthurian fantasy novel, with gold filigree and a tapestry illustration of a man and woman on horseback. "Do you have a specific goal? Or are you just asking which one I *like* more?" I ask, thoroughly trained by now to quantify my response to even a question like "blue or red?"

"Just, what strikes you about each one?" Lorna says. I know Lorna a bit from group happy hours, where she never seems exactly pleased to see me and reacts to anything I say with poker-faced silence. At first I wondered what I could possibly have done to earn the hostility, but then I started to notice that she was like that with others too, and that it wasn't hostility, but more like a mix of shyness and a complete disinterest in charming people. As if the drive to ingratiate that I've leaned on my whole career had somehow just skipped over her. Since then, I've been fascinated by and envious of her sangfroid. But it's still unnerving to have her focus turned on me.

"Let's see," I say, looking from blue to red and back again. Quick, what are some emotion words? "The red cover makes me expect more action, maybe? A faster pace? Whereas the blue is . . . stately. The blue says there's, like, more feeling and possibly romance inside." I tap the tapestry horse, who looks hand sewn and imprecise. "I know blue is a masculine color, but the needlework makes it read feminine here." As the words come out, I realize I mean them, and it feels like speaking a language I thought I'd long forgotten. "What *is* this, by the way? If you can tell me."

"Amazon is going to publish this book," Lorna says.

"It's all happening!" adds Ron. Then their meeting room opens up, and before I can ask anything else, they're gone.

————

4:00 p.m.: Calista gives me a reassuring wink as Mitch enters the room. "Hi, guys!" he says, all smiles. A copy of the document is already at his usual place. I say my line: "Shall we read?" "Absolutely!" Oh, this is exciting now that it's finally happening.

When we presented this plan to the North American execs, it took them about twenty-five minutes to read through the doc and make notes. Mitch barely picks up his pen and is done in less than ten. When he finishes, he pushes his chair back from the table a couple of inches. "Looks like we're ready to discuss!" I say, and he nods. "Any comments on the overall document?"

"Yes. It's stupid," he says.

I was prepared for a range of reactions, but not this. A cube of ice blooms in my chest. "Oh," I say. "Okay. Can you say more about your concerns?"

"I just told you my concern. My concern is the stupidity of the entire proposal."

"No, I understand," I say. "It's just that Wilke and his VPs are overall very supportive of it, so understanding where it falls flat for you would be really—"

"Then they didn't read it," he says. "If they liked it, they didn't read it."

"Mitch, they read the doc," Calista breaks in.

"No they didn't," he says. "They just pretended to, or they would have called it stupid."

"With all due respect, that's not true," Calista says. "They read it and we had a detailed discussion." Normally, I'd be concerned about her speaking up for me this early in a meeting. I should be able to manage these conversations on my own, even hard ones. But this isn't a normal discussion. Something is dangerously wrong.

Mitch ignores her and turns back to me. "How many merchandisers do I need in each international territory to be a fifty-billion-dollar business?" he asks me. "That's what your job is. To give me one set of numbers. Not this garbage about *oh, let's hire good writers.*"

My jaw is wobbling so hard it must be visible, and I just hope I don't sound as if I were talking through a box fan. "I hear you," I say. "So that I can meet your expectations, could you talk more specifically about—"

"How much more specific can I be? One set of numbers. How many merchandisers do I need in each territory? I'm asking you for this specific information right now." I'm now doing facial isometrics, trying to retract my eyeballs far enough into their sockets to keep the tears from being bumped off the ledge onto my face. Forget everything I thought I'd learned about concentration doing twists and unsupported headstands. *This* is the yoga. I am spoon bending, becoming the mountain, moving the river.

"I don't have that number offhand," I say. "But I will get—"

"Because you're stupid."

"*Mitch,*" Calista says. She looks ashen in a way I've never seen her, and it comforts me a little to know that she's in shock too. I can't tilt my head to look at the document without getting tears on my face, and it's no longer safe for me to even attempt to speak. I know some men are spooked by tears and back down, but Mitch might tear my throat out. And anyway, my lungs feel flat and hard as PVC. I let Calista carry it from here, and though she tries to salvage the discussion by asking him what he *does* want out of the merch role, and he gives her a scrap or two, I can't really hear it. When I was in elementary school and my father thought I was acting up, his standard

MO was to ask, "Who the hell do you think you are? Who?" over and over, waiting for a real answer while I, a first grader, stood frozen by the enormity of the question. When I steal glances at Mitch's face now, I also see my father's face, and my body has gone cold and rigid in that old familiar way.

Eventually it does end. "Thanks, guys!" he says jauntily as he leaves the room.

5:00 p.m.: I'm bent over double in the corner restroom stall. Women shuffle in and out to pee or touch up their faces before heading to the bus or happy hour, but I'm not worried they'll hear me crying, because I'm not making any noise, just sort of sweating tears. It feels like molting, like weight loss. It's the flow state we all dream of. I'm still holding my copy of the proposal, and when I unfold it, I see that the notes I took are just isolated words like "bad" and "no" and "bad" and "help."

6:00 p.m.: I run into Calista in the lobby, where she takes one look at my face and sweeps me into a hug. "Hey. We'll figure out where to go from here," she says.

"I know," I say as we get in the elevator to the garage.

"I partially blame myself for how it went. I clearly misread him on this topic."

"It was so surprising," I say. I should tell her I'm talking from some place so far away that nothing I say has meaning, but it's too hard to explain.

"I know this is very small comfort," she says as the door opens on her floor, "but he wouldn't have talked to you like that if he didn't think you could take it. He treated you like the leader you are."

"True," I say. As soon as the door closes, without a second

to think about it I bite the skin on the side of my index finger hard enough to make a weeklong bruise, and then I get into my car and reach under my pencil skirt and scratch my thigh methodically—one, two, three times, until a little blood comes out. Now I can breathe. Now I'm okay to drive home.

16

INFERIOR ALIEN BRAIN

Because Mitch gets to throw toddler fits while I'm not allowed to show emotion at all, I am angry but I think it's shame. Every morning I feel a little sick when I get on the elevator, as though I ate just a bite of something rotten, so I am angry but I think it's IBS. I have to put my worst employee in the bottom 10 percent to make the curve, even though she's still pretty good, so I am angry but I think it's softness. My best employee is a quivering wreck and my praise goes right through her, her eyes darting in mistrust until I'm half convinced I *am* lying to her, and I am angry but I think it's lack of compassion. I'm about to join the demographic known as "over forty," and I am angry but I think it's body dysmorphia. All the money is starting to seem normal and not like winning a prize every day, and I am angry but I think it's ingratitude. John gripes that it's distracting to have cleaners in the house and I read it as him saying I should be doing the cleaning myself, and my office is noisy and crowded all day long and John works in an empty house for all but the six hours a month our cleaners visit, so I am angry but I think it's lack of focus. Whole Foods has just four lanes open at rush hour, and the lines back up into the aisles, and I am angry but I think it's failure to be in the moment. We're losing the engineers again and I don't even really know why, and I am angry but I think it's stupidity. I used to like sex but now after a day at Amazon it feels like under-stimulating activity, like a word search or a local newscast I once saw in Vermont, and I don't know how to talk about it so am resigned to having boring sex for the rest of my life, which people say is normal anyway *after forty*, and I am angry but I think it's hormones. I think it's going to be one conversation and then the men make it a different one, and I am angry but I think it's lack of foresight. When my father asks how work is and I say, "Honestly, it's really stressful," all he ever says in response is, "Well, Jeff Bezos is a smart guy," and I am angry but I think it's not enough therapy. When my mother asks and I say, "I'm not sure I can make it much longer," and all she ever says in response is, "But how will you earn a living if you leave," I am angry but I think it's not enough therapy for *her*. Maybe I *am* stupid, just a little, but just a little is way too much, so I am angry but I think it's shame. Mitch hasn't apologized, and I am angry but I think it's entitlement. Mitch probably doesn't even remember, so I am angry but I think it's mediocrity. I hold my face still as though it were propped up with toothpicks, and I am angry but I think it's poise. All the books for women say not to smile or nod too much, so when I feel like smiling or nodding, I have to stop and think through the ramifications for my career, so I am angry but I think it's denial. One night John asks what I think about a local ballot referendum, and instead of just telling him, I find myself composing a paragraph free from ambiguity or feeling words or rhetorical gaps he could nail me on, and I realize I do it all the time now, translate myself into Amazon-speak even when

I'm the only one listening, and I am angry and sad and maybe scared, but I think it's just assimilation. Because I know that Amazon is the god to be pleased, and Amazon is men, and thus all men are Amazon, I am angry but I think it's just my brain, my inferior alien brain.

17

GINZA IS SILENT

I know after the Mitch debacle that I'll be leaving his organization, not because I think he'll push me out—he probably forgets I exist within days—but because a tiny spark inside says anyone who talks to me like that doesn't deserve me on his team. Plus, while my role still offers "room to grow," Mitch killed the global-change part, and the prospect of sticking around to run Dads & Grads sales and A/B test headlines is less than thrilling. The spark scares me a bit, because expecting humane behavior isn't exactly the Amazon way. Maybe I'm acting like a spoiled brat, I worry.* But the spark is insistent, and so I heed it. Within a few weeks of my decision to leave, I see an email from Lorna of the Book Covers on the women@ alias, asking for referrals for a marketing role in her mysterious new venture.† I'm still pretty sure she doesn't like me, but my curiosity wins out, and just days later I shuttle from Columbia Center to Amazon's nascent new campus a few miles away to meet with her. For decades, the neighborhood at the end of Lake Union has been populated mostly by

---

* I know. But I really did worry.
† Directly recruiting via the aliases is frowned on, so hiring managers ask for "referrals," knowing people will refer themselves.

warehouses and loading docks, but now the first four or five mid-rise Amazon buildings are up and connected by courtyards and sidewalks. There's retail space on the ground floor of each one, most of it still empty, and standard amenities like benches and bike racks that feel lavish by Amazon standards. The building lobbies are airy and fitted out with the kind of furniture a real, grown-up company would have, and some sort of algorithmic gizmo by the elevators tells you which one to get on to arrive at your floor fastest. Upstairs, the actual work spaces still suck, but informal meeting spaces are placed here and there, along with tiny conference rooms we can use for interviews.*

A handpicked committee (including Calista) has come up with a name for each building that ties in to Amazon's history. Jeff sits in Day One, reflecting his adage that "It's always Day One at Amazon." Nearby is Rufus, named after the corgi whose paw pushed the button when the website launched in 1994. The building where I meet Lorna is called Fiona, for reasons I don't yet know. Only people who work in Fiona are allowed on the upper floors, so Lorna and I meet in the coffee shop off the lobby.

"We are starting a publishing company," Lorna reveals, which confuses me because Kindle Direct Publishing already exists. "KDP is self-publishing," she clarifies. "This is more like the traditional New York model, where we pick and choose what to publish and give the books professional editing and cover design and all that stuff KDP authors do for themselves." What differentiates Amazon Publishing from the

---

* Though for some reason many are furnished with Adirondack chairs that turn an interview into an awkward *lounging* situation for candidate and interviewer alike.

New York model, she says, is that APub can use all the data garnered from all those self-published books as a slush pile—finding the best ones, giving them a professional polish, and republishing them with the full power of Amazon's marketing might. "Also, a lot of authors have had bad experiences with traditional publishing," she says. "Unless you're Stephen King or James Patterson, you get lost in the shuffle. We want to treat authors like a new kind of customer, and gauge our success by their happiness."

I immediately love all of this, especially the Amazon spin of finding new books from inside our own house. "But to be completely up front, I don't know much about publishing," I tell Lorna. "I mean, I read constantly and I used to be a writer, but that's as far as it goes."

"I'm not concerned about that," Lorna says. "You know how Amazon works and how to get things done here. The specific subject matter can be learned." I find her nonchalance surprising at first, but then it starts to make sense. After all, I came to Amazon not knowing how to write software requirements, throw people off a lifeboat, stand in the path of a Beijing taxi to make it stop for me, or write in the voice of Jeff Bezos. Surely I can figure publishing out, too. Maybe publishing will be the place where I really find my feet and lose my fear. And while such a context shift might seem random, at Amazon it's pretty normal. For every person I know who has pursued one type of job on a vertical path through the ranks, there's another who's hopped more widely, from Retail to HR to Community back to Retail. Amazon has big plans, after all, and, to Lorna's point, needs people who know how to do things at Amazon. So if you want to carve out multiple separate careers here, no one's going to stop you.

Marnie and Andy come over for dinner that Friday, and I talk to them and John about it while I stir the risotto. Well, first I bitch about how much nicer the new campus is than Columbia Center. "The lobby furniture isn't torn," I said. "There's a cafeteria with a salad bar with *farro*. I almost died." By tech standards it's still the land of austerity: no employee gym, no free snacks, no loaner bikes. In such a landscape, access to whole grains represents a big step forward. "Here's the question," I continue. "Am I crazy to take a job in a field I know fuck all about?"

"Why not?" Marnie says. "It's not like I knew anything about video games when I started in my role." She and Andy recently left Chuck's team to become the category managers for Video Games and Small Appliances, respectively. "And it's been fine. Retail is retail."

"As you can see, Marnie has a real passion for the space," Andy says. I can't tell if the two of them are here together or *together* and it's making me crazy. They've certainly been hanging out a lot lately. "Andy came by and we went for a bike ride as friends," Marnie will say, or "Andy and I went to a movie as friends." I've asked her if this involves some special paperwork, or wearing paired shirts that read "FRIE" and "NDS." "No, it just means we're both nervous all the time and waiting for the other one to do something."

"I have a passion for finally getting promoted," she says now. "It's been seven years." Leading a retail category is the surest path anyone knows to getting the nod. "John, how is *your* work going?"

"Not bad," John says. "Things are steady. Growing a bit."

"He's giving a talk at the Apple store in Ginza next week," I say. It's starting to bug me how much John downplays his career. "I'm a coder," he says when someone asks what he does for a living, as if he were a junior web dev instead of the founder of a rapidly growing start-up. Maybe I'm being sucked into power-couple fantasies, or maybe there's just something about his refusal to cop to being successful that makes me feel alone in this new life. Maybe it's the innate male confidence that eats at me. He doesn't need to puff himself up, because no one's invested in tearing him down. Whatever the reason, I wish he'd knock it off.

"For a few friends," he says, shrugging.

"I'm really just piggybacking on his trip," I say, referring to the annual visit to Amazon's Tokyo offices I've arranged for the same week. I may be thinking of jumping ship, but that doesn't mean I can coast in the meantime, especially not in my weakened state.

At least I know *how* to do Tokyo this time around; one upside to my string of world tours is that now I know the little things no one tells you, like where the U.S.-friendly ATMs are in Tokyo (7-Eleven) and which clear, colorless liquids in the office vending machine are actually water versus a ricey-tasting impostor (the two on the far right) and how to avoid packed subway cars (you cannot; you can only evolve to be at peace with bodies pressed into every inch of your own). But I missed the fact that Tokyo hits 100 percent humidity in August. In Seattle, summer temps above eighty make the local news, and our clothes start coming off. But on the streets of Shibuya people are still in formal work wear, some with jackets neatly folded over their arms in deference to the staggering swampiness. Midway through our week there, I leave the office at six after eleven half-hour meetings in a row and head back to the Cerulean Tower, stopping in the train station to pick up the green-tea Kit Kats my team loves and, on impulse, a notebook with the words "ROCK CHEER" in bubble letters over a photo of young Prince looking worryingly glum. John's been in Shinjuku all afternoon, meeting with the local reseller of his company's software. I spot him by the lobby umbrella stands, looking dazed and soaked.

"Prince looks bummed," is all he says in greeting. We're right under an air-conditioning vent and in silent agreement we just stand there watching each other deliquesce.

A smiling staff member approaches and sets a small bench beside me. "Oh. Domo arigato!" I say, and drop my bag onto it. "It's a purse bench," I explain to John. "What? It's a thing they do here. It's normal."

"*Seems* normal," John says, a single sweat bead dropping off his earlobe. "Let's go upstairs and lie on the vents until dinner."

This round of country visits *should* feel like a victory lap. The content system we've been fighting for three years to keep on track is finally launched, and the merchandisers are pretty happy, by disgruntled merchandiser standards. We've cut the time it takes to make a new marketing campaign by almost 40 percent. But I don't feel victorious. Yes, I've taken a terrible situation and made it better. The software is no longer actively hostile. The merchandisers have access to critical metrics for the first time. We've even gotten some of the co-op kings to change how *they* work.

But the job still sucks. And though the North American VPs reacted enthusiastically to my proposal to de-Frankenstein it, when push came to shove, no one wanted to spend the money, and I have no authority to make them do it. I've elevated merchandising to less bothersome background noise, and I have enough ideas to keep edging it forward indefinitely. But none of it's going to add up to a story that will get me promoted, or even necessarily thanked. Granted, that's the Amazon way: promotions, most notoriously the one I'm in line for, are scarce and mysteriously granted, and still having a job counts as thanks.

Not getting promoted doesn't make me weird.

But it does make me *not me*. I am a promotion getter, goddamn it. I've built my entire life around this central fact. I just didn't know how *fuzzy* the whole notion was going to be here. In year one, Chuck told me I was right on track. In year two, Calista said my performance was there but the job itself needed broader scope. By year three, the scope was there but I hadn't quite gotten my arms around it. Now, post-Mitch, we're not talking about it at all. Calista did her best to dust me off and keep me moving forward, but I can tell she's cooled a little on me too, and I can't blame her, what with my signature project going up in smoke. I haven't yet told her about my meeting with Lorna, but I'll have to as soon as I return. Lorna's invited me to formally apply for the marketing role, and when I do that, Calista will get an automatic notification, which is not the way I want her to find out. She deserves a real conversation, though I suspect it will sting when she doesn't beg me to stay.*

When we arrive in Ginza half an hour before start time, the Apple store auditorium is already half-full. "Huh," John says.

"What happened to a talk 'for a few friends'?" I tease,

---

* She doesn't, and it does.

bumping my hip against his. For all he's downplayed this event, I half expected his speech to be delivered guerrilla-style to six people by the wall of chargers and covers.

"What did Shin do to get all these people here?" he says. Shin, his Japanese reseller and also John's translator tonight, spots us and waves from the stage.

"Go find out," I say. "I'll find you something to drink up there."

Ginza's big shopping street closes to car traffic on weekend afternoons. It's nearly 6:00 p.m., and most of the pedestrians are gone now, too. I didn't really take it in during our walk from the subway to Apple, but now the silence and stillness descend on me. I head for a food hall across the street, but midway I just stop and stand alone on the center line of one of the most expensive and famous streets on earth. It's the closest I'll ever get to being Tom Cruise in *Vanilla Sky*. But the moment has its own singularity, too, as though I've frozen time and space.

Dorothy, we are not in Michigan anymore, I think. I might have learned to navigate these far-flung cities, but the unlikeliness of being in them at all can still bring a lump of gratitude to my throat. Amazon shoved me into the wide world, and now I know I can stand on my feet in it.

The Apple auditorium fills up, and though the audience receives John's talk in unnerving silence, at the reception afterward there's a line out the door to meet him and give him small cloth-wrapped gifts and invite him to speak in Hokkaido and Kyoto. I hover by the sides of the room with my harsh red wine and grab Shin when she comes my way. "Is this normal?" I ask her. "All these people?"

"No," she says. "John is famous." The man next to her says

something in Japanese and Shin laughs. "Kojii says John is the Paul McCartney of calendar software."

"Does he *know* he's famous?" I ask. Across the room, John is heads down with three guys showing him something on a legal pad.

Shin shrugs. "Now he does, I think." As she heads to the restroom, my phone pings with texts from Marnie:

> We kissed!!!!
> It was good
> We've agreed to keep doing it

Two hours later, I return from the subway station restroom to find John chatting in Spanish with a man and woman holding a tourist map. "Toma el metro a Yotsuya," he says, pointing to a spot near the middle, "y sale al norte. Uh, creo que sí."

"Gracias! Thank you!" the couple say, and head for one of the exits. The man glances back to confirm it's the right one, and John nods vigorously and waves. "Obama!" the man says in farewell with a thumbs-up.

"Obama!" we respond in unison.

"Hey, babe," John says. "I'm hungry. Do you want to get some room service back at the hotel?"

"Sure, but first can we back up just thirty seconds or so to the part where you were giving random people Tokyo transit instructions in Spanish?" I ask.

"They're here on vacation from Mexico," John says. "They were in Seoul last week. It sounds cool, we should go." I just keep looking at him. "All my old Spanish just kind of came back out of nowhere," he says.

"Who *are* you?" I say as we board our train. "Did you realize you were sort of . . . big in Japan?"

"Not really," John says. We sink onto a bench at the end of the car.

"People came from all over the country," I say.

"It's weird, right?" John says. We ride in silence through two stops. "It makes the future feel bigger somehow," he says. "Not that it felt small before. It's just—you don't always know when things are changing."

"Yeah," I say, taking his hand. I will go home to Seattle and get that job with Lorna, I think. I'll jump into one more unknown space and figure it out, because I know I can, and because I never want to feel stuck again as I did at AMG, as I did in Ann Arbor. I want the world to stay wide, and if that means reinventing myself again, sign me up. "How confident do you feel about the directions you gave those tourists, by the way?"

"Hopeful?" John says. "I feel hopeful about the directions."

PART III

DROWNED

2011–2013

18

EVENTS IN THE HISTORY OF FEMALE EMPLOYMENT

2011: As the new campus expands, stands of umbrellas—
Amazon orange, of course—appear in building lobbies. I assume they're for visitors only until I see employees taking and
returning them and no one telling them to stop, and then
the idea that someone somewhere at Amazon spent company
money to help me stay dry in the rain comes very close to
making me cry.

2011: The team is managing an exploding volume of author
contact information via Post-it notes, private mnemonics, and
phone numbers scrawled on the backs of their hands. A handful of Salesforce licenses would actually be life changing, we
realize, but the dev team balks: *We wouldn't be able to modify
the code to add new features.* That's okay, we say, Salesforce has
all we need. *But what if* someday *we need a new feature they
don't support?* Like what? *That's the point! We don't know! It
could be* anything! What we do know is we're drowning *now*,
we say, and making stupid errors. *But what if Salesforce steals
the data from us and uses it for their own benefit?* This fatal case
of Not Invented Here Syndrome goes on for weeks, until we
blink first. We'd be fine with one built internally, we say, but
the dev team balks: *Our road map is full. The idea's not a game*

changer. Coders don't get promoted for projects that simple. Two years pass and nothing changes.

2011: A Pennsylvania newspaper publishes a horrifying news story about a Lehigh Valley Amazon warehouse where temperatures soar to more than one hundred degrees in summer. So many workers suffer heat exhaustion and heatstroke that Amazon has paramedics on call. Production quotas aren't reduced in extreme heat, and employees too blurry-eyed to see straight have been fired for failing to meet theirs. The people quoted in the story are mostly veteran warehouse workers who know what's par for the course. Amazon is worse than anywhere else they've worked, they say. At other warehouses, the loading dock doors are kept open to provide a cross breeze, but Amazon keeps them closed on the assumption that it prevents employee theft.

I read this story on the shuttle, and my first thought is, *Oh yeah, we have warehouses.** My second thought is, *Yes, I can believe all this happened.* Amazon has never shut *me* inside an oven, but I'm familiar with its refusal to adjust productivity requirements in the face of human limitations. In later years, especially after I've left, there will be more reporting, so much more, about delivery drivers peeing in water bottles because they don't get bathroom breaks, about high injury rates and workers being fired by algorithm. Abuse of warehouse staff and drivers will become *the* Amazon story in the public eye. Some corporate employees will take matters into their own hands and start communicating directly with warehouse staff

---

* I know, I know. But that's how walled off my career has been from the part of Amazon that packs and mails stuff to people's houses.

about resistance and revolt. But here in 2011, I think, *This is indefensible*, and then I get off the shuttle and get sucked back into my own productivity and anxiety vortex and the warehouses vanish from my mind for another few years.

2012: It's an election year, so time for a new round of "Women: Are They People, or Just Host Bodies?" This year, we are blessed with the bonus topic of what constitutes "legitimate rape," as a congressman from Missouri has assured us that the bodies of legitimately raped women will automatically prevent a fertilized egg from implanting. Elsewhere, Rush Limbaugh calls the law student and contraception activist Sandra Fluke a slut who has to take lots and lots of birth control pills because everyone knows the pill is something you pop each time you fuck, sort of like taking Lactaid before an ice-cream social. I had no idea at eighteen that my basic bodily autonomy would still be in jeopardy at forty-two. No one tells you it will never, ever stop.

2013: At performance review time, I notice that a man who works for me and is one level down in the organization makes forty thousand dollars a year more than I do. My thoroughly internalized shame almost talks me out of saying something. *It's not like you're starving*, I tell myself, as though that were the bar for dissatisfaction with pay.

I ask my HR rep if she knows what's up. "There are just so many factors that go into compensation," she says. "It's hard to say." She suggests I contact the comp team directly. "This is a really busy time of year for them, though." I wait until the review cycle wraps up and then I email them but I never get a response. The man is a poor fit for his job and impervious to my coaching and every time I see him I think about those forty thousand dollars.

2013: In a Payscale report ranking top tech companies on various attributes, Amazon falls near the bottom for median tenure (one year), pay, job satisfaction, and percentage of female employees (26 percent). But for "high work stress," we're outranked only by Tesla and SpaceX. So there's that. Internally, only the tenure data draws much attention; people point out that we're growing and hiring too fast for it to serve as a trustworthy attrition metric, which is true. Still, it feels as if they doth protest too much.

2013: Dave Eggers's *The Circle* is published. It's a novel about a tech company that coddles its employees until they are hopelessly enmeshed with their cultlike employer. Reviewers describe it as chilling and dystopian.

"No good?" John asks when I set it aside after a hundred pages.

"It's good," I say. "I'm just too jealous of the employees for having parties and nap rooms."

2013: Sheryl Sandberg's *Lean In* is published, and I skim it in an afternoon. "She wrote this whole book, when she could have just bought a Molotov cocktail for every woman in America," I tell John. "I'll never understand that choice."

2014: Speaking at a conference for women in tech, the CEO of Microsoft tells women that rather than ask for pay raises, they should simply trust the system. It's good karma, he says.

————

2014: Amazon and the publishing conglomerate Hachette get into a fight over who gets to set prices for Kindle books. It's hardly the first time Amazon has had a dispute with a publisher, but this time Amazon takes Hachette authors as hostages,* making their books difficult or even impossible to buy on the site. J. K. Rowling's new Robert Galbraith mystery novel is the highest-profile casualty; it isn't buyable on Amazon, which my brother-in-law's bookstore reacts to by hand delivering it to local customers on the morning of its release. Many Hachette authors are caught in the cross fire, along with their readers. The whole mess drags on for months and is portrayed in the media as a David-versus-Goliath battle. Hachette, a multinational behemoth, is no David, but for the second time in three years I find myself thinking, *This is indefensible.*

2015: Male Amazonians in Seattle file multiple hostile-environment claims with the State of Washington, alleging that the number of men's bathroom stalls is grossly inadequate for the size of the male population. (They're not wrong.) In California, the head of Amazon Studios attends an industry event where he tells a female television producer that she will love his dick, even though she didn't ask. For good measure, he also shouts "ANAL SEX" into her ear several times. The producer reports the harassment to Amazon, which promises to conduct an investigation. Like the vast majority of Amazonians, I have no idea any of this is happening. The warehouses aren't all that's walled off from us.

* Amazon would probably say Hachette took its own authors hostage. I disagree.

19

AMAZON SWALLOWS

On a warm night in May 2011, I'm drinking Sauvignon Blanc (my least favorite white wine, but I'm getting less choosy by the year, maybe even the month) on the roof deck of a hotel in Hell's Kitchen. "New York really *is* beautiful at night," I say to Vance, Amazon Publishing's most senior acquisitions editor. Vance is a fifteen-year Amazon vet, a former book buyer legendary for both his taste and his fearsome wit, and I'm nervous to be standing next to him. He's barely acknowledged me since I joined the team three weeks ago, and though I know that's just his way, I'm desperate for him to like me. But I know showing it would be the kiss of death.

"Well, that's Hoboken," Vance says of our view across the river. "But point taken." He looks back toward the bar, where it's still mostly APub people and Kindle execs milling around wondering if anyone who RSVP'd yes to our party is really going to show up. "I can't believe I'm missing *Clybourne Park* for this." Vance is a self-described theater queen, the closest thing I've met at Amazon to the older gay guys who used to smuggle my teenage self into over-twenty-one clubs, and he crams at least three shows into this annual trip to BookExpo, a giant trade show for the publishing industry. "Is *anyone* actually going to cross enemy lines?" On cue, the elevator opens and spills out a knot of women in wrap dresses and men in sport coats. Their doppelgängers arrive in subsequent loads, and within minutes the room is half-full of journalists and publicists and literary agents.

"Time to go make friends, I guess," I say, putting my empty glass on a passing waiter's tray.

Vance pats his head. "Just making sure I remembered to retract my horns," he says, and we wade into the crowd to act like people not bent on burning all of literature to the ground.

"Ignore the noise." That's what our VP, Ron, keeps telling us. Keep our heads down, do the work, pay no attention to what They are saying. But it's not as easy as it used to be. My job is no longer as inward facing, for one thing, so I'm automatically exposed to more of the noise than I used to be. Also, a lot of that noise is aimed directly at APub. Bloomberg runs a cover story about us illustrated with a book in flames. A publishing insider is quoted (anonymously) in *The New Yorker* likening our staff to Vichy collaborators. A guy I slept with a few times in college who now lives off the grid and sells weed messages me on Facebook to say he doesn't begrudge me my place of employment because "we all must keep a roof over our heads somehow."

My feelings are the usual tangle of guilt, defensiveness, and disbelief. I certainly get why Amazon's entry into publishing is perceived as a threat. I mean, not only do we have deep pockets; we also *own* the world's biggest bookstore. If I worked in New York publishing, I'd be antsy too. What bewilders me is the assumption that this is just step one in a malevolent plan. Their goal is to be the only publisher in the entire world, a blogger says. They want to systematically devalue literature until authors are working for free, says another. They want to control the very flow of ideas into the world.

From my desk, I can see the whiteboard we're using as a publishing calendar, and the junior staffer who spends a full week a month calculating royalties manually in Excel. There are fifteen people in the entire division. Some of us have grad degrees in literature; some are frustrated writers (or ex-writers, as I now call myself). We're all maniacal readers. And per usual, we're operating on gumption and partial information. It *feels* very much as if we were putting a show on in the barn, which I find exhilarating and fun. This is why I'm at Amazon, to do crazy things that sound impossible. So the vision of an encroaching, disciplined army doesn't square at all with what I see around me. And I don't *think* Jeff has a grand plan to control which ideas the world has access to. But honestly, how would I know if he did? Anything is possible.

Even if the team seems scrappy and humble, I know this party is still a big-swinging-dick move. Amazon's approach to trade shows is generally low profile and cheap. But this time we bought a pricey booth right at one of the entrances to the show floor, which five of us spent several sweaty hours setting up today. Also, most publishers bring just a few of their highest-profile authors to BookExpo, to sign galleys and sit on panels. But we flew in *all* of ours* and are putting them up at this hotel that's significantly nicer than where we'd be staying if they weren't here. It's all a bit nouveau riche and social-climby for my taste. But the authors seem thrilled, and the rooftop bar is probably approaching fire code limits, so what do I know.

* Granted, there are only about fifty at this point, but still.

Wretched but necessary Sauvignon in hand, I move through the crowd in the spike Manolos I wear far too seldom to handle with any grace. I'm looking for the biggest swinging dick of all: Arthur Adler, the old-school publishing titan we've just hired to run our New York office. Arthur is so much of the elbow-patches-and-martinis world that he strikes me as a weird Amazon fit. But the plan is that while Seattle focuses on the Kindle slush pile and genre fiction, Arthur's office will publish big, splashy original manuscripts, which presumably means we'll need his Rolodex and charm. The announcement of his hiring ran in the BookExpo daily newsletter this morning and spread fast, with the general online reaction being what I'd expect if Yo-Yo Ma joined AC/DC.

There he is with his martini and blue blazer, listening in apparent fascination as Nate, the VP of Kindle, describes a recent skiing mishap in Banff. I sidle up in the way normal people do at parties and wait for a natural pause in the conversation so Nate can introduce me in the way normal people also do at parties. He glances at me, but just keeps talking and talking. I'm a little surprised because Nate, while widely feared and dreaded, has always been pretty cool to me; he's in my likable-asshole category, which in the Amazon context is a compliment because it means he at least has a personality. But tonight he ignores me long enough to start pissing me off.

I'm contemplating whether to slink away as though I've mistaken Nate and Arthur for the men I *meant* to say hi to when Arthur turns to me and introduces himself. I welcome him aboard and tell him I run Amazon Crossing,* the im-

* I didn't get the marketing job I first applied for; Lorna decided to hold out for someone who had actually marketed books before, a hard stance to

print for literature in translation, and suddenly I have his rapt attention. Oh, so *I'm* Kristi. He's been hearing all about me. Translation is what will put APub on the map, and I sound like the perfect person to lead it. I don't see how he could possibly hold these opinions yet, or even how much he could have heard about me, but that's fine. I understand that publishing is a glad-handing business, and frankly I could use some glad-handing. He's really good at it, too. For reasons I will spare you, I once spent twenty minutes in conversation with Bill Clinton's brother, Roger, and for those twenty minutes I felt like the funniest, smartest, most fascinating person on earth, and I thought that if the Clinton charisma was this overpowering via Roger, three minutes with *Bill* would probably end my life. Arthur isn't quite Roger Clinton (who is?), but he's closer than anyone else I've met. We make plans to have lunch when he's in Seattle next week, and my work here is done. "Nice to see you, Nate," I say, tapping him on the shoulder. "I'll let you two get back to it." As I walk away, I glance over my shoulder and note with satisfaction that Arthur's eyes are still on me. Whether it's for the right reasons, I can't say. But I've made an impression and I'll build from there.

I spot Lorna in a small group near the fire pit and am headed her way when a cluster of men and a few young female APub employees come rampaging out of the elevator. Though most of our authors were self-published before we came calling, we've also signed a few who either were dropped

---

argue with. But two weeks later she offered me this role instead. Did I have any experience running a translation platform? Had I ever even considered it? No and no. But it was Amazon, and I was me. So of course I took the job.

by their publishers or left because they felt neglected, and the three biggest names are leading the merry band who've just arrived. Calhoun is a performatively schlubby thriller writer who made a ton of money in self-publishing in the interval between leaving his last publisher and signing with us. Dumoni, slick and glib where Calhoun is ostentatiously downmarket, writes what Vance calls straight-guy-on-a-plane spy novels and swoops his hair back a lot. And Laird, a promising but lesser-known horror writer, hardly talks at all, just follows the other two around and giggles at everything they say.

I first noticed the three of them drinking in the lobby bar around 2:00 p.m. By three, seven other men from our list had joined them and they were audible all the way to the front desk. "Fucking *no* other publisher would do this," Calhoun was declaiming. "*No one* ever brought me to BookExpo, much less paid my fucking bar bill." The other men hung on his every word. "You know what you get out of other publishers, besides fucked in the ass? Lunch. *Maybe* you get lunch." Draft beer gave way to whiskey and tequila shots. Crossing the room, I spotted Lorna working on her laptop at the bar. "Should we be worried about the girls?" I asked her, "the girls" meaning the mostly young and junior women who work as author relations managers, or ARMs. Authors at other publishers have been known to complain that there's no one around to take their call or answer questions, so we dreamed up the ARMs as a competitive advantage—someone to help you decipher your royalty statement or remember your favorite cigars to send on publication day or just talk you down from an anxiety attack. Or socialize with you at industry events where your writerly self might feel ill at ease.

"I'm having some food sent over there to soak up the booze," Lorna said in response, not moving her eyes from the laptop screen.

"The guys are *really* drunk," I said. "And Mitzi is actually sitting on Calhoun's lap?" The other ARMs might have been relatively young and green, but they knew how to handle themselves at a work party. But Mitzi, who complains at work about her hangovers in a way that makes it clear she's proud of them, made me nervous. I certainly didn't think Mitzi was going to *set out* to fuck one of our authors, but I also wasn't sure what state she might be in if one of our authors decided to fuck her. And when I watch the three friends, I automatically cast them in the frat-party film where Calhoun is the one who fucks the passed-out girl, and Dumoni is the one who says "Hey, man, that's not cool" but doesn't do anything to stop it, and Laird is the one who watches quietly from a corner and is racked with guilt that he takes to his grave.

"I figure they'll say something if they feel uncomfortable with how the guys are acting," Lorna said, continuing to type. Lorna and I were about the same age, and at least a decade older than the author reps. *Will* they say something? I wanted to ask her. Would *you* have, at twenty-eight? But she was clearly focused on other work, and she'd been in the books business for years, and me for three weeks. Maybe the norms were different in publishing. Maybe I should enjoy it.

Nearing midnight on the rooftop, the chucklehead trio and their acolytes have reached the stage of drunkenness where drunkenness itself is the primary topic. "I am so fucked up," owlish Laird says, confirming he has the power of speech. Dumoni, clad in a black trench coat despite the late-May

warmth, comes back from the bar holding four martinis between his fingers. The whole group, Mitzi and one other
ARM still in tow, streams past Lorna.

"Rock and roll," Calhoun says to her in passing. "Best
fucking publisher ever."

I'm not going to be the Mennonite who expresses worry
again, so I don't say a word as I join Lorna and two other
women on the management team, women I've known since
my first days at Amazon. Bess, the leader of the ARMs, is
the hyper-competent, sunny southerner I hired to replace
George way back in my first role, and Sally, now the head of
Acquisitions, has had her fingerprints on almost every part
of the Books business. "I heard the band is getting back together!" people kept saying when word spread about the team
Lorna was assembling. We're all seasoned vets who are *still* in
over our heads in this new space, but it's fun and cozy to be
there together, and we're thrilled (and shocked) to be an all-
female leadership team.

"People came!" Bess says as I join the group, clinking her
glass to mine.

"They really did!" I say. "And they're being nice!"

"That part's so weird!" Sally says. Lorna shakes her head
as if she doesn't know what we're on about, but she's smiling
and I feel a tinge of what I imagine—hope—she's feeling right
now, to know that she and Ron took this from one medieval
fantasy novel to an operation that has a large swath of Manhattan completely freaked out. *We* may be just getting started,
but it's already been a long road for her.

"Has anyone checked in privately with the girls?" asks
Sally then, nodding toward the group who have drifted peril-
ously close to the pool. Mitzi and Laird are playing a shriek-

ing game of keep-away with something. "I don't want these guys treating them like concubines."

"I think it's fine," Lorna says again. "They know we're here if they need us." But I'm thinking about the porn room at AMG, and the porn rooms in Vegas, and whatever other porn or porn-adjacent rooms I've forgotten I was ever in. I didn't know *need* was possible, or at least acceptable. Why would they?

Breakfast the next morning is quiet. Lorna, Sally, and I switch between greeting the authors who've made it downstairs this early and swapping celeb sightings. They both arrived two days before me for agent meetings all over town, giving them an unfair advantage. Sally saw Jon Hamm in the East Village. "He said 'hey' and did a little wave," she says, demonstrating. "It was an epochal experience."

Lorna saw Christopher McDonald at Babbo. Christopher who? Sally asks, and Lorna and I say "Darryl from *Thelma and Louise*!" in unison.

"Oh my God, Darryl," Sally says. "Do you think Darryl remarried?"

"Yes, and *fast*," Lorna says.

"What is this unquestioning assumption that Thelma and Louise definitely died?" I say, and they both look at me with pity. "What? We don't see it! Something unexpected could happen seconds after that freeze-frame."

"Oh, honey," Sally says.

"I'm just saying we don't know for sure. Please let me have this one thing," I say.

Bess joins us with a giant take-out coffee, looking drawn. "So. It got worse last night," she says. "The guys were all starving after the party wrapped up, so a bunch of us went to that terrible diner by the Javits Center. We took up about four tables and it was just *loud* and then it got all quiet just in time for me to hear Calhoun say something to Mitzi and Jane I'm not even sure I can bring myself to repeat."

"Spill it," Lorna says.

Bess lowers her voice. "He said, 'Other publishers spit. Amazon swallows.' Right to their faces."

"What the *fuck*," says Sally. "This is not okay. We have to do something."

"I did," says Bess. "I told him right then and there I thought it was crude and ugly. He wasn't listening to me. No one was listening." Her eggs arrive and she picks up her fork and puts it back down.

"For some reason that kind of thing rolls right off my back," Lorna says. "It just doesn't bother me."

"Well, it doesn't bother me *personally* either," Bess says. "But I don't want him talking to my team that way."

"Yeah, *I* can handle it, but we're probably wide open for a hostile-environment claim," Sally chimes in.

"That's my concern," I say. "I'm sure *we've* all dealt with much worse than what he said, but legally we're vulnerable." Just three Gen X women scrambling to make it clear that *we* would never make waves over a harmless workplace cum-ingestion joke, but these kids today: they're soft; we must protect them.

"I guess I could say something," Lorna says.

"I don't think they're going to listen to a woman," I say. "We should ask Ron to talk to him."

"We could," Lorna says, but the repetition of "could" versus "should" tells me that even if Lorna declines to intervene, we're not going to go over her head and ask our VP to. We're going to do what we've always done: move body first into the world whether we like it or not and be unflappable. Look at Calhoun and his chucklehead buddies—when we must—in a way that says, *I know you know I know, and I could fuck you up, but instead I'm letting you get away with it, for reasons that seem inescapable but also make me hate myself nearly as much as I hate you.*

20

THERE ARE NO WHEELS

6:30 a.m.: Wake afraid. Make the magical green smoothie that no longer feels quite so magical now that I'm drinking at least a bottle of wine every night. "It's not even 7:00 a.m. and I've already ingested two superfoods," I brag anyway as I pass John's office, then realize he's on speakerphone and by the sound of it I've just told a bunch of Aussies about my breakfast.

8:00 a.m.: Yessssss. I-5 is backed up, a secret relief. It means more time to prepare myself for the maelstrom, not to mention to enjoy the BMW John surprised me with on my birthday last year. I've always appreciated a nice car, but I was never a *car person* until I drove this one for the first time. Maybe this is how it feels when a woman who never cared much for babies meets *her* baby and falls in love at first sight. It's just so *heavy* and solid and safe, like having a really good dad.

9:30 a.m.: APub is hiring at warp speed; my first interview of the day is my fifth of the week. The candidate's name is Caitlin—third Caitlin of the month—and from Instagram I know she's thirty and lives in Brooklyn with her husband of one year and their Boston terrier. From Sally's phone-screen

notes I know Caitlin has worked at Harlequin since right after college but wants a faster pace and a lower cost of living.*
"Can you tell me about a time you had to make a fast decision
based on only partial information?" I ask her.

"Great question," she says, then freezes. With gentle prod-
ding, she eventually comes up with an example of booking a
last-minute flight for her boss, but that was seven years ago.

"Anything more recent?" I ask, and she shakes her head
and apologizes. "That's no problem. Let's move on," I say.
Some people will cut an interview short when it's clearly not
a fit. I can't bring myself to do that, especially because she's a
solid candidate in many ways. But in my head, it's over. It's
probably Harlequin's fault, not hers, but if she can't make hard
decisions on the fly without help, she's doomed here.

10:30 a.m.: Ron's biweekly staff meeting. Lorna and her all-
female team are on one side of the table and the Bon Vivants
on the other. Bon Vivants is my private name for Arthur Adler
and the other two men who directly report to Ron. All three
of them started out in New York publishing, and they seem
to have transferred that lifestyle—long lunches, hand-wavy
goals, blazers—to Amazon, while the women run around
frantically with a checklist in one hand and a protein bar in
the other. It's not that the Bon Vivants don't do any work; it's
just unclear what that work involves.

Today we're reviewing a press release and FAQ written
by Bess. The PR/FAQ is Amazon's newest viral document

---

* It's fun to hire New Yorkers and San Franciscans because their perspective
is so fucked that they think Seattle is cheap and go around for the first year
saying things like "I'm thirty-nine and this is the first time I've lived without
roommates!" and "I can't believe my house came with a yard!"

craze, a mock press release that forces teams to imagine how they might present their project to the world *before* they dive into building it. It's really useful for identifying blind spots and weaknesses, and also really hard to write. Bon Vivant 1, who to the best of my knowledge has never even taken a stab at a PR/FAQ, is on his laptop the whole time. Bon Vivant 2 breezes in twenty minutes late, puts his feet on the table, suggests an option cited and dismissed in the document he's barely glanced at, and then says, "Bye, kids, I've got to hoof it to Beijing," and leaves. "Why tf is he going to Beijing," I text Sally. "Who tf knows," she texts back.

Arthur, Bon Vivant 3, is on speaker from New York, and his main contribution is to warn us that if we on the West Coast don't start paying bigger advances for high-profile books, we will fail as a business. This is Arthur's thing in every meeting, regardless of the agenda: that we are not spending enough money for books, that our experiment seeking out dark horses rather than household names is insane. Who knows, maybe he's right. But we've already had some mystery and romance hits by previously unknown authors, while Arthur's New York team has paid hefty advances for celebrity memoirs and a seven-hundred-page James Franco novel. Arthur had so much autonomy in his previous jobs that I think he's forgotten what it's like to have a boss or be told no, and I'm sure it's frustrating, but it's also frustrating for me that he's been here for more than six months and can't comment on any other aspect of our business but the size of the checks we write. That's not okay at Amazon, or not unless you are a Bon Vivant. It's not that the Bon Vivants are bad men. They're nice enough, or at least fun. They just live in a better world than we do.

11:30 a.m.: I stop by the kitchen to put the lunch I've been carrying around all morning in the fridge and hopefully kill whatever microbes have grown on it since I left home. Just as I don't *quite* believe that warnings about mixing alcohol with certain medications apply to me personally, I also tend to forget that my body is infectable. Lorna is there refilling her coffee cup and asks how the interviews are going. "Honestly, the candidates are starting to blur together into one promising young Brooklynite who wants to 'shake up publishing,'" I say.

"Same here," she says. "They're good. But they're getting hard to tell apart."

"Also I'm starting to resent them slightly before I've even met them?" I say.

"Me too." We discuss whether we should ask Recruiting to slow down a bit, or just keep pushing through to finish sooner. For now, we'll keep pushing.

12:00 p.m.: As of 9:00 a.m., there were two noon meetings on my calendar. Now there are four. I text two of my senior people in case they're available to cover, but they're double booked too. So I choose the meeting I know is closest to Ron's heart: brainstorming ways to use Kindle data to help authors engineer their books to be bestsellers. For instance, data aggregated from across multiple top-selling mysteries could suggest the perfect chapter length, or the ideal number of words in a sentence, or how far in the book the first murder should occur.

I think, with every bit of heart I have left, that this is the worst idea in the world. I can't imagine anything more depressing than making a bestseller by telling an author to make their first kill at 33 percent. I may be an ex-writer now, but I still remember how much satisfaction came from feeling my way into the material, slowly uncovering what it wanted to be. And if I had ideas for doing this *better*, I would say so. But my only idea is "NO, NO, NO, IT'S GROSS, STOP IT," which is going to put me on the wrong side of Ron's vision and possibly make me sound like a snob, too. So I keep my mouth shut.

1:00 p.m.: A debrief for one of last week's candidates, yet another Caitlin. I desperately want to hire *this* Caitlin, who has edited some of the top names in romance and made a few tough decisions under pressure. But the Bar Raiser, a Kindle ops manager, is very much against it. "She admitted she doesn't even know how to do a vlookup in Excel," he says. "I just don't see her succeeding at Amazon. It would be a bad move for *her* as much as for us."

"I hear you," I say. "But it doesn't actually *matter* if she can do vlookups. We need her to acquire and edit romance novels. That's it."

"It doesn't matter *now*, maybe. What happens when she wants to change roles in a few years, though?" This keeps coming up with Bar Raisers, that the people we're interviewing aren't *fungible*. It's a holdover from when we were mostly a retailer and the conventional wisdom was not to hire anyone we couldn't imagine in at least three different Amazon roles. I get why this is hard for him, but he's not going to veto my chosen Caitlin.*

* And anyway, I doubt I seemed all that fungible at first either, and now look at me.

"Here's the thing," I say. "She's probably *not* going to do anything else at Amazon. She's going to acquire and edit romance novels either for us or for another publisher, maybe for the rest of her life. That's her career path."

I swear he pales. "Can't you find an internal candidate who's a romance *fan*? Someone with a passion for the space but an analytical mind?"

"No," I say. "We need professionals, not fans. And she *has* an analytical mind. She knows where a manuscript isn't working and why. She negotiates contracts. That's all analysis. It's just not *math*."

I can tell I've almost got him. "I just want to reiterate that the vlookup thing threw me," he says. "That's basic, basic stuff." It's tempting to confess that I also don't know how to do a vlookup, but this probably isn't the moment.

2:00 p.m.: I cross the courtyard for coffee with Fritz, an editor visiting from the New York office. We've never spent one-on-one time together before, but in group interactions he generally seems disgruntled and a bit frantic. Also, the subject line of his coffee invitation read, "Chaos."

Mid-afternoon at any Amazon coffee shop is a mob scene, but I spot him right away with his bow tie and attaché case. "Hiiii! How is Seattle treating you?" I say with elevated cheer, because a certain kind of crabby guy inspires resistance in me.

"It's like being in a lovely, sleepy village that closes up by nine," he says with a half smile.

Oh, goody, he's one of those. "Spoken like a true New Yorker," I say.

"Not really," Fritz says, playing with the empty sugar

packet in front of him. "I was born in Maryland and we didn't move to New York until I was two."

"But you've lived there ever since."

"Oh yes, for thirty-five years. But only people born in New York can really call themselves New Yorkers."

"Huh," I say. "I've only lived in Seattle for six years, and I still consider myself a Seattleite at this point." Fritz shrugs as if to say, *Well*, Seattle. *Who* knows *what kind of strange customs are accepted in this diurnal Scandinavian hamlet?*

I *definitely* have more questions for him about his residency rules, but the subject of the meeting is chaos, so I figure I'd better get to it. "The wheels are falling off," he says. "I'm working on twice as many books as I managed at Crown. We still don't have a clear acquisition strategy, because Arthur can't focus for ten straight minutes. The publishing process itself is a *nightmare* of hacks and manual work. They're falling off, Kristi. The wheels are *falling off*."

Just an hour ago I had to persuade a veteran Bar Raiser to envision a changing Amazon, and now I have to break it to a newbie that some things will probably never change. "So, the thing about Amazon is that there are no wheels," I say. "They were never there. What you're experiencing is just how it is here. Absolute chaos."

"So how do you get anything *done*?"

"With great difficulty, usually." I think he's looking at me in disgust, but it's actually the unaccompanied schnauzer behind me he's squinting at. "Oh, that's just Poppyseed," I say. "Poppy for short. Her mom's over by the window." Poppy's mom catches my eye and we exchange waves. "Your new short hair is so cute!" I call. None of this seems to make Fritz feel any better.

Maybe if I could tell him Poppyseed's a native New Yorker he'd feel more at home, but I don't know where she was born.

"Things *have* to change," Fritz says.

"Then my sincere advice is to pick something that's not working and start making it change," I say. "Write a one-pager. Propose a new process."

"I don't want to be the guy who says, 'That's not my job,' but that's not my job."

"Keeping this house of chewed-on Popsicle sticks glued together is everyone's job," I say. "You'll get used to it. I mean, you'll have to." I give it three months tops before he quits.*

3:00 p.m.: As Fritz and I wait to cross Mercer on the way back to our building, he reads one of the bright yellow flyers that started popping up on neighborhood telephone poles a few weeks ago. It's a quiz to find out if you are something called an Amhole. "What *is* this?" he says. "I didn't sign up to be *hated*."

"Fritz, you're from the *book* industry," I say. "How did you not realize people hate Amazon?"

He sighs. "I guess I didn't think it would be so *personal*," he says. "Will I get used to that too?"

"Not really," I say. The light changes.

4:00 p.m.: Heading to my office for the first time today, I pass a clutch of co-workers in the hallway, apparently continuing the conversation from a meeting they just left. Cassie, the senior product manager on my team, waves and jerks her head ever so slightly to the right, where Arthur, also in town from

---

* He makes it for four.

New York this week, is giving one of the ARMs in the group a shoulder rub. I automatically check the ARM's face. It's neutral, neither traumatized nor pleased, but that doesn't tell me much.

Cassie stops by ten minutes later and closes the door. "He's giving a *lot* of unsolicited shoulder rubs this week."

I sigh. "Did he do it to you again?"

"Oh, but of course." It happened to her for the first time three months ago, and when she brought it up, I asked her if she wanted to report it. "I'm not sure what I'd be reporting," she said after a moment of thought. "It's more annoying than overtly inappropriate. I mean, it's always out in the open. I don't even think he means it in a sexual way."

My own view was as fuzzy as hers. The rubs, which he rotated among maybe half a dozen women (I was spared), weren't outright *horrifying*, but that still didn't make them okay. But whenever I thought about raising the issue with Lorna, I remembered how she shrugged off the Chuckleheads and decided maybe I was being too sensitive, especially if my own employee didn't care to press the issue.

"Did you say anything?" I ask Cassie now about the latest uninvited massage.

"Not a word. I merely removed his hands from my shoulders without even turning around to face him."

"Streamlined and elegant," I say. "I wish I could have witnessed it."

"Oh, I'll make sure to take credit for it in my performance review," she says.

5:00 p.m.: The draft offer for Caitlin-who-can't-do-vlookups arrives from Recruiting. It's solid. I'm sure she'll say yes. But the Bar Raiser's worry still nags at me. Are we giving her a job, or a chance to fail wildly? What happens when she thinks a romance manuscript has a propulsive, smoking-hot story, but Ops says we're 4 percent heavy on romances for the quarter, and Marketing thinks the big plot turn should happen at Kindle reading location 4323, not 4651? Who wins? *Productive tension*, I remind myself. Productive tension is fine. And what is a job anyway, if not a chance to ruin your life? "Looks great," I write back. "Let's go get her!"

Right before I leave for the day, my doctor sends results from my annual blood work. Everything is in the ideal range, she says. I guess I should be happy, but my first thought is that maybe those ideal ranges are not so ideal, if I fall within them. Maybe the bar for health is way too low. Or maybe my doctor's asleep at the wheel. Because *something* in me is worming itself closer to the surface, and if my doctor was looking, surely she'd see it. Surely anyone could.

21

THE AMHOLE QUIZ

Here is the self-test Fritz saw on the telephone pole:

Answer yes to one or more of the below: BOOM!
You are an Amhole.

1. Think this neighborhood started with your arrival?
No.

2. Do you walk six people wide on the sidewalk chatting about Amazon crap and not let others pass?
No? I mean, when walking on the Amazon campus with generally one Amazon co-worker, we do sometimes discuss matters related to Amazon, so I guess this is a partial yes, sorry, I will prepare a list of other topics for future walks, such as melons, the death of the electric car, what to do when Sunday nights = nausea.

3. Can you barely resist snapping your fingers at service people in the area?
So, this is embarrassing, but I can't really snap my fingers? I've tried to learn since childhood but I can manage maybe 5 percent of the time, same as with cartwheels. So no, I don't snap my fingers or do cartwheels at service people, by which I assume you

*mean waiters and waitresses, who are part of my lunchtime life
three or four times a year, tops. So: the final answer is no but due
to skill and opportunity conflicts I can only take partial credit.*

4. Do you think sexy is contrived casual attire, arrogance, and
talking/smelling like a used car salesman?
*Well, no. But I also think some sort of conscious dress style and
the gift of gab wouldn't be the* worst *thing to happen to the men
of Amazon. I mean, when I try to picture the sexy-aspiring population you are describing, my mind's eye seizes up. Amazon
is in fact the most asexual place I have ever worked, I haven't
even had a decent work crush in several years, let alone wanted
to* smell *anyone, and I have to say I miss it, I miss the sense that
giddiness is a possibility, but I also understand that whatever
blood flow would be going to the giddiness organs has been redirected to, you know, daily survival and I can't argue with that
prioritization. So to circle back, my answer is no. But I would
love to want to smell a neck.*

5. Do you not realize that you are working for an updated version of Sears and Roebuck so you should check yourself?
*I have to say that this is phrased as more of a comment than a
question. Also, are you visiting from yesteryear? Because there's
also the Kindle, there's web hosting, book publishing, and so on.
But if you are asking if I'm aware that people can pay Amazon to
send them products in the mail: yes, I realize that, and am duly
chastened, I guess.*

6. Do you believe for a second that you are not a highly ex-
pendable cog in the corporate Amazon machine?
No.

22

A GENIUS OF THE NOTHING FACE

It's midnight and I have a 6:00 a.m. flight to New York to represent APub at a benefit for literature in translation that *someone* thinks I shouldn't go to, maybe because I'm recovering from a food poisoning so severe that the bile stripped my vocal cords and is starting to take my voice. "You do not have to do this," John says.

"I *do*," I say, huddled under a blanket in the TV room. "It's not just the gala. I have meetings. I can't bail on everyone for no reason."

"No reason? You were violently ill yesterday."

"Yes, and now I'm recovering," I say, eating another saltine corner to prove how robustly that recovery is going. John just stares at me. "It would be irresponsible to cancel this late," I add, which doesn't make the stare any friendlier but also makes my inner Taurean toddler dig in deeper.

"'Responsible' would be taking care of yourself," John says.

"*Duh*," I admit. "But this is my year, John. I'm finally in the right job at the right time to get promoted and I'm not giving them *any* reason to blink. It's time to get this fucking thing done once and for all, and I'm not going to risk it because *in the past* I had a stomach flu."

"This is madness."

"Yes," I say. "You're right. It's absolute madness and I'm still doing it. I'm going."

"Fine," John says, but he's shaking his head no.

It's true. This year, 2013, is my peak point of Amazon success to date. Well, and forever, though I don't know it yet. For one thing, Amazon Crossing recently became the world's largest publisher of literature in translation. If you think that must mean we published *hundreds* of translated books, ha-ha, no. Fewer than 3 percent of books in English are translations from other languages, so we became the industry leader with a list of just twenty-nine. Naturally, people are mad about it. The blogosphere claims we machine translate the books and publish whatever the program spits out, though in reality we hire the same freelance translators other publishers do and let them do their usual thing. At a London Book Fair panel, a highly respected translator says we've been great to work with and men in the audience yell "Plant!" at her as Cassie and I watch from the back of the room, knowing any word out of our pieholes will only make things worse. I know there's no outrunning the stain, but wearing it gracefully gets harder and harder. When I meet new people who know where I work, I sometimes find myself method acting the role of a decent human being, doubling down on smiles and warmth because I assume the stain is what they see first.

But for all that, running Crossing is *fun*. Obama does a Kindle-exclusive interview that year, and on a dare from Ron we translate and publish it into eight different languages in eight different countries in one week, just to see if we can pull it off. Authors from Germany and Iceland and Spain find substantial English-language audiences for the first time in their careers. Lorna writes in my performance review she's ready to start having serious discussions about how I can get promoted.

In addition to my achievement peak, this is my peak year of Amazon happiness. It's a very Amazon happiness, tenuous and a little guilty and heavily contingent on drinking—with authors, with colleagues, with myself at night when I need to forget that in nine hours I have to get up and do it all over again. It feels weird to be happy working for a company so intensely loathed. And feeling happy also makes me worry I'm just not paying close enough attention, that I've become blind to my own inadequacies and now they'll lead to my doom. But I wasn't blind. I was great at my job, and the happiest I would ever be at Amazon. If I'd known it, maybe I would have been better prepared for all that followed.

By the time I get to the airport, my voice is shot for real. The TSA agent is not amused when I only make silent mouth shapes in response to his "Good morning." My seatmate jokes to the flight attendant that I just don't want to talk to him, which is not entirely untrue. By baggage claim I'm fully mute and opt for the long train ride into Manhattan rather than deal with the usual cabbie wanting to know why a pretty girl like me doesn't have children and if I've accepted Jesus Christ as my savior. My hotel is close to Eataly and I often get dinner to go there, but I'm a little feverish after check-in and instead I order room service by taking the elevator twenty-three floors down to the lobby, showing a menu to the concierge, and pointing at my throat and then the chicken salad. He looks bewildered. Though in his defense, *I've* never seen laryngitis quite this bad, either. Where previous bouts just made my voice creaky, this time it cuts from creaky to just *gone*, like a twisted typewriter ribbon.

I didn't know a voice could do that. But then before this week, I also didn't know you could get laryngitis from throwing up. And I didn't know Edward Albee was still alive, so hopefully my mime face doesn't look too surprised as he's introduced to me now under the *T. rex* in the American Museum of Natural History. As we shake hands, I manage to say "laryngitis" and gesture at my neck, so he knows not to wait for whatever astounding bon mot I would otherwise bestow upon him. It's a nice moment. I'm glad he's still alive, though I would not mind being dead myself.

In fifth grade, my class attended a college production of Albee's *Seascape*, in which a couple sunbathing on a beach end up in deep conversation with two human-sized lizards about, I don't know, Society or something. I pre-panicked about the lizards for weeks in advance. I knew they'd just be actors in green makeup; still, they sounded scary and I was afraid one might come into the audience and slime me. "You don't have to go," my mother said. But I did have to go. If I didn't, I knew the lizards would just keep getting scarier in my mind. So I waited anxiously in the alarmingly small theater until they finally showed up at the end of act 1 and I could see that they really were just people in green unitards.

That's the vibe I try to conjure now, wobbly and feverish in my stupid cocktail dress at the PEN gala for literature in translation. Edward Albee is just a normal guy in a suit, and so is Tony freaking Kushner next to him. There's regular gal Francine Prose taking a champagne flute from a tray, and carpool mom Toni Morrison admiring someone's earrings. I may lead the world's largest imprint for translated books, but this is their planet and *I'm* the lizard who crawled from the muck of Amazon. The upside to my bile-eaten larynx is that this way fewer people will know it.

By the time we're seated for dinner, I've rallied enough to remember that while stressful, this whole deal is also pretty cool. *I'm standing under a dinosaur's neck in a famous museum in New York City*, I think. I never even crossed the Mason-Dixon Line until after high school, and I was thirty-eight before I'd been to New York. Everything in New York feels glamorous to me, including the rattan-cane chairs around the tables, standard-issue event furniture that since childhood has signaled Maximum Fanciness in my mind. I wave across the table at Jane, top editor in Arthur's office, and at Bon Vivant 2 in his tux. Bon Vivant 2 and I knew each other a bit back in Retail, where I found his insouciance charming; he made Amazon seem like an easy, no-big-deal place to be. But this time around he seems kind of red-eyed and spackled together. Every time I run into him with his dog, he introduces her as "my longest successful relationship," which was cute the first time but now sounds robotic and sad. And I'm definitely sick of hearing him say "I haven't read the document fully, but . . ." before derailing a discussion with whatever random idea just crossed his mind. Maybe his charm has degraded, or maybe I'm just less charmable than I used to be.

Arthur and his blond-bobbed, Chanel-suited wife, Nancy, are seated on my right, and as always the sight of Arthur sparks both affection and profound fatigue. The New York office is his kingdom. Ron has told him not to meddle with the Seattle office's book acquisitions, which means he's *constantly* meddling with them. One agent in particular, a cigarette-voiced woman on whose person I once counted seven separate Versace lion heads, seems to have a merciless grip on him when it comes to bidding more, more, more for a manuscript. Unfortunately for us, she represents a number of romance authors the Seattle office is negotiating to publish. Over lunches with Arthur, she talks him up from whatever the romance editor has already offered into a ludicrous advance and extravagant marketing package, negating my editor's work. Of course Finance always says no to the overinflated terms, as Finance should, but Arthur is never the one who has to walk the offer back; instead, the editor has to make the phone call, and the Versace lady yells so loudly about our incompetence and unprofessionalism that I can hear her an aisle away. "Why can't he just *stop*?" one editor asked me, confessing that calling the lion lady gave her daylong stomachaches. "Why can't he at least call me *before* he ups the offer, so I can do my job?"

Because Arthur has spent decades doing exactly as he pleases, that's why. "I'm Arthur's manager. Ignore the noise and let me worry about him," Ron says in his cheerfully reassuring Happy Dad tone whenever anyone complains about the chaos he causes. And I believe Ron *does* worry about Arthur; it's just not clear that he's *acting* on the worry. When Arthur hijacks Ron's staff meetings with long, off-topic speakerphone monologues, Ron becomes absorbed in his phone until Lorna or sometimes Sally jumps in to redirect the conversation. Arthur might be Ron's direct report, but he's ours to manage, and we're failing.

And yet as much as I want Arthur to, you know, leave Amazon and never come back, I also *like* him. When he catches my eye, winks, and reaches past his wife to pat me on the hand, I instantly feel a little bit better. Arthur is twinkly and avuncular and calls me brilliant and inspiring and other things the lonely daughter inside me is dying to hear. As long as he's going to be around—and at this point I can't imagine what could get him fired—I'll play the Inspiring Up-and-Comer role for him, especially if it means his VP endorsement of the promotion I think I might finally, really, actually be up for next cycle.

"Kristi is a fellow Michigan alum," he tells Nancy. Arthur and Nancy met at Michigan as undergraduates, and he often ends our conversations with "Go Blue!"

"How about that!" says Nancy, whose bouclé jacket I'm pretty into. I guess I could afford my own Chanel suit by now, but the gap between me and someone who has one and actually wears it feels unbridgeable.

"Just for grad school," I croak. "My MFA."

"Oh, are you a writer?" she asks.

"I used to be," I say. "But then I realized I'm better at helping other writers publish their books." I've told myself this over and over, which hasn't yet made it true.

"Very few make it," Nancy says. "And you came to Seattle after school?"

"Actually, I stayed in Ann Arbor for over a decade after graduation."

Nancy gapes at me. "But *why*? Why would you do that?"

People don't usually react with such horror when leafy, liberal Ann Arbor comes up. "I liked it?" is all I have by way of response, though it happens to be true.

"You *did*?" Did I accidentally say I spent a decade living in a drainage pipe and loving it? I don't think so, but I *am* feverish and on my third glass of wine.

"I take it you didn't?" I say with a smile.

"Well, it's just not a place you *stay*," she says.

Fortunately, the speeches start then and I don't have to explain why I stayed someplace you don't stay. My new friend Edward Albee gives a short speech that makes Arthur tear up, which touches me (damn it, why am I so *susceptible*). Then Tony Kushner, the keynote, talks for *five years*. Back when we lived in the hellmouth of Ann Arbor, John and I saw all seven hours of the *Angels in America* touring production in one day, one of *the* great art days of my life. I try to live in that day now as he talks and talks about the dangers to free speech until the audience starts *heckling* him to finish up, which I frankly did not realize could happen at a high-minded black-tie event.

Then he names Amazon as one of those dangers, and half the room turns and stares at our table—even if the rest of us could slide under the radar, Arthur is too well known to go unnoticed—and a few of them boo at *us*. It's not great. Arthur looks stunned. Bon Vivant 2 is chatting with the table next to ours and doesn't notice. And I assume the look of pleasant neutrality I learned in my first year at Amazon: shoulders and brows relaxed, mouth corners just barely turned up. Not defensive, not ashamed, not laughing like a good sport. Just . . . nothing. I've become a genius of the nothing face.

Eventually, it does end, and I walk out with Arthur and Nancy and turn toward the cabstand. But not a single taxi is waiting, only hired black cars. "Do you know of any other cabstands nearby?" I croak to Nancy as nonchalantly as I can manage. It's after midnight, I'm blazing with fever and a little drunk, and being back on my feet reminds me that the vamp of my shoe jams my toes forward painfully. I'd been counting on collapsing into a backseat and being ferried back to my hotel.

"Well, we have a car waiting right over there," Nancy says. "Where are you going?" Chelsea, I say. "Oh, that's too bad," she says. "We're headed uptown. But if you just wait on Columbus, I'm sure someone will come along any minute."

"Piece of cake," Arthur says, and kisses my cheek. Then they're off.

Harsh, I think. Would it really be so hard for them to give me a lift? But I mince obediently to Columbus Avenue and watch off-duty cabs whiz by for twenty minutes. There's always the subway, but in these pre-iPhone days I'm actually not sure where the station is, and anyway it's after midnight and I don't love the prospect of riding the train alone in a tight black dress. Just when I'm coming to terms with the idea that I might have to start the three-mile trip on foot and look for a cab along the way, an in-service taxi rolls up, but a man in shoes built for human ambulation beats me to it. I stop short, look at the ground, tell myself I'm not going to cry.

"Hey," he calls. "Do you want to share?"

I look up. "Yes," I mouth, nodding wildly to bridge the gap, one hand at my throat. "Thank you. Thank you."

An hour later I'm in bed, having one more glass of wine—that's a normal thing to do at 1:00 a.m. when you're sick, right?—and emailing John. "Amazing night at the PEN event," I write. "Feeling tired but on the mend. Love you." I need John to think this trip was worth it, and if that means lying to him, so be it. I can't have him bailing on Project Kristi Gets Promoted now, not when it might finally be in sight.

I follow that email with one to Lorna and Ron: "Just a note to say that the PEN gala was a success, not to mention an inspiring reminder about the power of translation to bridge cultural divides. You may see mention in press recaps of Amazon's table being heckled, but it was just a brief moment near the end of the evening and the whole team handled it with grace. Happy to follow up with more detail when I'm back in the office next week." I set the email to send at 8:00 a.m. so I don't appear *too* maniacal, and pass out.

As a follow-up to Lorna's comment that I'm ready for serious promotion discussions, a week after returning from New York, I have a meeting with Ron to get his take. "Hey, there," I say with calibrated nonchalance at the appointed time, sliding his door shut behind me. "Thanks for making the time. Lorna suggested it would be a good idea for us to start talking about this."

"I couldn't agree more!" he says, breezy as ever.

"Have you had a chance to take a quick peek at the document I sent yesterday?" I ask. I spent the whole weekend writing a self-assessment of my skills and experience against the official HR requirements for L8 employees. Amazon promotion proposals are dense, data-packed documents that are required to include reasons *not* to promote along with the case for promotion. I've taken the same approach in my self-assessment, hoping I can map my weak spots to projects that will help me improve.

"Yep!" Ron says. "Good stuff."

"Great!" I say. "So as you've seen, I have my own take on where I'm already promotable versus areas where I still have work to do. I'd love to get your perspective so I can build the right kinds of growth opportunities into my goals for the coming year."

"It's easy," Ron says with a sweep of his hand. "Just change the world."

I look up from my steno pad. "Sorry, what?"

"Change the world," he repeats, "and when I go into that roomful of executives to make the case for you, it will be an easy sell."

The faces of men in this org who've recently been promoted past me drift through my mind. Most of them seem more than competent, but I'm not aware of anything *world changing* they've done. There are only so many chances to invent the Kindle, after all. "Do you have thoughts about what that might *look* like in my role?" I ask. "Like . . . how will we know I've done it?" We've already become the largest translation publisher on the planet. We're managing translations through proprietary software that as far as we know is the first of its kind. We are in the planning stages of expanding into eight other language pairings. If all of this is too small, then I need help knowing what big enough looks like.

"We'll know when people are bringing us *wheelbarrows* full of money," he says, grinning.

Ron is saying my promotion will take place in a fairy-tale universe to which I don't have a map. For one hot second I want to slap that smile off his smug, complacent face. *Why did you take the meeting if you can't be bothered to have an actual conversation with me?* I want to yell. But seconds later, shame chokes out my anger. Maybe it's me, I think. Maybe I should have swanned in here like a Bon Vivant and said "My good man, it's high time I got kicked upstairs" instead of presenting an earthbound, Amazonian document. Maybe I need to be a swashbuckler, not a workhorse. Honestly, I don't know at this point.

"Well," I say. "Change the world! I guess I have some thinking to do." I have rarely felt as acutely female as I do at this moment. So careful and domestic when there should be sea wind in my hair.

Ron has already half turned back to his monitor. "I have every confidence you'll get there," he says. But the only thing I'm confident of is that it will be a long while before I talk to anyone about promotion again.

23

I HAVE NO INFORMATION

I may not talk about promotion anymore, but I do become slightly obsessed with proving I can change the world in a way that would count with Ron. People have been publishing books for hundreds of years. But what if the Kindle could emit an old-book smell when you turn a page? What if airports had tiny private Amazon reading lounges rentable by the hour, with recliners and Keurigs and bitchy cats? What if we turned one of our sci-fi books into a live-action role-play game involving, say, a million players around the globe? Two million? *Seventy-five million?* What if we could pipe narration directly into customers' brains? That last one might actually do it, but I don't know quite where to start—explain that I need to hire an ethically flexible neurologist? I must demonstrate that I have maniacal ideas without seeming maniacal myself.

I start to worry I've become the thing Calista once warned me about: someone who wants a promotion too much. "They can smell it on you, and if they can smell it, they won't give it to you," she said. "It's not fair, but it's true." I need to pretend that external recognition is just a cute little extra bonus and that consistently delivering world-changing greatness for Amazon's benefit is its own intrinsic reward. But everyone I know here is trying to get promoted. True, most of us grew up as hyper-achievers. Amazon didn't create our yearning for recognition, but it exploits it for maximum return by holding the rat pellet just out of reach and then frowning on any rat who looks hungry.

In July, Lorna is sent to a weeklong off-site leadership development program,* and on the last day she texts from the bus back to campus asking if I'll meet her for a drink that afternoon to talk over an idea she's excited about. Lorna doesn't use words like "excited" lightly, or much at all. "Yes!" I reply. Bring on a fun side project, hopefully one that will bring back my swagger. I arrive at the Brave Horse Tavern a few minutes early, order a glass of Rioja, and settle in, looking casual yet also ready to alter the totality of life on earth forever.

"So I've been thinking a lot lately about what's next for me," Lorna says ten minutes later. "Circling around the idea of taking a sabbatical and working with a literacy NGO, maybe in Latin America. But in the last few days I've landed on something different." Her wine arrives and she takes a big swallow. "I think it's time for Amazon Publishing to open an international office, and I want to be the one to do it. So my tentative plan is to move to London for a year, get it established and staffed up in all the EU countries, and then come back to Seattle and figure out what I want to do after that."

"So we'd be acquiring foreign-language originals?" I ask. She nods. "Wow, that could be huge for Crossing, having access to unpublished books from Europe. I mean, we'd need

---

* Marnie and I attended it the previous year as the only two women in our cohort of twenty-four.

to think hard about how much risk to take on." We currently only acquire Crossing books that sold well in their native languages; it doesn't guarantee they'll succeed in translation too, but it mitigates the risk. "And I'd want to make sure my editors have close ties to yours, because it could get messy having two separate teams publishing books into a market. But wow, it's really exciting."

"Well, that's why I wanted to talk to you before I even suggest it to Ron," Lorna says. "Because my plan would be to take Crossing with me."

"Oh! Do you mean *I'd* need to move to London, too?" I try not to look *too* excited, but I love London and would take any excuse to move there.

"No," Lorna says. "I'd hire someone a level above you to run APub International, including Crossing."

"Oh," I say again. "I'm sure you've already considered this, but you know, as we've chatted about before, I'm pushing hard toward *being* that person." *Chatted.* Why can't I just say "discussed" when it comes to conversations about my own goddamn career? Why do I always make it sound so casual?

"And you'll get there. But I want to get started this year, right away, and I need someone who can hit the ground running at director level."

"Okay," I say.

"You've done a great job with Crossing."

"Well, thank you," I say. "Can I just ask what you think this would mean for my next move? I mean, it sounds like my job will be going away."

"I don't know what it means for your future," she says. "I haven't gotten that far ahead. First I need to sell Ron on the whole idea. So to that point, it's really important that you don't tell anyone this is even a possibility. I don't want to destabilize people until we have solid news for them."

Maybe I don't count as people, because Lorna has just destabilized the fuck out of me and doesn't seem a bit bothered about it. A nitrousy numbness is moving down my neck into my upper back. "Of course," I say. "Not a word. Is there any way I can be helpful to you and Ron in arriving at a plan?"

"Not that I know of for now," Lorna says.

"Okay," I say yet again, as if this were all just fine. "Well, obviously this is unsettling news for me. I love running Crossing, but more generally I love being at APub, so I really hope there will still be a place for me here." A tiny, deadpan nod from her. "I guess I'll just wait for more information, then?"

She nods. "Appreciate your patience and discretion."

"Do you have a timeline for when I might know more?"

"Not yet. It will probably be a couple of weeks."

Driving home afterward, I replay various shake-ups I've been part of at Amazon. At times, I've been the one delivering the news that someone's job or boss is changing; at others, I've been the recipient. But there's always been a clear plan in place. Sometimes even the schedule for telling people is laid out to the hour, so we get to them in the right order and minimize rumors. No one has ever sat me down and said, "Hey, your job is probably going away and that's literally all the information I have for you, and we're not going to involve you in the planning process, and by the way this is a secret." Even at Amazon, that's just not how you treat people.

Maybe it's a sign of respect, I tell myself, like when Mitch told me I was stupid and Calista said it meant he knew I could take it. Maybe Lorna knows a pro like me can handle having her career upended with no plan B or any real show of caring in sight. Maybe it means I'm a real leader in her eyes. After all, great leaders always put the organization ahead of their own interests. Saying what was really on my mind—that I was alarmed and needed reassurance that Lorna had my back—could have made me look weak. Instead, I look tough and stoic.

This is the narrative I sell myself, and I buy it the way I'd buy a hyped new anti-aging serum: not quite believing, but grasping at anything that might stave off collapse.

Maybe by playing it cool and not saying what I'd wanted to—*this sucks, and you should* know *it sucks, and you can't even be bothered to pretend you care what happens to me*—I've proven myself worthy of her respect. Thank God I didn't say what I *really* wanted to, which was that I saw my whole career coming to an end before my eyes, that if even my manager couldn't be bothered to care, surely no one else at Amazon would, either.

I decide to sell myself the sign-of-respect narrative, and I decide to sell John on it too. "Lorna's planning a huge reorg to deal with her midlife crisis," I tell him when I get home, rolling my eyes and pouring myself a huge glass of wine. "It's possible Crossing will get moved overseas without me."

"Huh," John says. "That seems like a terrible idea."

"I don't disagree," I say. "But it's just more Amazon Boggle. They'll find something good for me to do." I hate myself for lying to him and I also hate him for being so easy to lie to. But it has to be this way. One word of sympathy and I'll cave in. I top up my wine as he takes the pork chops out of the fridge. The bottle is nearly empty. "Hey, pop another Chardonnay in there to chill," I say.

———

Two weeks pass, and then four with no news. For a while I check in with Lorna at our weekly one-on-one meetings. "I don't have any information for you yet" is her standard, expressionless response. She doesn't elaborate, and if I press, all I get is a paraphrase: "A lot is still up in the air" or "Nothing concrete to report so far." I start to feel awkward for even asking, like a stage-five clinger in need of hourly reassurance. *Organization first*, I remind myself. *Be a leader.*

Around this time, I also notice that my yoga practice no longer buffers my work worries, that even in the middle of savasana or a pose that requires all my focus, part of me is thinking about whether I'll have a job next month. Clearly this is yoga's fault. I need a more difficult practice, one where I could *die* if I'm not paying attention. Suddenly it seems obvious that my longtime neighborhood studio is geared toward sad and lazy people who don't want to work hard. I embark on a sort of Hostility Tour of other studios around town, looking for one that can instill the fear of God in me, wiping out my fear of unemployment.

Wouldn't you know it? It turns out *every single yoga studio* in the Greater Seattle area is for cowardly pussies. "My body is going to *devolve* with this level of lowest-common-denominator instruction," I tell John, who wisely does not argue. I wonder if running, something I've avoided since eighth grade, might provide the level of distracting agony I require, and, boy, am I right. At first I pursue the sublime misery three times a week. But if three is good, five can only be better. Soon my right shin starts kind of *squeaking*, but I ignore it.

By month two, I've stopped asking what's going to happen to me and switched to maniacally demonstrating my versatility and breadth of knowledge. In a technically focused meeting, I ask questions that remind people I've been a PM and understand the software development process. In acquisition meetings, I speak up more often about non-Crossing books the editors want to buy, to show that I can be smart beyond my own domain. And I never miss an opportunity to brag about a Crossing success, whether it's signing a prestigious translator or one of our books scoring a five-star customer review average. If nothing else, I'll leave here with every human and dog in the building knowing I was good at my job.

I get a gut check from Marnie one weekend as we shop for the dress she'll marry Andy in. "Am I just being a delicate flower?" I ask her, idly trying on veils as she gets changed. "Like, should I feel *sanguine* about the situation?"

"No," she says over the dressing room door. "It's not normal to be left hanging for so long. I'd be just as freaked out."

"I keep telling myself she's only doing it because she knows I can handle it," I say.*

"That's exactly what Amazon wants you to tell yourself. I don't know what you should do about it, but I just want to validate that it's fucked up."

Eventually I even break down and tell John how worried I am. "She just keeps repeating the same thing, like Bartleby the Scrivener or something," I say. "I can't get *anything* out of her. It's like my future at Amazon is entirely irrelevant to the person who's supposed to help me shape it."

"Fuck her," John says. "Do you even *want* to stay under these conditions?" We're at a club on First Avenue waiting for Spoon to take the stage and I'm drinking white wine from a plastic cup to convince myself I'm not too tired to be here.

---

* Even though I cannot, in fact, handle it.

"What choice do I have?" I say. "I've had, what, four jobs in six years? I don't have it in me to start over at Amazon yet again. I need some kind of stability." I've been browsing the internal job board, but the postings are full of words like "relentless" and "tireless" and "obsessed" and there's far too much bragging about foosball competitions and Beer Tuesdays. It's probably all very exciting if one is a Soylent-chugging college boy, but I don't make career decisions based on who has the best Nerf wars.

John shakes his head. "I don't mean something new at Amazon. This city is packed with good jobs."

"John, no one outside Amazon is going to hire me. I've been doing weird, random shit at this weird, random company for years. My career narrative looks *insane*." I shift my weight to my other leg. Running five times a week has produced what I've diagnosed as "a tiny adaptation issue" in my right shin, and it's sending up shards of pain.

John sighs. "Don't do this. Your career narrative says you're a goddamn Green Beret at this point. It's this fantasy of being unemployable outside Amazon that's insane."

"I heard Nordstrom won't even hire Amazon people anymore because we come barging in like assholes who know everything," I say.

"Yes, you've told me that thirty times," John says.

"And I heard Starbucks has an *official deprogramming process* for us because we arrive so fucked up." It looks for a moment as if the show were starting, but it's just roadies laying down more duct tape.

"So you'd get deprogrammed! If that's even really a thing."

"Look, the fact is I can't afford to leave Amazon," I say.

"*We* can't afford for me to leave Amazon." Stock makes up two-thirds of my compensation by now, and because the value has risen wildly since the shares were granted, my annual income is well above market rate.

John sighs again. "We have *plenty* of money. And my company grew *double* last year. And your new job would pay plenty of money, too."

"Maybe not Amazon money, though."

"Who gives a fuck? If you don't have to put up with working at Amazon, do you really need to make Amazon money?"

That's the million-dollar question. "My husband was horrified by what this bag cost," Sally told me last week about the Marc Jacobs hobo she pulled the trigger on after weeks of contemplation. "But when you work at Amazon, you have to give yourself a present now and then." Every Amazon woman I know has an equally high-achieving spouse, and also every one of us is outearning that spouse by a lot, just because of the batshit stock. John has never shown the slightest macho insecurity over it. Neither have most of the husbands; they're evolved and smart enough to just feel lucky. But what's too hard to explain to them is that we don't *feel* overpaid. Amazon could be depositing a million dollars a month into my checking account and I would think, *Yes, this seems about right, given the fear and the chaos and the ugly surroundings and the endlessly escalating demands and the way no one ever says thanks.*

"I just can't contemplate leaving Amazon right now," I tell John. "It's more than I can get my head around."

"Fine," he says. "Just stop bullshitting yourself that you *can't*. You can leave anytime. You're choosing to stay."

He doesn't get it. He *can't* get it. And fortunately Spoon are taking their places right this second, so I don't have to go through the futile exercise of trying to explain.

In month three of limbo, Lorna and I are both in Germany for the Frankfurt Book Fair, a massive gathering of international publishing pros for business and cocktail parties. "Want to get lunch today?" she asks one morning as we cross paths (painfully in my case, because walking now hurts too) on our way to separate meetings. Ooh, I think, maybe she has some news. At one, we grab prepacked salads in the expo lobby and then spot the snow leopard of book fair phenomena: an empty bench. "Holy shit," Lorna says.

"Is it a trick? Will we be electrocuted if we sit on it?" I ask.

"I'll take that risk," she says, and down we go, unelectrified. "There have been years here where I swear I've eaten every meal sitting on the floor."

"I did so much lobby-floor eating the year AMG sent me to Sundance," I say. "Though one day I looked to my left and Tilda Swinton and her friend were also eating on the floor and it was the greatest moment of my life."

"No way," Lorna said. "Tilda Swinton?"

"Swear to God," I said. "Perched like an exotic crane in this wild origami coat." I open my Greek salad's dressing, which appears to be straight tahini.

"How's your fair so far?" Lorna asks. Good, I say. It's hard to be a lot more specific about book fairs; they're more about saying hello to remote contacts in person and making plans to make plans to make a deal next month than about doing actual business on the spot. She says hers is good too, and then we fall into silence over our plastic clamshells and I realize she isn't going to bring up the matter of whether I'll have a job much longer. Just don't ask, I tell myself. Talk about Tilda some more, oh, or tell her about how you passed John Mellencamp in an empty lobby and he said "hey" and you said "hey." That's quite a saga, she'll love it. But I can't help myself. As we toss the remnants of our lunch into overflowing bins, I say, "Being here makes me wonder if you have any updates on the changes we chatted about back in summer?" Very casual-like, as though only being smack in the middle of the world's largest international publishing fair brought it to mind.

"I don't have any new information," she says. "Sorry."

"No problem! Can you just give me your point of view on one thing?" I ask. "Should I be looking for a new role outside APub? Or do you think something internal will work out? I don't want to end up unemployed—I'm sure you can understand that."

"I understand," Lorna says. "I hope something will work out. I just don't know yet."

My whole face, even my jaw, feels stretched with packed-in tears for the rest of lunch, but I can't risk losing it in public. I leave the expo and march, wincing, to a small, empty park by the nearest metro station. I can't allow myself to outright sob the way my body wants, but I do let the tears sort of push themselves up and through my eyes like water from a backed-up drain. I watch pigeons mill around and wonder how, of all places in the world, I wound up in *Frankfurt*— probably a nice-enough place to live, but you wouldn't want to visit—walking around a convention center saying, "Wonderful to put a face to a name!" over and over on behalf of a boss who seems almost comically indifferent to my hopes and fears. The more my skull empties of tears, the calmer I get. This has all gone too far, I decide. I will leave APub, and maybe Amazon too. I have contacts at plenty of other companies. I'll start putting feelers out to them tomorrow and trust that someone somewhere will be willing to take a chance on me and that this time maybe I'll land someplace where life could feel a little less punishing. I wipe my eyes and check the time. It's three thirty, probably a great time to have the hotel gym to myself. I hobble to the metro to get in a few miles on the treadmill before my dinner meeting.

Back in Seattle a week later, Lorna pulls me into her office on ten minutes' notice. Her visa issues have been worked out, she says, and her new role in London will be announced soon. Sally will be stepping into Lorna's job as publisher. Would I like to take over Sally's role and run West Coast acquisitions? "Wow," I say, both to buy time and out of genuine surprise. One voice in my head says, *This is the job. Running six imprints instead of one. Enormous influence. A chance to really make my name.* Another voice says, *NO. Leaving is your only smart move. You are so saturated in fear and anger by now that you're one more bad day from it puddling around you for everyone to see. Fuck this place. Save yourself.*

"Absolutely," I say. "What an amazing challenge, and I'm so honored that you thought of me. I'd be delighted."

24

THE LOVE BUILDING

I stare in horror at Vance's PowerPoint slide and then hear his voice down the aisle and decide I need to lay eyes on the man himself. He's in his cube, showing his 1974 high school yearbook to the new marketing manager. "Here I am in show choir. Oh, and this is me in French Club. As you can see, I had *quite* the impressive collection of dickeys." He slams the yearbook shut dramatically when he sees me. "Oh, it's *her* again. What is it *this* time?"

"Your slide for the agent summit," I say, leaning on his cube wall. "It's very . . . elaborate."

"Well, isn't that the sole purpose of PowerPoint? To do stupid jazz-hands things to information that belongs in a simple Word document?" Maisie, the King Charles spaniel from the next cube, has wandered over and Vance scoops her up. "I love this baleful little face," he says.

"I mean, where did you even find that font? Did you *commission* it? Why is there animation? Why are the book covers tilted at a jaunty angle? Do you hate me, Vance?"

"I do love a strong serif," he says. His laugh is rolling and gravelly, one of my favorites. "Look, this is what happens when people in a non-PowerPoint company are suddenly forced to use PowerPoint. We lose our minds."

"I know, I know." I can count on two hands the number of slide presentations I've either made or seen in seven years at Amazon, and I don't miss them. But literary agents are different—very different—from Amazonians, and it has slowly—unforgivably slowly—dawned on us that if we want to make deals with them, we need to speak their language. Hence my request that Vance and the other imprint leads who report to me each make a plain, basic slide highlighting their big books for the year and give me a short, punchy sales pitch for each one. I grab a marker and draw on Vance's whiteboard. "See? Just boxes and lines. Clean, simple, boring."

Coco, the romance imprint lead, pops her head up from her cube on the other side of Vance's. "Hey, have you looked at my slide yet?" Not yet, I say. "Great. Don't! I'm making you a new one right now." She says it with a laugh, but Coco has the most severe case of Brilliant Self-Flagellating Woman I've dealt with in my Amazon career, and I know she's now sure I want to fire her, that she'll almost certainly knock on my door later to ask if I've lost confidence in her ability to do her job. As I've told her several times, of all my directs, Coco is by far the most prepared to do *my* job. But sometimes it feels as if assurances and compliments actually make things worse. If I say that there's nothing to be afraid of, she thinks I just haven't found her out yet. If I say I'm always here to give her air cover, she thinks a higher-up wants her head on a pike. Sometimes my stomach reflexively cramps when she knocks on my door.

"Can we agree that this whole endeavor is insane?" Vance says. "Flying to New York for a two-hour meeting with agents who could just as easily look at our website? And with you crippled!" He points at the black ortho-boot I'll be wearing for at least another six weeks.

"I'm not *crippled*," I say. "I'm just maybe a little bit *hobbled*."

"You're like Tiny Tim."

"I'm fine."

Fine? No. I'm not fine. On paper, sure. I used to run one imprint, Crossing, and now I run six*, the biggest leap of my career. The people who work for me are smart and funny and kind. We get paid to publish the kinds of books that make plane rides fly by and keep people up past their bedtimes reading just one more chapter. On any given day I might be asked to weigh in on the potential of a sci-fi series or cast the tie-breaking vote on whether a romance cover shows too much nipple. Authors are so damn grateful—for the first or second chance they get with us, for the higher royalty rates, for the exposure they're getting all over the website. They send us cupcakes and flowers and some of them tell us we've changed their lives.

The only problem is that I can't actually *do* the job. It turns out that sextupling my scope of responsibility overnight, with no transition period or training or ramp, is not as simple as my Amazon-skewed brain thinks it should have been. And at the same time I was stepping into Sally's job, she was taking over Lorna's, and she's too frantic trying to keep on top of *that* to spend much time helping me to acclimate. Also, we've both worked at Amazon a long time and are used to jumping into confusing new roles, so I suspect that like me she didn't think increasing the scope of my job *times six* would be, you know, as hard as it is. Sally carries around a steno pad with a running list of tasks and questions and worries, and during our

* Five? Seven? Six and a half? Honestly, it seems to change by the month.

one-on-ones she flips from page 2 to 6 to 1 to 9, looking for things to ask me about. The sight of her hands fluttering reminds me of fifty-two pickup and my heart begins to flutter along with them, and I feel as if I were doing to her what Coco does to me, as if an endless chain of Amazon women were clutching at the jeans hems of the one above, desperate for reassurance. When I tell her I feel as if I were failing to get my arms around the job, she says, "That's because the job is like *sand* falling through your fingers," meaning it's the role, not me. But how do I make it *not* like sand? I don't know, and I'm ashamed for not knowing, so I don't ask. I just keep trying to figure it out day by day, but it's like solving a jigsaw puzzle where every third piece is missing and also the underlying picture changes every night. Six months in, I should be at full steam, but I'm still trying to make a landscape out of tattered cardboard shapes.

In rare moments of perspective, it's clear that all of the women here are working so hard just to hold it together and manage our jobs that we have very little time or energy left for helping each other the way we used to. Sally isn't giving me what I need, and I'm not giving Coco what she needs, and Coco's probably letting her team down, too. *Put on your own oxygen mask before helping others*, the saying goes, but ours got lost or ripped along the way, and Amazon doesn't care. "Ron said his job is to keep throwing things at me until I tell him I'm drowning," Sally tells me. "Why do we have to live that way?" Sally is as battle hardened as Amazonians come. For her to complain is no small thing. But she can't stop the deluge that cascades past her onto all of us.

I've also taken this job just as multiple problems have all started to come to a head. Each editor now oversees about a hundred books per year—in a normal publishing company, it would be more like twelve or fifteen—and they're working with Scotch-taped tools and manual hacks. Sales are slumping and Marketing is too swamped just covering the basics for all these books to pay special attention to books that need extra help. "Your job is to find bestsellers," Ron tells my team in a comically hectoring tone every chance he gets, and God knows we're trying. In the meantime, a sense of failure wafts over the team, which leads the editors to second-guess themselves into paralysis, which makes finding blockbusters even harder, which means even more speeches from Ron about how we need bestsellers *right this minute*, and so on. Vance is a deeply gifted editor with skin even thicker than Sally's. When he tells me expectations have shot way past reasonable, it means we are well and truly fucked. As the leader, it's my job to make the editors' jobs doable, but I can't find the thread to pull that would start to ease the whole, and bit by bit I start to carry that whole inside my chest like an impermeable gray rock. It takes a bottle of wine and two Benadryl to fall asleep most nights, and I wake up feeling as if I've already failed the day, because I have.

Of course Vance is right that the trip to New York is insane, and of course I go anyway, hobbling through fifteen-degree wind tunnels in my ortho-boot and light coat and no hat or gloves because I forgot that the weather might be different three thousand miles away. I meet with the agents, who all seem faintly disgruntled, and then I head to the building with the Love sign to see the New York team, but they all seem disgruntled too. Actually, it's worse: they seem *depressed*. Their books aren't selling either, and publishing celebrity memoirs means tolerating shitty treatment from people like the actress turned director who lit a cigarette in a closed cab next to our hugely pregnant publicist, glanced at her belly as though seeing it for the first time, and said "Oh, you're pregnant. Well, I don't give a fuck" before exhaling in her face. They're burning money, they know it's a huge fucking problem, and they don't know how to turn it around. *What can we do to make things less chaotic?* they want to know. *What does Ron want from us? What does Sally want from us? Why is Arthur allowed to jerk us around so much? Why won't Ron rein him in?*

All I can say is "I don't know." *If even you don't know, then we're fucked.* Well, yeah. I don't say it, because I don't need to. I flash back to merchandising, the last time people really needed my help and I ran out of it, and the shame cuts through my belly like a hot knife and I don't even try to resist it, because I'm useless and useless people should be ashamed.

At day's end I go back to my hotel, drink a whole bottle of wine, and watch a movie where Helen Hunt is a sex surrogate to a man in an iron lung. Oh right, sex still exists. Fucking John was once a reliable way to shed my daily worries. But lately I have to drink my way into wanting it at all, and even then it takes being shoved around or pushed to my knees to feel anything. If I come out without rope marks or bruises, was it even sex? The man in the iron lung brings tears to my eyes. *I'm cut off too*, I think in my wine fog, and am disgusted by my own self-pity.

In the morning, I forget to put the boot on before I step out of bed and the hairline crack in my shin lights up, but even that feels better than my staticky hangover. And anyway, this is just what I do: make things better and then turn right around and make them worse.

25

PROFESSIONAL HELP, REVISED

By day I learn Amazon, and at night I seek out articles and listicles and TED Talks on femaling in the business world, just in case there are tips or hacks or something that could help me do it better. This is how I know I should lean forward in my chair far enough to show warmth but not cleavage. But also sit with my shoulder blades against the chair back and my feet on the floor. That I should stand with my hands on my hips but never cross my arms. Make eye contact for at least two seconds but never more than five. Look at a man's forehead and eyes—a.k.a. the business triangle—but never his nose or mouth, the social triangle. Listen with attentive interest but without nodding or tilting my head. Speak naturally, but never end on an upswing. Speak assertively, but don't interrupt. When interrupted by a man, insist on finishing my thought, but charmingly, so he won't feel as though he did anything wrong. Don't volunteer to take meeting notes, because it will seem secretarial. But do volunteer to take meeting notes because it's the only way to make sure my contributions will be captured. Do negotiate for more money, but don't let on that money motivates me. Be an advocate for women at work plural, but not myself as a woman at work singular. Always take credit for my accomplishments, but also

~~let my accomplishments speak for themselves. Raise my hand~~
~~for new assignments to be *helpful*, not eager. Dress to embrace~~
~~my femininity but also to de-emphasize my boobs, shoulders,~~
~~waist, hips, legs, lips, and hair. And smile. But not too much.~~
~~Less. Less. Yes, like that. Now hold.~~

Sit in whatever way allows you to not think about your body.
When entering a room with chairs at the table and along the
wall, take a chair at the table. Speak however you speak. Your
natural speaking voice got you this job and it has not magically
gone wrong since then. Arrange your head on your neck however you like. If it tilts, it tilts. You stand fine. You walk fine.
Do consider the power of the three-inch heel, the solid kind
you can stride in. But feel free to dismiss it, too. Don't apologize for making money or wanting more of it. Don't apologize
for making decisions. Don't apologize for using your leverage
to make things happen. Don't apologize for not knowing an
answer right away. Say you will get the answer and then do it.
Don't apologize for asking a question, but try not to ask the
same question more than once. Write down what you learn,
process it later, integrate it, let it lead you to your next, slightly
upgraded question. When you *do* need to apologize, do it sin-
cerely and do it just once and move on. Never hire someone
you wouldn't be willing to work for. Never hire someone who
isn't smarter than you in at least one key way. If you're nervous
before a meeting, write the two main points you want to make
on an index card you can refer to under the table. Spend the
most time with your best people, and if you are putting off
dealing with your worst people, be aware that your best people
know it and are waiting for you to do something. When firing someone, remember it's *infinitely* worse for them than it

is for you. Always look for ways to bring other women into the room, but be wary of creeping volunteerism: it is not your job to serve on every single committee meant to help women advance. Pick one and feel free to recommend men for the others. Without men, such programs are closed circuits anyway, and never touch the real layers of power. Worry less about actually overcoming impostor syndrome—everyone has it, even men—and more about acting in spite of it. Learn to talk sports, or not. Have opinions about the Marvel universe, or not. *Never call anyone stupid.* For God's sake, wear what you want.

26

HONOR BERRIES

I think about drinking all the time now. I think about what bottle I should open tonight and what tricks I might employ to stop myself from drinking the whole thing and how I know I'll drink the whole thing anyway. I think about how much fun it used to be and how strange it is that it's now no fun at all and yet I keep right on doing it as if I signed a contract or something. I think about whether drinking this much will shorten my life and how I might not care. I'm desperate to stop thinking about drinking, not only because it exhausts me, but because every moment I spend thinking about drinking is a moment I'm not thinking about how to be better at my job. *So just stop*, I tell myself, meaning stop the rumination. For the next few months I try to become a more carefree, thoughtless drinker, but the rumination never goes away, and though I haven't gotten any worse at my job, it isn't getting easier, either.

One night in June, John is away for a week and I'm sitting out back with our golden retriever, about to go into the kitchen and open the bottle I know will lead to more worry, when it occurs to me for the very first time that *another* way to reclaim the mental space I spend worrying about drinking would be to, you know, not drink anymore. The idea infuriates me, but there is a certain logic to it. I still drink that night, the whole bottle plus a bit more, but when I open my eyes the next morning, I decide the no-drinking thing is worth a try if it will get me off this treadmill of shame and regret. Something in my body relaxes as soon as the decision is made, as though it's been longing for this day. But contemplating a happier future is way too scary. Instead, I think, *I'll finally excel at my job*.

By the time John gets home five days later, I'm in a state of very fragile euphoria. The absence of chemical depressants from my system probably has something to do with it, or the good sleep I'm getting. But mostly it's the euphoria of *success*. Every day I don't drink is a day with a big win in it, and I've had five big wins in a row. It's been a long, long time since I've felt this successful. My Amazon brain wants to discount it as something anyone should be able to do, but I know that way lies danger. "Remember when Linus was potty training and we had to fall all over ourselves praising him every time he remembered to pee outside?" I ask John. "I'm Linus now. I have to treat myself like a conquering hero just for managing this one basic thing."

John is quietly happy for me, which is how I want it. I can't handle the pressure of *him* treating me like a conquering hero. He immediately stops drinking at home, though I tell him he doesn't need to on my account. I tell Marnie offhandedly and she gives me the great gift of reacting in kind. Otherwise, I keep it to myself, which is tricky at work because publishing is a boozy profession and some kind of toast or happy hour always seems to be happening at one of the makeshift bars on our floor. But I pass beneath the radar, distracting myself from temptation with fantasies about how if one of the bottles broke and a co-worker accidentally stepped on glass and needed to go to the ER, I could leap into action as the designated driver.

Or that maybe on the way home from work, a cop will pull me over for a busted taillight or something and will ask if I've been drinking and I'll say, "My last drink was ten days ago, Officer," and he'll smile slowly and say, "Ma'am, I'm proud of you." A man who reeks of alcohol is often slumped at the corner of First and James on my downtown running route, making mumbly conversational salvos at people waiting for the light to change. I usually wear earbuds and ignore him, but one evening it occurs to me that we're kind of alike and I find myself giving him a half smile. I never knew I could feel so ordinary and so thrilled at once.

But even four months later, I'm not actually much better at my job. I'm calmer and sharper and better rested and starting to believe in my own strength, having done the one thing I thought I could never do. But it means fuck all at APub. Our yearly goals change every month or two. We're told to acquire more books, then fewer. Ron requests documents exploring new imprints and programs and then changes his mind. Things get harder because other publishers have caught on and are now shopping the website for successful self-published authors to sign. Wait, we think, what if we could find the books on the site that no one else will notice because they're not successful *yet*? With the help of a PhD statistician on loan from another team, we start working on an algorithm to surface obscure books that are on a trajectory to break through a few weeks or months from now.* We nickname the project Under the Sea. Ron, understandably excited by the prospect of finding a whole new gold mine under the other gold mine,

---

* Yes, we're trying to use an algorithm to predict the future. Yes, it's crazy.

tells Sally he wants 75 percent of the year's acquisitions to be Under the Sea books, which would be great except that the books the algorithm is recommending are mostly not good. *Really* not good.

Things are rough on the non-acquisition side, too. Some series acquired in APub's early days have "reached the end of their natural life cycle," according to our marketing director, Mia, meaning after four or five books sales have slumped and we haven't been able to goose them back up. And because those dying series make up a lot of our list, we aren't producing bestsellers the way we used to. "I'm declaring the house on fire," Ron says, because his only two urgency settings are "all good" and "cataclysm." "We need new bestsellers *now.*" So it's on my team to find new ones, which is fine. Except it takes a *long time* to publish a book. A finished manuscript still needs a contract and copyediting and proofreading and a cover and page layout and printing and so on. Most publishers need at least nine months. In bits and pieces, we've managed to get it down to six months. Faster, Ron says. Thirty days.

That's an 84 percent reduction off our current timeline, which I know because I'm so nonplussed to hear it that I have to quantify it for myself.

At the same time, Ron adds more and more criteria for acquiring a book until the decision tree looks like this:

> Will it earn back its advance in six months or less?*
> Can we get the rights to publish it in the U.K., France, Germany, Spain, Italy, Japan, China, and Brazil?

---

* Conventional wisdom says that only about 25 percent of books *ever* earn back their advances.

Is it commercially viable in the U.K., France, Germany,
    Spain, Italy, Japan, China, and Brazil?
Is Amazon Studios interested in developing it?
Could it also be adapted into a comic or graphic novel?
Is it fan fiction friendly?
Can it be marketed with existing automated programs?
Does it fit squarely into one and only one genre?
Is it adaptable to musical theater?
What about puppetry?
Will it inspire a viral dance craze?*

Oh, and is it a good book?

Ron doesn't understand why acquisitions have slowed so much. "I have zero doubt this team can find the right books for us!" he says, smiling as always, to a roomful of carefully blank editorial faces.

At rush hour in London and Tokyo, sometimes the subway car would be so packed that I couldn't reach a bar or strap, and I'd play a game where I used my core muscles alone to stop from falling into other passengers when the train stopped and started. Lately my abs feel the same soreness as I try to make the center hold, the center that's like the bubble in a lava lamp, moving constantly, spawning bubbles that look just like it, until my synapses are all tangled and my attention keeps landing on the wrong one. At least half the bubbles are failure bubbles, and when I mistake them for normal bubbles and touch them, they pop and poison the water.

---

* My imagination may have entered the chat for these last three. But the rest of it's real.

———

In the midst of all this, I'm speed walking back from the cafeteria with my salad one day when I run into a co-worker I last saw five or more years ago. She's French and wears red lipstick with no other makeup and wears silk scarves without looking as if she were cosplaying a 1970s stewardess, so I find her almost unfathomably glamorous. "It's so nice to see you!" I say, realizing in the moment that I don't actually remember what we worked on together.

"It's so nice to see you too!" she says, and then we just stand there smiling at each other, and it occurs to me she might not remember, either. Finally she gestures to her tray of sushi and nods toward Mercer Street. "Well, I'm heading to the lake to eat lunch."

Wait, what? I stand there clutching my plastic clamshell and watching her walk away. I mean, I know Lake Union is just across the street, but it's never occurred to me that I could *go* to it. Well, she *is* French, I think. Maybe all the French employees meet up and have lunch in swan boats while drinking Pernod and reading Balzac out loud. Anything could be happening over there.

In the middle of a meeting to review the ninth iteration of a six-pager with Ron, I schedule "go to lake" in Outlook for eleven thirty tomorrow. When the time comes, I stride out of the building as though I have a legitimate excuse, cross Mercer's six lanes and streetcar tracks, and stand at the southern tip of Lake Union. It's a sunny day and toddlers are bumbling through motion-activated sprinklers, shrieking with glee each time they get sprayed. Just across the plaza is the Museum of History and Industry, another place I have never thought of as visitable, and beyond the museum a marina and tiny beach. People are all around me, mostly tourist types but a sprinkling of people with Amazon badges around their necks too, alone or in pairs.

I walk slowly toward the beach, hands empty—I forgot the lunch part of this appointment—and spot one of my editors splayed out on the lawn, reading a book. When I see her, I turn around and head in the other direction—not because I'm afraid she'll think less of me for being there, but because I'm afraid she'll be afraid I think less of *her*.

On the other side of the museum is a place John likes called the Center for Wooden Boats, which turns out to be just a few repair pavilions and, you know, some boats. I don't particularly care about boats and what they're made of. But now that I'm here, I see that they're kind of beautiful and vulnerable, especially compared with the fiberglass cabin cruisers in the marina. *I guess I like wooden boats*, I think. One is the caramel color of my hair and I wonder if it feels just as warm in the sun. Down a few steps is a covered dock with just one small, shiny teak boat tied to it, and on the deck is a card table with a dozen pints of small neon-red strawberries; $3, says a handwritten sign clothespinned to a carton full of singles.

I'm flooded by a desire to eat a strawberry, but I don't have any money on me. So I just look, thinking about how growing and picking and packaging and transporting these berries is someone's *project*. I've always admired people with projects. I used to try having projects myself (knitting, baking, viewing every film in the Criterion Collection) in a failed attempt to become a moderate drinker, but the project and the moderation always died together. Maybe I can have another one now, if I can figure out what it should be. *Look at you, crying over strawberries*, I think, wiping tears from my eyes. *You made it back. You're so alive.*

Days later, twenty-five of us are gathered for the weekly pitch meeting, with another ten on speakerphone* from New York, London, and Munich. I run this meeting, but Ron has started attending too, which I assume reflects his lack of faith in the editors' ability to spot all those blockbusters he knows are right under their noses. As always, I take my seat with an air of brisk cheer and a stomach full of acid.

Things get off to a good start, with the romance team pitching a woman/merman love story (in this post-*Twilight* world, romance authors have started going pretty far afield in search of mythical beings who fuck). Marketing thinks it's an easy sell, Amazon Studios likes it, world rights are available, the financials look sound. "Love it!" says Ron, looking up from his phone. "Is this an Under the Sea book?"

"It's not," the editor says. "I'm looking at anywhere from eighty to a hundred Under the Sea titles per week, but nothing has popped yet."

"Well, just don't forget that 75 percent goal," he says, as if anyone could.

Next up is Jared from sci-fi. Everyone's a bit jealous of the sci-fi editors, whose books are the most likely to check all the Studios/graphic novel/fan fiction boxes. Jared has a great eye for the kinds of meat-and-potatoes space operas that hard-core genre fans devour. He looks a bit nervous today, though. "I'm presenting an original debut manuscript," he

---

* Literally speakerphone; as of 2013 Amazon has no videoconferencing technology that I know of.

begins. That could explain the nerves: "debut" means the author has no sales track record for us to examine, and "original" means it's still just a manuscript, not a self-published book, so it won't count toward our 75 percent. "I know that's not our focus right now, but this book is really something special, the best thing I've read in ages. Think China Miéville meets *The Corrections*."

Two thoughts cross my mind simultaneously: that I'm dying to read this book, and that it's never going to fly. Too literary, too cross-genre, too untested. Too *new*.

The guy on the marketing team who handles sci-fi says, "It's great." He looks pained when he says, "I genuinely loved it. I'd read it again. But it's definitely on the more literary side, where we have struggled to make books break out."

"It's *accessible* literary, though," says Jared.

"Accessible doesn't mean much if we're not able to market it effectively," Mia says. I know she's just doing her job, protecting her own overstretched and exhausted team. And yet there's something glib about the way she says no that makes me angrier each week.

"Understood," Jared says, his face tight. "I just want to point out that even if this book isn't a bestseller out of the gate, I think it's a legitimate Hugo and Nebula contender, and a nomination *would* be an easy marketing and PR win."

"Sales, sales, sales," chimes in Ron. "We want prizewinners that are *also* bestsellers, and there is no team on earth better positioned to find them."

"Okay," Jared says, and from the look on his face it's a blessing that he doesn't say more.

My phone buzzes with a text from Sally, who is at the

other end of the long table: "Why is J presenting an unpublished ms? He should be acquiring from Under the Sea."

"He's looking," I text back. "Slim pickings."

"In what way?"

"Incompetently written to the point of being editor-proof" is how Jared described his latest Under the Sea options to me, and I sampled enough to confirm it for myself. "They're beneath the minimum quality bar," I text.

"Why isn't the algorithm surfacing better books?" We've been over and over this, but that's just how it is with Sally now. She's been out a lot with a series of brutal upper respiratory infections, and when she's in the office, Ron has her on enough side projects to add up to a second or third full-time job. Our relationship has been winnowed down to me delivering the same bad news she's already forgotten from last week and her replying, "We have to fix that right away," as though I were not already killing myself trying, as though anything *can* be fixed in a landscape where new top-down goals and business models land on us constantly.

"We're experimenting with the algorithm every week," I reply. "It isn't getting better. But we won't give up." Since the day we met back in Retail, Sally's been the most voracious reader I know. Like me, she taught college-level literature until the need to eat and have health insurance won out.* I do not believe for one goddamn minute that she really thinks the algorithm is going to save us, or that passing on great books

* Sometimes I imagine an America where people didn't have to make career decisions based on access to health care, and the possibilities break my fucking heart.

that need a little extra marketing love is smart. But that's how she's playing it, so that's how I have to play it too. There was a time when Sally and I could talk about books we love for an hour. I miss it.

For the second week in a row, we leave having rejected almost every pitch. I close my office door and hope no one will knock for a little while. I don't know what to tell Jared, and if Coco comes in for a new round of *Am I going to be fired? I know I'm going to be fired*, I'm afraid I'll lose my temper, something I've never done at Amazon and have no intention of doing now.

Lorna has already emailed me, with no subject line, CC'ing Sally. "That was the most frustrating meeting I have attended in a LONG time," she says. "Why has our decision-making become so strangled, and what specific steps are we doing to make it better?" Never mind that she knows damn well what the issues are, that Ron's reach makes its way across the pond, too; it's the most words I've heard from her since she moved to London and I'm instantly washed in shame, a childhood-grade shame not so different from the day in kindergarten when I colored in that phonics worksheet wrong. It expands in my upper spine and my throat. Tears press up from my stomach the way vomit would, in a wave that advances a bit more with each cycle. Peristaltic crying. I can't stop it and I can't risk a dash for the lobby doors in this state, either. I just round over my lap and sob as invisibly as possible and give myself this little pep talk:

You are a shameful person. You're weak and indecisive. You have no guts, no backbone. You let your team down every day because you're not strong or smart or brave enough for this place. And don't pretend you haven't always known this day would come, when everyone would finally see that you don't belong at

Amazon. This is when the system starts to reject your sad, dull-minded, misbegotten self. It won't spit you out today, or even this year. You've got too much fake cred for it to happen that fast. But you'll stop mattering. People will lose whatever hope they placed in you. And eventually you'll slink away and be replaced with someone who has a functioning spine, someone who can please without needing to please, someone who doesn't give a single fuck about consensus or feelings or caution. Someone who acts less like a goddamn useless woman. *And you'll deserve it, because you're a mediocrity who should never have gotten in the door.*

The sheer force of the evisceration stops my tears, and I take advantage of the lull to slap on my sunglasses and walk around the block a few times, where my mind gets quiet enough to let the underlying thought through, the one I've been fighting off all morning:

Maybe I should start drinking again.

I know I won't actually do it. Even the notion of putting alcohol in my mouth is viscerally repulsive by now, even bizarre, like drinking watered-down antifreeze. But the impulse is devastating all the same. I cross Mercer with a bunch of boys in their twenties, junior devs on scooters and hoverboards. I hit the docks and start pacing along the marina. *What are you going to do?* I ask myself. *You can't have a job that makes you want to drink.*

It hits me like brand-new news that I could just leave. I could even leave *right now.* Just drive away and never come back. John wouldn't care; if anything, he'd be delighted. *I'd be a failure*, I think. But suddenly the word looks so small. *Okay, let's say you run screaming and become a failure. Do you care? What if you just . . . let yourself fail?* I almost laugh out loud at the notion of *deciding* to let myself fail. But it's inside me now, even if it sounds absurd, as physically impossible as willing myself to drown.

But everyone would know *I failed*, I think then. *If I leave this job before I've nailed it.*

So? Let's say two hundred people write you off as a failure, but meanwhile you're sober and not crying all the time. Would that be a fair trade-off?

I don't know. The word "failure" is starting to look big again and I have to back away from it. But I store away the idea that failure could be exactly what I need. I add it to a mental list I started compiling the day I discovered the strawberry stand and realized I was interested in myself: *You like wooden boats and flaky salt and having dahlias at your desk. Sometimes you tell yourself mean things when you run. You feel calmer when you go outside at lunchtime. If you don't sleep well one night, you usually do the next. Having a whole mystery series to read makes you feel safe. You always thought you weren't tough, but you are. You really do believe failure goes on some sort of permanent record. You can get weirdly absorbed in cleaning out a drawer. You try so hard to be good at things you don't actually want to do. You never ask yourself if maybe you should just stop doing them.*

27

WHAT WE THINK WILL MAKE US HAPPY FOR ONCE

I don't run screaming right away. I want to hold out for the right next role, so I need to be solid enough at this one to buy myself some time. For the next month I overprepare for meetings, though it often doesn't matter because by the time the meeting takes place, Ron's changed his mind about whatever we're doing anyway. When Arthur visits, I listen thoughtfully to his complaints about advances and I say "Go Blue!" back. Lorna comes back from London for two weeks and I try to avoid running into her, because if she treats me coldly I think it could actually break me this time. With my directs, I'm all painted-on calm helpfulness. I think Vance knows something is wrong, because he takes to belting his own version of "Rose's Turn" from *Gypsy* at me in our one-on-ones. "I have a dream / I dream it for you, Kristi!" But the others don't seem to suspect I've declared myself a dead woman walking, even though I've pared down my office to what will fit in one tote bag. No more tchotchkes. No more three extra pairs of shoes. Certainly no more gifts of wine from authors. Just a lacquer in-box, a pair of headphones, a coffee mug, and the wooden musical merry-go-round someone gave my mother the day I was born. I could be out of here on fifteen seconds' notice, and knowing is enough to keep me here for now.

———

But outside work, something else is happening: a rapacious curiosity about everything around me. Strawberry-boat moments come along often now. I see modern dancers on television and wonder where the line between plain old movement and dance first began. Captivated by the spice aisle at Whole Foods, I bring home four varieties of salt and force poor John to do a taste test with me. "When you get right down to it, what even *is* salt?" I ask him. John has also quit drinking by now, though I doubt the salt tastings had much to do with it. I think about my childhood fascinations: mermaids, sticker albums, Trixie Belden books. What happened to that bookish, gawky girl in the Mork from Ork suspenders and sad perm? Is she still in here somewhere, underneath all the spreadsheets and meticulous highlights and lipstick painstakingly chosen to look exactly like, well, my lips? It's not that I want to fully be her again. But maybe we could meet in the middle.

One Saturday afternoon, I'm puttering around the house and start to think about all the years I spent wanting to be a writer. More to the point, all the years I spent actually *writing*, from age four to twenty-eight. Poems, three-act plays, a third of a novel, essays, two full short-story collections. The living room has two walls of built-in bookshelves where I keep copies of the little magazines I published in on the bottom shelf. I sit on the floor and pull out the story Amy Hempel chose as first runner-up in a contest.

I'm all set to cringe, but it's really not half-bad, if a bit thin and overly controlled. I start spotting lines I'd change if I could, and then a whole section near the end catches my attention, a tricky section that I never quite nailed. *Ooh, I know*

how I'd fix this, I think. I haven't written creatively in more
than a decade, but I've read a *lot* at work and home and I guess
I've picked up some knowledge of how to make a story work.
And the idea of fixing it sounds *fun*, too. My body feels the
way it does on a favorite amusement-park ride: awake, attentive, only the happy kind of nervous.

I still have a few old books of writing prompts, and I take one
to a quiet coffee shop in the neighborhood, along with a notebook and pen. I feel *unlicensed* and in danger of being found out,
but I riffle through the book until I find a prompt I like, and
then I write a page of a story about a man and a woman snowed
in together the same day they've broken up. It takes me a couple
of hours to write that one page, because of all the considerations
I'd forgotten, like sentence rhythm and starting the dialogue in
the right place and being clear about place and time. There are
a hundred decisions to make and it turns out I still remember
how to make a lot of them. Maybe I can learn the rest, I think,
and the aperture in my mind's eye switches to wide-screen.

Nothing on the Amazon job board piques my curiosity, and
though I begin returning headhunters' calls, the notion of
starting over entirely is exhausting. But one day Brian, the guy
who led my Executive Development retreat, mass-emails the
alums asking if we know a good candidate for a junior program
manager to handle logistics and contracts for his program, and
it sparks an idea.

John and I go to dinner at Marnie and Andy's new house,
a glass-and-steel box like a small but dazzling airport hangar.
Andy and I have never talked about my sobriety, but when
we arrive, he's making elaborate alcohol-free cocktails from
homemade rhubarb syrup and some sort of smoked-wood

infusion, which I find enormously touching. John huddles at the far (and I do mean *far*) end of the counter with him while I tell Marnie what I'm thinking. "Would it be completely insane if I went to work for Brian?"

"No, because you told me on our last day in the program that you wanted to work on it someday," she says, slicing leeks into thin circles. When I don't say anything, she looks up. "Don't you remember?"

"Not at *all*."

"Well, you did," she says. "So if you still want to do it, it can't be that crazy?" Andy hands us martini glasses filled with pinkish-red liquid that tastes like a smoky Campari. "So we have some news," Marnie says, and I immediately wonder if she's pregnant. The wedding isn't for a few more months, but I know they'd like a kid and no one is getting any younger.

"We're moving to San Francisco," Andy says, and they both look so damn happy about it that I guess I can't throw the screaming tantrum I want to.

"Wow. Why?" I say in a tone that probably conveys the same idea.

"Because San Francisco gets 260 days of sunshine a year and Seattle gets 152," Marnie says. I wait for more reasons, but that's it, I guess.

"Are you sure?" I ask. "Because you know, fog, plus remember how bitchy Mark Twain got about the weather there, and he normally had a more positive attitude."

"Mark Twain?" John says.

"What?" I say. "He found San Francisco to be a terribly uninhabitable place."

"He just said it was cold, not dark," Marnie says. "You've seen how it's been for me. I used to need one sun vacation to get through winter, then two, and now it's three. It's getting *expensive*. Plus, the Bay Area is only a two-hour flight from here! And we'll have a guesthouse with its own full bath, so you'll always have a place to stay."

"So you're both transferring?" John asks while I pull out my phone and attempt to discreetly disprove that San Francisco is sunnier than Seattle.

"No, that's the other thing," Andy says. "We're both leaving Amazon."

"We've slowly come around to the idea that working for Amazon is kind of a drag," Marnie says. "I'm going to get my MSW and become a therapist for women in toxic workplaces."

"And I have no idea what I'm going to do," Andy says. "But there are like ten thousand start-ups down there that could probably use an Amazon vet if they want to scale."

Google has confirmed the days-of-sun thing, because Google sucks. "But you *just* bought this house," I try.

"Yeah, selling it will probably be a wash," Andy says.

"But in a way, who cares?" Marnie says. "We're going to live in a place with daylight and not work for Amazon. And you should go work for Brian if you want. Haven't we all slogged it out long enough to do what we think will make us happy for once?"

At home that night I email Brian. "Obviously your open role is too junior for me, but what would you think about using me in some other way?"

He replies within ten minutes. "Can you meet tomorrow morning? 9 a.m.?"

My last day at APub comes five weeks later. John and I are going on vacation in Oregon, and then we're picking up Ella, the ten-week-old golden retriever puppy we've adopted as a kid sister for Linus, and then I'm moving two buildings away to start my two-year term as the inaugural Leadership Development Fellow on Brian's team, a role we invented together in the course of one coffee date. As a career move, it's pretty zigzaggy. It's certainly a two-year step off the promotion path. But who cares? I just want to learn new things and have a chance to feel valuable again. And I want kindness. My team members take the change in stride like the veterans they are, and if anyone senses how desperately I want out, they don't comment on it. Lorna in London says nothing. Ron also says nothing, so I request a short meeting on my last day to say goodbye.

"Big changes!" he says.

"Yes!" I say. "I really wanted to thank you for the opportunities I've had here. I've learned an insane amount in these three years." My larynx feels wobbly and I have a flash of frustration that I'm in my mid-forties and haven't learned how not to almost cry.

"Glad to hear it!" he says, grinning. This would be a good time for him to thank me in return for being flexible and brave enough to take on three separate whole-ass jobs in three years and nail at least two of them. But he just sits there smiling.

"If I could offer one bit of advice for going forward," I say, "it would be that I think people could use some re-inspiration, which is something you're so good at." I really am starting to judder now, so I say the last bit fast: "I think people need to hear a little more often about the things they're doing right. I think it would make a real difference."

"Great!" he says as if I've delivered a huge compliment. "I will certainly take that into account."

"Well, thanks," I mumble, and flee in the slightly shamed hermit-crab shape my body will still assume a decade later when I think about how it started and how it ended and the dignity I will never get back.

PART IV

DRY

2014–2015

28

PR/FAQ

**Amazon.com veteran Kristi Coulter joins
Executive Development Faculty as inaugural
Leadership Development Fellow**

*Coulter to teach Amazon's theory and practice of business
management to company executives*

SEATTLE—JANUARY 15, 2014—Veteran Amazon.com
employee Kristi Coulter has joined the company's Executive
Development Faculty as its first Leadership Development
Fellow, reporting to program leader Brian Simmons. During
her two-year appointment, Coulter will co-develop and teach
Amazon's theory and practice of managing at global scale to
company executives from around the world.

Amazon's Executive Development training is a six-month
engagement in which high-potential company leaders come
together for a carefully structured series of off-site retreats,
simulations, 360-degree feedback, individual coaching, and
peer collaboration. Each participant brings a real-life Amazon business challenge from his or her job to use as learning material, and works with faculty and other students to

design a solution based on Amazon's theory of replicable, self-improving mechanisms.

"Going through Executive Development training myself was a highlight of my Amazon career and made me a better leader," said Coulter, who most recently served as West Coast Editorial Director for Amazon Publishing. "My time at Amazon Publishing has been an unmitigated joy in every respect, and it's hard to leave. But I can't say no to this opportunity to use my Amazon business experience in service of its brilliant leadership theory and curriculum."

FREQUENTLY ASKED QUESTIONS
(*for internal use only*)

Q. So this seems like a bit of a career zag for Coulter?
A. Amazon is proud to offer a culture where employees can explore a wide variety of interests that allow them to utilize all their natural strengths and develop new ones. Coulter is thrilled to come full circle and put the totality of her skill and knowledge to work on behalf of Amazon leaders and, indirectly, the Amazon customers they serve.

Q. Can you be more specific about why she's making this change?
A. Recent personal developments in Coulter's life awakened a desire to repurpose the skills and energy she has been putting into Amazon Publishing toward a new end, and joining Executive Development offered the perfect opportunity. "I just can't imagine anything more satisfying," she says.

Q. Is that true? Can she really not imagine anything more satisfying?

A. When asked for confirmation, she nodded and smiled.

Q. And why now?

A. With seven months of sobriety under her belt, it occurred to Coulter that it would be easier to stay sober in a job that did not flood her with anxiety and despair. "I've gained a fair amount of clarity in sobriety, and spent a lot of time reflecting," Coulter says. "One thing that became clear through that reflection is that Amazon Publishing is a teeming clusterfuck where I don't want to spend one more second of my time on this earth."

Q. Oh, so it was all Amazon Publishing's fault? Sounds like a serious lack of Vocal Self-Criticism.

A. No, of course it wasn't all Amazon Publishing's fault. It was also not the right role for Coulter, who is temperamentally unsuited to making as many decisions on the fly as the job required of her. The jump from running one imprint to six overwhelmed her, and the larger business's rapidly changing strategies and goals sometimes disturbed her equilibrium. And also, Amazon Publishing was "a carnival of chaos, missed signals, and male entitlement," and the idea of dealing with it any longer made her want to lie down in the road.

Q. Coulter had been focused on Amazon Publishing as her path to a long-desired promotion. Did she consider gutting it out for that purpose alone?

A. After she was told the criteria was "changing the world"? "No," says Coulter.

Q. He *really* said that?
A. "He sure did," says Coulter.

Q. And yet she stayed on the team.
A. That's not a question.

Q. Wait, is this Kristi talking now? Where did PR go?
A. Yeah, it's me. I asked PR if it was true that Jeff just bought the sky and they went running to find out.

Q. Why did you stay on the team?
A. I thought no one else would want me.

Q. And your sobriety altered that perspective?
A. Yes. I had long assumed that getting sober would mean finally facing head-on the abyss of my own inadequacy. Instead, I realized that I like myself and deserve to work somewhere less reminiscent of a goat rodeo staged on a rusty Tilt-a-Whirl.

Q. Fair. But still—why swerve into an entirely new domain?
A. If you've been paying attention, you know that swerving into new domains is kind of what I do. Also, the two weeks I spent as a participant in the Executive Development program were the most valued I've ever felt at Amazon. Like a human full of strengths and potential, versus a person-shaped, sad-macramé knot of tasks and deficits. I want to help give fellow Amazonians that same experience. And based on the interview loop, I think Brian and my other new colleagues are worthy of my time and energy.

Q. *They're* worthy of *your* time and energy? Noting a lack of humility here.
A. [*Laughter.*]

Q. Why are you laughing?
A. Because you think I give a fuck.

29

ACTIVE REST

"Try a few more beats of silence," Brian says softly as our students disperse for the mid-morning break. "Next time you ask the group a question. Just give it another five or ten seconds before you answer it for them."

"I can *feel* myself jumping in too fast," I say, "like it's my job to prevent awkward silences." Brian is a giant with a sonorous baritone voice, and even at five feet nine in my heels it's as if a friendly tree has folded on itself to chat with me. But I'm slowly getting used to it.

"It happens to everyone," he says. "Play around with something new and see what happens."

Ten minutes later, the cohort has reassembled in the banquet room and I'm standing in front of them again, gesturing at the big screen. "So, before the break we were talking about which of these management levers leaders tend to underuse when managing on a global scale," I say. "Let's look at the flip side now: In your experience, which of these have you seen *overused*? Or overused yourself?" I look out at twenty-four impassive faces—twenty-two of them male and two female, same as when Marnie and I were students five years ago. It seems clear that they will never, ever speak, but I wait. Why can't a few of them at least make dramatic thinking faces? I wait a little more. Brian winks from the camcorder at the back of the room and I think, *Boy, do I hate that guy.* The answer starts to inflate my lungs, but I give it five more seconds.

"I guess I'd say org structure is overused?" ventures a product manager from the Sydney office to nods and murmurs. "Reorgs especially. Sometimes they're necessary, but sometimes I think we use them as a magic pill. 'We' including 'me.'"

I smile to acknowledge his openness, and secretly at my tiny triumph. "I call reorgs Amazon Boggle," I say, miming the shaking of the cube. "You know you'll end up in a slot, but in the meantime it's loud and bumpy." That gets a laugh, and just like that I don't feel alone in the room anymore.

When we break for dinner, I linger in the classroom, which is actually the grand stone-and-beam event room at Sleeping Lady, a retreat center two hours outside Seattle. It's snowy on this side of Stevens Pass, and the view outside is woody and idyllic, like a Pacific Northwest spin on Currier and Ives. "So, that was possibly the most useful feedback I've heard in my entire Amazon career," I tell Brian once the last student has left.

"Say more about that," he says, which is his response at least half the time anyone says anything, it being a trainer's habit to keep people talking once they've started.

I think. He waits. "Well, it was practical," I say. "You suggested something I could *do*, versus just 'be better at drawing students out.' And it was in the moment, so I could try it out right away. Now that I've tried it, I won't be too nervous about doing it again. It was honestly very helpful to me."

Brian smiles. "That's how all feedback should work," he says. "By the way, the time from when you asked the question to when Daniel responded was just ten seconds. I clocked it."

"That's insane," I say.

"Time can be that way."

It must be said that I sometimes find Brian a bit loony too, or at least wildly un-Amazonian. Because Amazon is so over-meetinged in general, there's considerable discipline at the individual meeting level, with clear agendas and scheduled times that rarely extend past an hour. But Leadership Development is a quiet cul-de-sac where Brian can schedule four-hour meetings, essentially free-form rap sessions, whose sole agenda item is something like "Curriculum improvements." If he swings by my desk and says, "Got a minute?" he could actually mean a minute or he could still be rambling happily two hours later about what we should teach at 3:00 p.m. on Wednesday of week two. And all elements of the job seem to have equal weight in his eyes; I've seen him segue from thirty minutes on a point of management theory to ten on whether we have enough dry-erase markers on hand without the slightest change in tone. Working for Brian sometimes feels like being trapped with the nattering professor who Explains It All at the end of a disaster movie. As perfectly suited as he seems for this Amazon role, I'm pretty sure he would crash and burn in any other.

He's also a bit in love with his own thinking. I find myself asked to "pressure test" his ideas, only for him to decide every time that he was right after all. We go back and forth for twenty minutes one day about the definition of the word "innovation." Brian insists that unless any new thing in the world kicks off a self-perpetuating continuous improvement cycle, it isn't truly innovative. I think this is picky to the point of being batshit, and also it's 2:30 p.m. and I'm badly in need of my 2:00 p.m. coffee and a little grouchy about it. "By that definition, if TVs were still big boxes with antennas like we had as kids, they wouldn't be considered an innovation," I say. "If the wheel hadn't become attached to a car, it would just be some round thing. If heart surgery hadn't become something a robot could do, we'd consider it no big deal."

"All good points," Brian says. "But I think what you're describing is the quality of *being innovative*, while I'm talking about *innovation*."

My next logical line of argument is, *WHAT THE FUCK, BRIAN?! What kind of maniacal hairsplitting* is *this?* But it occurs to me just in time that I don't really care that much. I already know I'm not going to change his mind; my job in pressure testing Brian's ideas is to be just tough enough that he can think he's legitimately confirmed them. I've done that, and now I'm tired and ready to move on. I roll my eyes, but with a smile to signify it's all in fun. "Brian, you are parsing those words to a *very* fine degree. But I haven't really thought about it that way, either. Maybe I should sit with the idea for a day or two."

This is my way of reminding him I'm an introvert, something we've touched on several times since the one-on-one where I identified it as a fatal flaw. He'd asked if there were development areas I'd especially like his help on, something I'd never been asked before. "I guess my introversion?" I said. "I think it makes me less likely to have big public debates and think fast enough on the fly. So I feel like I need to at least be better at faking being an extrovert." I tell him that at APub, I got anonymous peer feedback saying that introversion—in general, not just mine—didn't square with good leadership.

"Well, that was ridiculous peer feedback," Brian said,

drawing up taller in his seat. "Was Abraham Lincoln a bad leader? Rosa Parks? Is Warren Buffett a bad leader? What about Bill Gates? Elon Musk?"

"Elon actually does seem pretty bad," I said. "But good point about the others."

The next morning he dropped a book about introversion on my desk: *Quiet* by Susan Cain. I read it in one sitting that night, amazed to see so many of the traits I saw as weaknesses—like needing one freaking quiet moment to process new information, or feeling rattled in rowdy group discussions—reframed as just a different-but-equal way of being. "You know how I hate sudden changes of plan?" I asked John in bed later. "That's not me being a stick-in-the-mud. It's just introversion! You know how at family dinners I'm okay for a while and then I want God to end my life? I don't actually hate *all* of our relatives. I'm just an introvert! You know how I can't just pull ideas out of my ass on the spot at work? I'm not actually dumber than the people who can. I'm just an introvert!"

"Baby, I'm really happy for you," John said. "But I need to turn inward to go to sleep now."

Brian picks up on the cue I'm using now. "Well, I'll be very curious to know where your thinking leads you," he says. I don't actually plan to think about it, of course. I plan to walk away and let Brian be right. And I don't feel the least bit guilty about that, either, though the dutiful girl in me knows I should. If I can admit that I need space and time to do my best thinking, then I can also admit that what I need this year is what runners call active rest, or walking even though I could probably force myself to run. Because active rest is for recovery, and I am in more kinds of recovery than one.

———

Brian has the floor for the afternoon session, an introduction to the business simulation we've built the whole week around. I'm running a few minutes late from conducting a Bar Raiser debrief by phone and then slipping on a patch of ice outside my cabin; like those of everyone in our group except a few avid skiers, my clothes and shoes are unsuited to real winter weather. I enter via a door next to the giant stone fireplace just as Brian is asking the group to name some great leaders.

"Churchill," one guy says as I enter. Churchill always comes up early.

"Patton," says the guy in a blue-and-red-striped sweater that triggers an association in my mind I can't quite name.

"Certainly. Who else?" Brian says.

"MacArthur," a burly bald guy says. "Grant."

"Sure," Brian says. "Any *non*military examples?" *Ernie!* I think. The blue-and-red sweater is a Muppets sweater.

"I know she was controversial, but Margaret Thatcher," says one of the women. *Oh, c'mon, don't disclaim your own choice in advance*, I think.

"Thatcher made a lot of mistakes," says Churchill guy. "A lot." *Like Churchill didn't?* I want to ask, but maybe I shouldn't lay into one of my own students first thing.

"Let's just name them," Brian says. "Not debate them."

Silence. Then a guy who arrived from Chennai just hours before the training kickoff says, "Should I be the nerd who says 'Jeff Bezos'?" and everyone laughs.

At dinner, conversation at my table centers on whether Sleeping Lady is too pleasant a venue for Amazon to use. "I mean, I'm eating lamb risotto," says the man who earlier mentioned Patton. "Which is great, but feels almost *wrong*. Like this is money we could be spending on a better customer experience." Heads nod all around the table.

A certain kind of Amazonian loves to gripe about non-Calvinist surroundings. The lobbies in our new South Lake Union buildings are no fancier than those in any real company, but I still hear people cluck about them as though they featured Jacuzzis and rare white tigers rather than just non-sagging sofas and current magazines. At times I think it's harmless nostalgia for the dorm couches in our old lobby. But sometimes I think bare-bones ugliness has become a fetish for us, a complement to the CrossFit boxes and Spartan races that have become trendy in Seattle. Maybe some employees like the contrast with the custom granite countertops and wine fridges and kids' playrooms in their five-bedroom Eastside houses.

The thing is, Sleeping Lady isn't even all that fancy. It's more of an elevated summer camp than the kinds of resorts I have no doubt these guys frequent in Banff and Kona. The rooms are on the basic side, the food is all buffet-style, and the gym was apparently teleported from someone's 1986 basement. It's just *comfortable*, designed so that people can be well rested and well fed enough to focus during the twelve-hour days in store for them. I'm not even sure how much of the grumbling is real and how much is performative, a Frupidity Olympics rich men stage for each other the same way they tried to one-up each other with war leaders this afternoon. "You know, there actually *is* a bunkhouse on the property," I say. "I think it sleeps twelve. Just in case you really want to hear each other snore."

After dinner a bunch of them head for the Grotto, Sleeping Lady's bar. "Coming along?" someone asks me. From my own student days I have fond memories of drinking lots of wine in that bar and flirting madly with an irreverent Jeff Goldblum–esque exec from the entertainment division. And for bonding purposes, some bar time wouldn't hurt. But nine months sober, I still dread the moment it becomes clear to others that I don't drink, the quick calculations and adjustments I see—or think I see—pass over their faces, and the follow-up questions that feel intrusive no matter how kindly or casually they're meant. If I go along, I'll end up feeling less like part of the group, not more.

So I'm glad to have the excuse of an 8:00 p.m. meeting with Brian to debrief on the day, even though I'm also kind of irritated by it (seriously, can't it wait?). As we settle into a corner of the cafeteria with our decafs and crème brûlées from the legendary dessert bar, I tell him about the frugality panic.

He shakes his head. "There's always someone," he says. "They're welcome to sleep on the bus if it helps."

When we wrap up, he asks if I'm heading to the Grotto. I shake my head. "I haven't been not drinking for long enough to feel comfortable in bars yet," I say. I haven't managed to use the word "sober" out loud yet; this awkward negative gerund is the best I can offer.

I flush a little as I say it, but Brian just nods. "Cool," he says. "See you in the a.m., then." He doesn't know it, but I'm practicing this on him, too.

The next morning at 7:57 I'm back in the events building, this time on the staircase overlooking the huge lobby, watching the cohort hive around the ground floor. Some of the men are tapping on their phones, some flipping through the packets of fake emails they were given last night. A few of them are commiserating about hangovers from that trip to the bar. In a far corner, the two women are talking intently.

Brian comes out of the classroom behind me in the purple shirt he always wears on day one of the Glass Factory simulation. "I'm very, *very* curious to see how this plays out," he says, steepling his long fingers. "You've got a little puddle around you, by the way."

"It's from the snow," I say. My jeans hems picked it up on the walk from my cottage to the lodge. "Wait, how do you *not* have a puddle?" But it's 8:00 a.m. now, time for Brian to execute his magic trick for silencing a large and scattered group of people: he silently raises his hand in the air. As soon as he does, I raise mine too. A man facing our direction sees our hands and raises his, and the men near him raise theirs and stop talking, and so on. Within fifteen seconds everyone in the room is silent and has one hand in the air.

"Good morning," Brian says in his bass voice. "The annual executive meeting of Looking Glass Incorporated has now begun. Behave as you normally would. Run the company as you wish. We will convene back here in six hours."

The participants immediately skitter into new groups, gathering at the chairs and whiteboards set up for their preassigned divisions, while the executive team they elected yesterday enters the meeting room behind us on the landing. "I think I'll start in there," Brian says to me. "How about you?"

"I'm going to tail the auto-glass division for a bit and then maybe LCD," I say with a wave as we part.

Every cohort complains that it's silly to simulate running a glass factory. What Amazon does is far more complex than making glass, they say. Sometimes they argue there's no simulation in the *world* that can mimic true Amazon conditions.

But that's intentional. The goal is to observe their natural behavior under pressure, not how well they can out-Amazon each other. From my own experience, I know that being a fake glass plant manager will feel stilted and silly for about ten minutes and then the group will forget it isn't real and however they act at Amazon is how they will act here.

I spend the next few hours floating among conversations as they form and dissolve. As I predicted, the suspension of disbelief is total; these poor souls are running this fucking glass factory as if their lives depend on it. One guy is sharing data on the going rate for soda that isn't in anyone's packet; he must be one of the people in each cohort who take it upon themselves to spend the night before the simulation becoming Google experts on glass, even though we tell them there's no need. ("I assumed you were trying to trick us into underpreparing," this man will say later. We've promised them there are no tricks and no psyops, but some people think that's just part of the bigger psyop.)

On the other side of the room, three men are huddled in folding chairs. They glance at me as I pull up a fourth, but for once I'm actually meant to be ignored. There's something almost erotic about the power to insert myself wherever I want, knowing no one can question my right to be there or pull me into the discussion. My value here is in my gaze, and I can use it freely, watching faces and body language to a degree I'd never dare in the real world.

Just before lunch I see the two women and one man, a Customer Service site manager from Costa Rica, at a table near the buffet. I place a wager in my head as I approach. Yep, it's the diversity committee. Rumblings about rank-and-file diversity concerns are scattered through the simulation email packets, but there's no call to action and no one assigned to next steps. In some cohorts, no one picks up the thread; when someone does, Brian says it's almost always a woman.

You know who's *not* doing extra work these days, though? Me. Just regular work, which is still more than one normal person's job, but more than manageable for an Amazonian. And much of the work I've left behind is emotional. For the first time since I came to Amazon, I'm not managing anyone, which also means that for the first time in a decade I'm not trying to convince a brilliant woman that she isn't an abject failure. I didn't know how incredible it would feel to drop the weight of other women's self-loathing, to move around campus letting women's well-being be someone else's problem. I guess I should care, but I've given up. Giving up feels like the smartest way to go, for now.

By the time the sim ends at 2:00 p.m. the cohort is glassy-eyed and monosyllabic, but there's no downtime on the agenda; instead, we herd them to the breakout cabins scattered around the property. The one my group is assigned to, named Nuthatch, is charming but snug. "Whoa!" says one tall, ferrety tech director to his neighbor as our group of eight squeezes around a table better for six. "Careful with that leg. Don't make me file a sexual harassment complaint." The sim makes people pretty punchy, and I don't care about his dumb joke, but as the only woman in the room I know any reaction I have will carry extra weight. So instead of either laughing or ostentatiously *not* laughing along with the men, I feign enrapturement with my phone. Abstention: a girl's best friend.

Ten minutes later, he does it again. "Watch the elbow, buddy, this isn't feeling like a safe environment." This time

I give him a cool, level gaze while everyone else chuckles. By the third time, my gaze has expanded to cover the chuckling lot of them. It's not that I expect anyone to deliver a sermon about sexual harassment being no laughing matter. But could at least *one* of the jackasses not join in? The kindest explanation is that they think harassment is just, like, a *concept*, not something that might have actually happened to the woman five feet from them. That because they've never done it or witnessed it, it can't really exist. Or maybe they're so accustomed to women like me striving to pass as hybrids that they unconsciously assume I'll share their point of view. Or maybe they just don't see me at all.

Whatever the reason, it's not okay. It's not okay for these men to be so trapped in their own heads that they can't see the woman across the table as a person who actually has been harassed at work. When we break for the evening, I leave the cottage quickly, before Brian can make me hang around for yet another debrief, and head for a footbridge toward the back of the property. I push snow off the railing so I can rest my elbows on it and lean there in the dark. I know what I have to do, and I really, really don't want to do it.

The next day is devoted to peer feedback based on behaviors during the sim. We regroup in the cabin and follow a formal protocol known as Situation, Behavior, Impact. SBI is designed to prevent vague, unactionable feedback like "You suck at running a glass factory." Instead, the feedback giver might say, "Tom, in the situation where we discussed retooling your factory, you expressed surprise that glass is a man-made material, saying you believed it to be a form of magical ice. The impact of this behavior was that I questioned whether you have the right level of knowledge to run a glass plant, or whether in fact you might suck at it." The only thing the recipient is allowed to say in response is, "Thank you for the feedback." We pass a handheld recorder from person to person so the feedback recipient can later play it all back, perhaps on a continuous loop in his sleep.

When it's Sexual Harassment Guy's turn to hear feedback, the man next to him goes first. "Dan," he says, "the situation was the midday team check-in, when you suggested I talk with the auto-glass marketing director about work I was planning to take on myself. And the impact of your behavior is that you saved me some wasted cycles and mistakes."

"Thank you for the feedback," Dan says.

The next guy says, "Dan, my feedback is related to your role as leader of the plant-merger meeting. The situation was Jeff proposing we give up our physical plant and join his. When I voiced hesitation, you cut me off, saying we could revisit the issue later. But you never circled back, and the impact is that I felt unheard and also worried that we would make a decision without the proper due diligence."

"Thank you for the feedback," Dan says.

The recorder is passed to me. I try to take a deep breath without letting my rib cage or shoulders show it.

"Dan," I say, "my feedback is related to a situation in this room, not the simulation. The behavior is that you joked several times about being sexually harassed or accused of sexual harassment. They were lighthearted-sounding jokes and I didn't sense any malice behind them." I know that if I don't absolve him of evil intent up front, he might not listen at all. "But being harassed on the job is a common experience for women. I've been sexually harassed and it's made it harder to do my job. So one impact is that I felt alienated by the repeated jokes." So far, so good. Now for the kicker. "Also, it's easy to unconsciously assume other people have had similar life experiences. But if that assumption alienates your employees and co-workers, their mistrust could weaken your effectiveness as a leader."

Every cell in my body wants to end by thanking him for listening, or apologizing in case he felt uncomfortable. I keep my mouth shut.

The room falls silent, but thanks to Brian I now know how to withstand that, too. Then Dan says, "Thank you for the feedback." All the other men are staring at their hands, except for Brian, who has a slight smile on his face and is looking at me as if I just shape-shifted before his eyes.

"You're welcome," I say, and pass the recorder to my left. *Now* my heart starts juddering. Now the cortisol dams break. It's my usual pattern: calm through the brave part, a wreck immediately afterward. But better than the other way around.

At day's end, Brian and I stay seated as the men file out quietly. He turns to me as the last one out shuts the door. "Of all the times not to be videotaping," he says. "That was a *model* of courage and clarity. I wish I could play it back for you so you could see yourself."

"It wasn't too harsh?" I ask.

"*No*," Brian says. "Get that out of your head. It was flawless, and your masterstroke was to couch it as the leadership limitation it is. That could be a career limiter for him and he needs to hear it."

Does he really, though? I looked Dan up in the phone tool last night. His twelve direct reports are all men, and all but two of *their* forty-odd direct reports are men. His boss is a man, and so are all his peers on the team. It's likely that failure to empathize with women won't hurt Dan's career one bit. But I'm going to appreciate this moment anyway, the first time in my twenty-year career anyone has called me courageous.

Around sunset, I go for a run and pass another member of the group running in the opposite direction. "Nice work back there," he tosses over his shoulder. "Took balls."

The next morning, the jokester and I wind up at the breakfast bar at the same time. "These scones are my downfall," he says.

"They're so good," I say, and take this exchange as a signal that we are okay, though I'm surprised to notice that I don't particularly care.

30

WRAPPED IN PLASTIC

I called it. I warned Brian that if the cohort was scandalized by having a comfortable place to sleep, the prospect of traveling by seaplane to part two of the program would cause a full-on dark night of the soul. "How did you guys justify the cost of private planes versus a bus?" asks a man waiting with me near the window at Kenmore Air on Lake Union, jiggling change in his pocket. It's early June and the sun beating through the glass still feels novel and luxurious after a damp, dark spring.

"Easy," I say. "Alderbrook is an eight-hour trip by bus and forty-five minutes by seaplane. We're saving two whole transportation days."

"That makes sense," he allows. "The optics aren't great, though."

I hold my palms out like scales. "Bad optics versus wasting over three hundred hours of executive time," I say.

"Fair enough," he says, and we return to staring out at the lake. "I might just be antsy," he says a moment later. "I've never flown on a plane anywhere near this small before."

"I took a seaplane trip once as a kid," I say. "It was scary at first, but then it was fine. Don't worry." In truth, it was an experience of *pure terror*, because I was ten and we were flying to the Bahamas through the Devil's Triangle, subject of tabloid articles and *In Search Of* episodes about planes and ships vanishing mysteriously. I spent the whole flight waiting to be sucked out of time and space forever. Even now, I'm not *super* thrilled to be getting onto a plane the size of my grandfather's Buick. But as a faculty member, I think I probably shouldn't share any of this with a nervous student. In loco parentis and all that, even if he's about my age.

When we board, I realize the students are split between two twelve-seaters, while the four faculty members are all traveling together on our own tiny plane. "This seems weird," I muse to Brian as we follow our pilot down the dock. "If our plane crashes, who's left to teach the class?"

Brian gives me a funny look. "Do you think we'd just keep going as normal if only *half* the faculty died en route?"

"I guess I kind of did," I say.

"For better or worse, you are a true Amazonian," he says.

When we reach the plane, the pilot asks who wants to sit up front with him, a horrifying prospect I had not anticipated. "This guy does," I say, pointing to Brian.

A year into my rotation, I already know that a permanent gig on this team isn't for me. The aspects that initially appealed to me, like the sleepy pace and ivory-tower atmosphere, are pleasant but also make me feel vanished from relevancy into a dusty netherworld, like the basement office in *The Wire*. Most of the students are directors, and I'm acutely aware that I'm teaching people who managed the promotion I've been failing to land for a decade. Also, Amazon might have altered my DNA. I don't *mind* this sleepy life, but I know my destiny is to be back out there doing things that feel impossible even once they're done.

In April, John and I visit Marnie and Andy and their infant son in the Bay Area. Sitting on their deck after dinner one evening, I ask if they ever miss Amazon.

"Never," says Marnie.

Andy, who's now running a digital start-up, shakes his head. "There are a few things about the culture, like six-pagers, that I'm trying to introduce at my new gig," he says. "Amazon is really smart about some things. But I don't miss the constant grind at all."

"Why? Are you thinking of finally getting out?" Marnie asks.

John snorts. "She's always and never thinking of getting out."

I ignore that. "I don't know. I've been using this role to shop for my next boss, and it's been pretty uninspiring. It seems like almost everyone who comes through the program has some form of clinical depression. And of course it's 90 percent men, which says something about who Amazon is investing in." Toxic masculinity in Silicon Valley has been a mini-trend online lately, with stories in tech magazines about parties with models paid to attend and coercive boss/employee hot tubbing. But as always, masculinity at Amazon looks more like stoicism and duty than cocaine and ball-pit orgies. It's having months of work brutally torn apart in a meeting and saying, "Thank you for the feedback." It's calling into the WBR from vacation without being asked. It's the carefully neutral way you say "Good times" when things go sideways. I think maybe Silicon Valley hires the high-fiving princes of entitlement, and Amazon goes for the men raised to believe work and fun should be poles apart.

———

So far, no one in the seaplane cohort jumps out as the future boss of me. But I'm excited for the week anyway. In this year of our Lord 2015, Amazon has formed its first diversity team, whose first job is to quantify just how bad (or not) the status quo is. For weeks, rumors circulate around HR that the data on gender is, quote, fascinating. As it happens, Brian and I are looking for some data to use in class that will be outside the cohort's collective subject matter expertise. "I feel confident the average Amazon executive knows almost *nothing* about gender," I tell Brian, who chuckles and then gets to work negotiating access to the data and permission to use it in class.

A few weeks later, he drops a one-page summary on my desk. "Here's what we've been waiting for," he says.

"Oh my *God*," I say twenty seconds later, having finally become one of those people who can zero in fast on the key metric.

"Yeah, it's not great," Brian says. At entry level, Amazon's gender split is roughly equal. But by manager level, women have shrunk to a third of the population. At my level they're a quarter of it, and so on up the ladder above me: the bigger the job, the fewer the women. It's always *seemed* like that, but seeing it quantified is still jarring.

"What is *happening*?" I say, staring at the page. "Are we leaving, or just getting passed over for promotion into management? When we leave, are we going to other companies, or dropping out of the workforce entirely? What's the offer rate for external female versus male candidates? How does this distribution vary across SVP orgs?"

"All good questions that I don't have answers for," Brian says. "This is all they'd allow us to see. The good news is, we have the go-ahead to use it. Carefully."

Now that we've landed at our destination with zero lives lost, the time has come. Our home this week is a sprawling white-clapboard resort on the Hood Canal with Adirondack chairs and games like cornhole and badminton scattered around the grounds. "It just always sounds so wrong to call it 'cornhole,'" one man near me mutters as we pass, which may be the most in agreement I have ever felt with another human being. Our main classroom is basically a glassed-in gazebo, an amusingly feminine location for our latest group of dudes (plus one woman, a Finance director from Munich). Brian and I have agreed that he should take the lead in introducing the data, lest the men freak over hearing it from a girl. (I don't care if they freak, but it's not my call to make.) While Brian distributes copies of the data summary, I sit on my raised stool up front trying to look mild as a lamb.

"The goal of this exercise is to discuss what organizational levers you might pull if you wanted the data before you to look more like gender parity," Brian says. "We're not asking you to solve the problem today, or to debate whether it *is* a problem. Just what levers you would pull if you *did* want to solve it."

Everyone stares silently at their handouts for at least fifteen seconds. Finally, a Web Services director speaks up. "Pipeline," he says, hands up in a what-else gesture. "Start girls coding as young as possible." Yesss, I've won my bet with Brian that the pipeline would come up right away. One hundred percent of the gender discussions I've witnessed at Amazon have involved men agreeing we need to teach girl fetuses to code so we can hire them seventeen years later. This is one area where "move fast" does not apply.

"I violently agree. If we teach girls to see tech as a viable career path, logic would suggest they'll follow it," says a man in the front row.

"I think we're actually already *doing* this," says someone else. "We contribute to Girls Can Code, or whatever it's called."

"Girls *Who* Code," the Web Services guy says.

"Girls Who Code, yeah. We're already investing in that pipeline."

"I don't disagree that the pipeline is important," says a man I know a little bit from way back when I worked for Chuck. "But, you guys, what's happening at manager level? Just getting women into the pipeline is not going to solve for how they vanish into thin air as the levels go up."

"Work-life balance," says the AWS guy with a shrug. Here we go.

"Say more about that," Brian says.

"Women have children," he says. "Work-life balance is critical for moms." I catch the eye of the lone female cohort member, keeping my gaze neutral but wondering if she's as fascinated as I am by the mystical simplicity of "women have children."

"Okay," Brian says. "Work-life balance is a vague concept, though. What specific actions or resources would it take to move it in a favorable direction for women with kids?"

"Day care," says a man near the back.

"That's never going to happen," says someone else.

Fuck it, now is as good a time as any to jump in. "Remember, stay focused on what you think would be *effective*, not what you predict Amazon will or won't do," I say. I tell them quality day care is so scarce that I've known women to put their names on waiting lists in their first trimester of pregnancy. "And it's incredibly expensive, too. So if Amazon were to address both the supply and the cost issues, that does sound like a powerful lever to pull."

"Maybe," says the man who said day care would never happen. "But it would go against Amazon culture."

"Say more about that," Brian says.

"We're not like Google, with free massages and all that. Jeff's attitude is, 'We pay you well and *you* decide how to spend the money.' Providing day care for a subset of employees would go against that. It's more Amazonian to say, 'Here's your compensation package. If you want to spend some of it on day care, go for it.'"

Web Services guy is still thinking about work-life balance. "The problem is, Amazon doesn't support work-life balance for anyone," he says, to murmurs of agreement. "It just affects women differently, because women are moms. So . . . what do we do to support healthier work-life balance for *everyone*? That's the question."

"That's actually *not* the question," I say, tapping the document. "The question is which levers would you pull to achieve greater gender parity at Amazon."

"At what cost, though?" he asks.

"What?" I say, not trying to hide my irritation. "This exercise isn't about whether it's worth achieving gender parity. It's about how you would do it."

"With all due respect, it's un-Amazonian to accept a goal at face value when it should be questioned," says a man who hasn't spoken up before.

"This exercise has a specific purpose," I say, making eye contact with Brian and then breaking it so he doesn't perceive it as a handoff. "It's about how to use organizational levers to drive change, not whether the change should happen." I am dangerously close to being dismissable as a pedant, someone who just wants them to follow the rules. "But since we're here, say more about why this goal should be questioned," I add.

"I mean, I'm sure every person in this room would love to see more women in Amazon leadership roles." Heads nod vigorously as though these men have never craved anything more. "But what would it mean for us to become the kind of family-friendly company where that can happen? Would it mean moving slower? Having less aggressive goals?"

Brian's moving back toward the center of the room, so I hop off my stool and use the trick he taught me of walking into the audience to center attention on myself. "I just want to challenge an assumption some of you seem to be making," I say. "What data is *not* on the handout?" I wait five, ten, fifteen seconds. "There's no mention of parenting status. You're making assumptions in the absence of data, which could easily lead to the wrong solutions." *Am I a mom too?* I want to ask. *Is every woman you see someone designed to spend her life catering to someone else's needs?*

This is the moment it finally truly lands that I will never outrun my gender. Of course on some level I've known that for years, but never so starkly. I will never overcome the belief that the presence of women means a slower, softer, weaker Amazon. There is nothing I can do to make these men any smarter or less blind, because they're the norm and I'm a deviation. Or a deviant, a kidless mom, an outlier. A shock of energy runs through my body, but there's no place for it here.

"Fair point," says a fulfillment center GM from Cork. "There are probably any number of reasons women opt out of manager roles."

"Where does the data mention opting out?" I ask. "I'd call that another unknown."

"True," he says. "My point is just that not everybody wants the kinds of jobs the people in this room have. Honestly, it might be a sign of superior intelligence that a lot of women decide to do something else with their lives." That gets a laugh, of course. Those wise women, deliberately ceding all the money and power and opportunity to their inferiors. I catch the eye of the other woman again and raise one eyebrow to ask her if she wants to say anything, but her tight smile says she'll sit this one out.

"Nice work in a tough crowd today," Brian says when the afternoon session ends. "Debrief?"

But I'm already halfway out the door and pretend I didn't hear.

Back in Seattle the next week, we host a group of VPs for a "fireside chat" with Jeff Bezos, which as far as I can tell just means a meeting in a regular conference room where Jeff is guaranteed to be nice to you so you shouldn't be afraid. There's still a buzz of nervousness among the VPs, though, and from the ambient chatter I pick up while we wait for Jeff to arrive, I realize that a lot of these men (they're all men) have never laid eyes on Jeff before, much less met him. After all, Amazon employs about a quarter million people now, and the rumor is that Jeff has started to focus his time on a few specific pieces of the business, plus the whole outer space thing. The days of him meeting with merchandisers to talk about plogs are probably gone forever.

It's been three or four years since I saw Jeff, and my first thought when he enters the room with a smile and a "Hey, guys" is that he's *jacked*. Even his *head* looks more muscular. I lift weights too, but I am certainly not getting Jeff-level results.

The next thing I notice is that even now I'm not capable of seeing him as anything but a person. I try to see him through the eyes of one of the newer VPs, or a Facebook friend who thinks he should be in jail for unspecified crimes. I *know* he's wealthy to a degree I can't even conceptualize. I *know* his company runs on fear and superhuman expectations. I *know* he's the architect of practices that have harmed a lot of people and that he has done almost nothing with his unfathomable wealth to mitigate that harm. And yet I've been here too long to see him as the planet-owning villain or ominous cartoon character the world at large does. He's just the guy who runs this company and has made some decisions I support and an increasingly large number that I don't.

He even speaks the same way he always has, casual and aphoristic at once. I'm sure he's told these anecdotes a hundred times, but they still sound like ideas he's testing out on the fly. And I listen to him differently, more fully, knowing my presence here is incidental and there's no chance I'll have to speak. "People who are right a lot* are also people who change their minds a lot," he says at one point with a laugh, and I scribble it in my Moleskine like a koan to contemplate later.

Toward the end, someone asks what he perceives as the biggest threat to Amazon's future, and he says the two words that have already gone viral among employees in recent

---

* Are Right, A Lot Leadership Principle: "Leaders are right a lot. They have strong judgment and good instincts. They seek diverse perspectives and work to disconfirm their beliefs." I deeply wish I had known, oh, a decade earlier, that changing my mind was a legit part of being right.

months: "Social cohesion." If people just fall in line with each other instead of pushing for truth, he says, it will hamper Amazon's ability to find the right answers. Hearing this, I wish he could have witnessed last week's discussion about our gender imbalance. I have no reason to believe Jeff thinks Amazon's overwhelming maleness is a problem; if he did, we'd be taking dramatic action to solve it. But maybe the fact that not even one man was willing to buck the consensus would have appalled him. Maybe just by challenging their groupthink on principle, he could have woken a few of them up. I feel the missed opportunity in my chest. Because if not him, who?

At the same time, a new feeling has started to play around the edges. It's a giddy feeling, which is strange because it involves me not getting what I want, but it's undeniable, and this is what it says: *If you can never outrun your gender here, then you're off the hook for trying. If you're fucked, maybe you're also free.*

We spend much of the following month in Snoqualmie Falls, at a hotel known for standing in as the Lodge in *Twin Peaks*. "Diane, this pie is *incredible*," I say as Brian and I wait to check in.

"What's that again?" Brian asks, stooping as though he must have misheard.

"Agent Cooper? With his recorder?" No dice. "*Twin Peaks*," I say.

"Oh!" Brian says. "I always meant to watch that."

"The log is listening," says the guy in line behind us.

"The law is listening?" Brian says.

"The log," says the guy. "Also *Twin Peaks*."

"It's okay, Brian," I say with a pat on his arm. "You just had your mind on other things back then."

I've scored a room so close to the falls that the mist rises up to my balcony. All day I talk about management theory in the basement-level ballroom, and in the evenings I jog down to the base of the falls and cool myself in the fog, thinking, *She's wrapped in plastic.* There's a sign at the trailhead, warning that the climb back up is equivalent to twenty-six flights of stairs. Every night I convince myself this time will be easier and then trudge uphill with blazing logs for thighs and leaky lungs. *She's wrapped in plastic.* Laura Palmer died full of secrets, and when they did emerge, they were told by someone else.

My second soberversary falls at the end of our first week in Snoqualmie. I sit at the window that morning with my coffee and laptop open to an empty Facebook draft, wondering if I'm about to self-destruct. I'm connected to hundreds of Amazon colleagues here. What happens if I blow my rep for competence, control, reliability by coming out as in recovery? I feel a little silly for worrying—after all, who is steadier than someone who *doesn't* drink? Shouldn't everyone want a sober woman in their foxhole? But they've trained us to be on the lookout for hidden weakness more than visible strength. Maybe people will see me as a potential relapse, be afraid to put me in challenging roles.

I'm not at all sure this ends well for me. But I also don't think it ends well to keep leaving this huge chunk of myself at home, when there's already more than enough I can't share. And also, I want to take some credit for what I've done, to let people know that what may look like a few tweaks is more like a transformation.

You can always work *somewhere*, I tell myself.

"Today marks two years since my last drink," I type, and hit Post, and all day, when I'm not teaching, I watch the

Likes and hearts and well wishes appear, so many it's almost an animation, including scores of them from Amazonians I see all the time and ones I haven't seen in years. At dusk, I walk to the bottom of the falls and tell myself to please remember this day when just being myself did not in fact lead directly to doom.

I have plenty to do once the instructional season is over, managing our pool of executive coaches and writing case studies of pivotal decisions in Amazon history to be used in next year's classes and trying to devise a formula to predict which employees will get the most out of the program. (I get absolutely nowhere with the last thing but it's kind of fun.) Brian verbally delivers a performance review so glowing that I can feel the last traces of APub flop sweat vanish. It will set me up beautifully when I start interviewing for my next role, or at least it will once he types it up and enters it into the system, which he is always one day away from doing.

Within a few months I understand this is never going to happen; my best Amazon performance review is never going to be written down for me or anyone else to see. But I still need to find a new role in the next seven months, and the field of potential projects and managers is thoroughly uninspiring. The case histories have been so fun and illuminating to write, and the executives who are my sources so enthusiastic about them, that I start to fantasize about a role as Amazon's chief historian, assembling a whole library for both employees and outside researchers to access. But do I really want to invent *another* job for myself? It certainly won't get me back on the promotion track, and I feel as if I owe myself one more shot at that. Also, odds are it would mean working for Brian long term, and as good as he's been for me, I'm reaching the limits of what I can learn from him.

Out of the blue, Lorna invites me for coffee. I freeze when the invitation comes through, wondering what she could possibly want with me, especially given the frostiness of my last months at APub. I'm wary of being sucked back into worrying about whether she likes me or thinks I'm smart enough. But then I realize I don't particularly *care* what she thinks of me anymore. I don't work for her now, it's doubtful I ever will again, and my current job hunt is based on the assumption that I can't ask her for help. It would be nice if she respected me. I deserve it. But it's immaterial to my future.

Plus, I'm curious. "Okay," I murmur to myself, and hit Accept.

It turns out she's recommended me for a *job*, a really interesting job on a secret initiative.* "In full transparency, the VP approached me for it first," she says. "But it's too similar to my last few jobs. I told her she should talk to you, though. You could be a good fit."

At first I'm waiting for the other shoe to drop, but then I realize she's not doing this out of charity. Maybe she never washed her hands of me as thoroughly as I thought. Maybe there was more going on in her own work life back then than I knew, factors I couldn't see through my own desperation.

I'm tempted to ask. But she's still Lorna, not exactly a woman who invites confessions. So I just say thank you, that I'm happy she thought of me and will follow up with the VP. And then I ask how she's been, and we fill the rest of our time with talk of pets and vacations and what we've been reading.

---

* It turns out to be Amazon's physical bookstores, no longer a secret.

On the sidewalk afterward, we exchange a quick hug. "By the way," Lorna says. "A reporter from *The New York Times* contacted me about a story she's writing on Amazon culture. I think I'm going to decline to be interviewed, but can I give her your name? I'd like to do something to help her out, even though I don't want to talk."

"Sure," I say. "I might not talk either, but I'm happy to hear her out." Employees are forbidden to talk to the press without company permission, and even if I can do it without getting caught, it's still an act of disloyalty. The question is, Do I *want* to be a loyal Amazonian? What do I gain from that loyalty? What has it already cost me?

A few weeks later, a very pregnant Jodi Kantor meets me in the same café. "I want to be very clear that I'm speaking to you not just as an employee but as a *female* employee," I tell her before she starts recording. "Think of this as my testimony from alien territory."

PART V

GOING, GOING

2015–2018

31

EVENTS IN THE HISTORY OF FEMALE EMPLOYMENT

2013: Shortly before I leave APub, Arthur is sued in civil court for sexual assault by a pre-Amazon colleague. Sally and I read the news together over the phone, me at my desk and her in a cab to the airport. We're both gobsmacked. But an in-the-know colleague tells me it's been an open industry secret for years. "Everyone knew," he says. I ask if "everyone" includes the powers that be at Amazon. "I can't say for sure," he answers. "But it's hard to imagine them *not* knowing. The story was out there." I'm gobsmacked again* over the notion that Amazon might have knowingly hired a sexual harasser into a role where he had power over scores of women.

The silver lining is that the scandal accomplishes what two years of Arthur-driven chaos and mismanagement could not: he leaves Amazon. If the story hadn't broken, for all I know he'd still be there.

2016: Amazon begins construction on three giant geodesic domes, which Jeff really should have known the entire company would immediately begin calling Jeff's Balls. Jeff's Balls are meant to be a humid environment for rare native plants,

* Two gobsmackments in one day!

plus an equally humid "casual meeting space," plus home for a local bakery that sells five-dollar doughnuts. Meanwhile in the normal world, I badly snag a beloved Missoni pencil skirt on the bracket holding my door desk together. I also reach my tenth anniversary and am rewarded with a red stripe on my employee badge, if I physically go to the badge office and pick it up myself, that is, which I just cannot be bothered to do.

2016: Bar Raiser requests are coming in from far-flung parts of campus for teams I've never heard of. I ask Recruiting what's up and am told there's a new rule that every interview loop must include a woman, but a lot of teams don't have any women of their own to call on. I want to collapse into despair giggles when I hear this, but instead I say I'll pitch in as long as I can make it clear to candidates that I'm not part of the team they want to join. Separately, I have recently acquired one hundred pencils stamped "Smash the Patriarchy," and I leave at least one behind in every conference room* I visit as The Required Woman.

2016: I go see *Manchester by the Sea*, a film distributed by Amazon Studios. When our name appears in the opening credits, multiple audience members boo, and I hunch down in my seat lest they intuit I work for Amazon and pelt me with Raisinets. It strikes me as a key indicator of local sentiment toward Amazon that the booers presumably came here and paid money because they *want* to see this movie and yet they're still mad that we're the ones who released it.

---

* Along with various shuttle buses, public spaces, and, through methods I cannot divulge, a few men's restrooms.

2017: At one of those Bar Raiser interviews, when it's time for the candidate to ask *me* questions, his question is, "What will Amazon be doing in twenty years?" He's kind of a dick, both grandiose and evasive, and I think his question is dumb, but I give it a go. "I don't know," I say, "but I can tell you what *didn't* exist when I got here in 2006: the Kindle, Web Services, Amazon Studios, Amazon Publishing, Alexa, or Fresh, just to name the biggies." As I rattle them off, I'm a little awed by the scale of change I've witnessed. Maybe this was a good question after all. "So whatever it is, my guess is it'll be something neither you nor I have ever thought about."

The guy makes a game-show buzzer sound. "Wrong," he says. "It'll be hospitals."

2017: The #MeToo movement explodes, which is unfortunate for the Amazon Studios head who made big promises about his dick back in 2015. The producer he harassed talks to a reporter, the story makes the national media, and suddenly Amazon's private investigation isn't so private anymore and the studio head steps down. Hey, it only took eighteen months.

2017: At a coffee shop near my home, I overhear a start-up founder giving one of his young female employees a pep talk. "I know we're running lean," he says. "I can't offer the free massages and haircuts and three meals a day and Aeron chairs you could get at Amazon." My decorum wins out, but years later I'll still wonder how he got the idea that Amazonians got *any* of that stuff and whether I should have clued him in so he wouldn't feel inferior.

———

2018: On the Amazon intranet I call up the Old Fart tool, a nifty JavaScript thing someone built ages ago that reports your percentile for Amazon tenure. I enter my employee ID and learn that I've been at Amazon longer than all but 2 percent of employees. I don't know how to feel about that—proud, embarrassed, important, lost? Contrary to the tool's name, one thing I *don't* feel is old. I'm sober, I'm writing, I kind of like myself. What I am is tired. I'm too young to feel this tired.

32

NAKED GUY WANTS A COKE

"Imagine you have to explain something in writing that you barely understand yourself to millions of customers," says potential boss Josh, clutching both sides of our café table in gleeful anxiety. "It's new to the *entire planet*, so you can't even google it. And it's top secret, so even if there *were* experts to interview, you couldn't talk to them." He's grinning his face off. "How would you go about doing that?"

I have to laugh. "Um, with astounding skill, hopefully?"

"I know, I know, I'm being impossibly abstract," he says. "Believe me, I wish I could tell you more."

I've interviewed a bunch of hyped-up Amazon men to be my boss recently, but Josh is the first one who hasn't seemed as if he were on a death march. One guy thrummed his fingers on the table for the whole hour. "The opportunities for business growth are endless," said another, with an undertone of such dread that I wanted to hold his hand and tell him everything would be okay. All my boss candidates are pretty new to Amazon, which makes sense given that we've hired almost eighty thousand people in the last year. I know without having to ask that these men are in a state of shock, convinced they won't make it to the first stock vest, feeling guilty that they made their kids switch schools for *this*. I feel for them, but I'm also not signing up for anyone that transparently freaked out as my manager. I let those men know that whatever they're offering isn't quite the right fit for me and then I walk away.

Josh feels different. He's a little over-amped, yes, but seems as if he really loves his job.

"It's totally fine," I say. "Calista warned me."

Calista, who is now Josh's boss, boomeranged back from a whole ten months of retirement to lead this project. In fact, she's the one who first reached out to me. "I can't tell you what we're doing," she said when we met for lunch. "But I can tell you retirement was *fun*, so I wouldn't have come back for something that wasn't really exciting. And the role is practically made for you." There was a light in her eyes I didn't often see the first time I worked for her; she was as flinty and funny as ever, but more relaxed. Or maybe she was exactly the same, and I just grew out of my fear. I would love to work with her again, I realized, even if it wasn't directly this time.

"Even if you don't take the job, you and Josh should know each other," she added, and I see why now. Josh and I are about the same age and were both brainy art kids who somehow landed in oddball tech careers. He's one of the very few people at Amazon I can imagine having hung out with in college.

"Here's a hopefully helpful analogy for how bonkers this project is: think about when Henry Ford invented the combustion engine," Josh says. I nod as though I am familiar with anything about Henry Ford, jotting "combustion engine" in my notepad so I remember to google it later. "That one invention upended *centuries* of human behavior patterns. Which was amazing, but also terrifying, right? I mean, combustion engines can explode!"

I guess they can, now that he mentions it. "True!" I say.

"Well, what we're doing is just as fundamental a change to how people have always lived, and it has the potential to cause *profound* unease unless someone like you explains it to the world in exactly the right way."

This is not the first time the concept of mass consumer fear has come up in our thirty-minute conversation. "This doesn't involve, like, test rabbits, does it? Or actual explosions?" I ask. "You don't seem like the type, but I feel like I have to ask."

"No, no, no, nothing like that. Absolutely no bunnies," Josh says.

"And no one's waking up in a bathtub full of ice?"

"No organ theft," he says. "No microchips, no David Cronenberg stuff. It's a cool, good, benign thing that people will love once the best writer at Amazon has explained it to them and they realize there's nothing to fear."

Do *I* have something to fear if I take this job? Maybe. But my body feels abuzz in a way it hasn't since my best days in Amazon Publishing. The project sounds crazy and potentially scary, but in a *good* way that could bring back that only-at-Amazon thrill I love. When I got here, I figured I'd work in media marketing forever, but a decade later I've sold DVDs, built software, written as Jeff Bezos, interviewed over eight hundred people, run the world's biggest translation publisher, weighed in on whether a romance novel cover shows too much nipple, made adult men forget they don't really work in the glass industry. For a chronically anxious person, I seem to live for leaping into the unknown. "*I'm* the best writer at Amazon," I say. "So if you need someone to guide customers through a sea change, you need me."

I hadn't planned to say that, but I also think it's true. I look up to see if Josh is appalled and see that he's smiling bigger than ever.

"Do you think it's the bookstore?" John asks later. Rumors are flying that we're opening an actual brick-and-mortar bookstore in a shopping center near our house.

I shake my head. "A bookstore won't *shock* people, just enrage them." We roll through some other possibilities. Mail-order pharmacy? A bank? Health insurance? All would be news, sure, but hardly a rewrite of all human life as we know it.

"Amazon-made cars?" John guesses.

"Why would Amazon want to make a *car*?"

"Who knows why you people do anything? Why did you make that *phone*? A car might be stupid, but it would still be news."

"*Flying* cars would, maybe," I say. "Otherwise, come on, it's hardly Henry Ford's combustion engine." Having skimmed Ford's Wikipedia page after my meeting with Josh, I am now an authority.

"And you have to take the job *before* they can tell you what it is."

I nod. "Do you think that's crazy?"

"Yeah. But I also think it's cool."

I do too. In fact, I think the mix of cool and crazy might be what it takes to keep me at Amazon, the one thing it can offer me at this point that I can't easily find elsewhere.

Six weeks later, Josh meets me in his building lobby, where I have just signed a heap of forms promising not to spill the beans about whatever's going on here. We badge through a re-volving door off the lobby into a strikingly cold hallway, badge through another set of doors at the hallway's end, and then walk through a plywood mock-up of a turnstile into what looks like a pretend grocery store. Directly in front of me are shelves stocked with cereal and pasta and peanut butter, and to the right I see bins full of plastic fruit. Josh is watching me closely. "Whoa," I say. "We're making *food*?"

"Really good food!" Josh says. "Right here, all from scratch."

"Well, now I see what you mean about public mistrust," I say, but Josh looks confused. "Where are the ingredients grown? Are the farmers being paid fairly? Are we killing local restaurants? Is Jeff Bezos going to pay rent for all the waitresses and line cooks whose jobs he's destroying? Doesn't anyone care about the good old days when moms cooked dinner and the whole family sat down together? Is Amazon tracking what we eat and reporting it to our insurance companies so they can raise our premiums?"

"Oh," Josh says.

"Sorry. I've just worked here a long time," I remind him. We walk to the far wall, which is stocked with containers of Play-Doh pasta and meat loaf and hummus. I feel over-whelmed by how *personal* it is. After all, when I came here in 2006, Amazon didn't even want human beings to be writing copy anymore, and now, almost a decade later, we're cooking lunch for people.

"What *else* do you notice about this place?" Josh asks.

He trails me as I walk the length of the store. A few peo-ple are kneeling by one of the refrigerated shelves. Another group is talking about the ceiling, which seems to have a lot of *stuff* in it besides just lights. I pick up a box of cereal from the middle aisle and put it back. "Do the shelves refill automatically?" I ask.

"Nope, people do that the old-fashioned way," he says.

I go back to the refrigerated shelves, which are organized very precisely with plastic dividers. "How come there's Play-Doh food in the containers?" I ask. "That seems like a lot of work for a model store."

"It was," Josh says. "Why do you think we took the trouble?"

"Do they need to have weight?" I ask.

"You're getting warmer."

"Am I? I don't think I am."

Just then, Calista breezes out of a back room. "Yay, you're here!" she says, and gives me a big hug just before her phone rings. "Shit, I have to take this. Let's catch up soon," she says, grabbing a Diet Coke from a fridge case and exiting through a fake turnstile.

I watch her go. "Wait. If this was a real store, where would she pay?"

"She paid as she left," he says. "There's just no checkout. You take what you want and go."

"But how?"

"Because the store knows what you took," he says.

The Store Knows. It instantly takes on capital letters in my mind. Like Newspeak, or Big Brother.

"This is *incredible*. We're going to get *slaughtered*," I say with unmitigated glee. "Oh, wow. Thank you for giving me something truly insane to dig into."

Naked Guy Wants a Coke is the basic use case for Amazon Go. Naked Guy has no credit card wallet, no pockets filled with change, just a phone and his body. Naked Guy needs the phone to scan himself through the turnstile. But once he's in, he can even ditch the phone if he wants; he won't use it again. He just takes the Coke as though our store were his personal fridge, and when he leaves, the store will charge the card on his Amazon account and send him a receipt. Because The Store Knows.

Due to the secrecy of the project, we're housed in a generic leased building under the monorail tracks, a few blocks from campus. Engineers and scientists and designers and chefs have been working here for several years, but I'm the first and only writer and one of just a handful of people whose job encompasses every single part of the experience. The hub of a wheel, as Josh describes it, with many spokes plugged into me that rarely interact with each other. I have to design a system that makes it all speak in one voice, across screens and menus and stickers and signs and tutorials.

As I present initial concepts to the senior leadership team, I realize I've lucked into a rare trifecta:

1. My job is a perfect match for my talents.
2. My talents are critical to the success of the business.
3. The powers that be *know* my talents are critical to the success of the business.

It's surreally pleasurable to work for leaders who know that words matter. At one executive review, I suggest putting a sign over the exit that reads REALLY, YOU CAN GO! to reassure customers that even if they *feel* as if they were shoplifting, they aren't. Karthik, the widely feared VP of Engineering, is there. We've had a pleasant hey-how-are-you acquaintanceship for years, but I've never had to *work* with him before, and I'm surprised he's interested enough in the creative side to speak up. "I thought we usually avoided exclamation marks," he says, referring to editorial guidelines my team wrote the *first* time I worked for Calista.

"We do," I say. "But one or two in the entirety of the store is okay. And the sentence sounds kind of funereal without it. Even as Amazon's official Killer of Exclamation Marks, in this case I think it's important." I've never explained copy choices to a tech leader before, especially not one of his stature. And of course I have no data on customer preferences to offer him. I'm just riding mild rapids and hoping they stay mild.

He says the line aloud in a no-exclamation-mark tone. "Oh true, that's a bit grim. My other question is whether you considered adding the word 'just,' as in 'Really, you can just go!'"

"We did," I say, gesturing toward Megan, my counterpart for visual design. "But those four extra characters don't add much impact, and if anything I worry that they sound a bit impatient." All true, but I'm willing to capitulate on the "just" if there's much pushback.

There's no need, though. Karthik thinks for a moment and then says, "I can see that. Thank you. I don't have any other questions right now." I'm happy he landed on my side, but I'm downright giddy that he cared enough to question me at all.

My long Amazon history proves useful in unexpected ways, such as deciding how to message food expiration dates, a collective effort that takes several weeks of design mock-ups, reviews, and revisions before we're ready to present it for Calista's sign-off. "'Best by' is okay," Calista says in a way that tells me she's not crazy about it. "It's clear and accurate. But why did you decide against 'Enjoy by'? It's a little warmer." For the store to Know Things, the interior design must be simple and exact to the point of austerity. Words, hand lettering, and chalkboard illustrations have to do extra work to convey a happy human experience.

"'Enjoy by' was my initial favorite," I say. "But do you remember the Jeff Letter for Frustration-Free Packaging? When Jeff said we shouldn't presume to tell customers how they're going to feel? Telling our customers to enjoy the food might sound too much like an order. We should err on the side of just letting them know when it's freshest."

"I remember that vaguely at best," Calista says with a laugh. "But okay. I can get behind that reasoning." It's such a tiny thing to base a choice on, but it's those tiny things that tie me to the earth these days, the invisible net of words I'm making in hopes that our customers will feel safe and cared for in a way they never even stop to think about.

If only my day-to-day work life didn't remind me of how the merchandisers used to call themselves "monkeys." Leadership and my design peers may grasp that I'm doing real work, but most of the product managers treat me like a just-in-time service provider, someone who kind of slaps together copy for an audience of millions while they stand over me and watch. My desk is on an aisle, and four, six, even ten times an hour I hear the fateful words "Do you have thirty seconds?" to do something that will take at least thirty quiet minutes. Well, they're young and unused to working with writers, I reason at first; it's my job to teach them. I advertise daily office hours as the time I would be *delighted* to talk through ad hoc requests, but they go largely ignored. I offer a brown-bag presentation on the role of a principal writer and how to work with one and the PMs nod and then go right back to asking me to write complex instructions on the fly and without defined requirements. I start hiding out in phone rooms or Starbucks when I'm facing a deadline, but my meeting schedule is too dense to make fleeing the building sustainable or practical. So I resort to wearing big over-the-ear headphones as a signifier for "Please let me focus," to equally small effect. When I hit a record fifteen interruptions in a single hour, I march to Josh's office and tell him something's got to give.

"I'm being randomized," I say. "I feel like an abandoned game of Pick-Up Sticks." Josh came to Amazon just a year or so ago from the advertising world, and has told me explicitly that on top of my normal job duties, he needs me to be a walking Amazon role model for his other direct reports, who mostly grew up at normal companies and are struggling with the pace. They're being steamrolled by other teams, he tells me, and in response they try to work even faster, when instead they should be setting realistic, sustainable expectations and then meeting them. "I see now why the others are being walloped," I say. "There's somehow an impression that we're a real-time help desk."

"Yes, because Megan and the others have allowed that impression to form by never saying no to any outlandish request," Josh says sharply. If I'm not careful, he'll derail entirely onto the topic of how much his other directs are failing to act like Amazonians. Nice as it is to feel like the favorite, I don't want to talk smack about my colleagues with our boss. Also, the hard truth is that saying yes to every outlandish request *is* Amazonian. It may be ruinous and unsustainable, but Amazon as we know it wouldn't exist without a thousand tiny acts of self-destruction every day.

"I don't want to get sucked into the chaos they're enabling,"

I say now to keep us on track. "And I know *you* don't want me getting sucked into it, either. But all my boundaries are being ignored. I need a place to work that offers some level of physical protection, or I'm toast."

"What about coming in here when you need to focus?" he suggests, gesturing at his conference table. "I'd be happy for the company." It's sweet, but Josh has meetings in his office half the day. I take a deep breath and do something I can't recall ever doing before: ask for working conditions that actually enable my work.

"There's empty office space up and down the row," I say. "Why don't you just put me in an office?"

"I think those are all on hold for future L8 hires," he says.

"But they're empty now. So assign me to one and then kick me out when these future executives come along."

"Let me see what I can do," he says. "But I'll have to find someone to put in there with you. The optics of an L7 with a private office are not great."

"Josh, I don't mean this personally, but Amazon's arbitrary office policy is not my problem. Sure, give me an office mate, that's fine. But I'm not going to spend one minute worrying about the optics of being able to do the work Amazon ostensibly wants me to do." Within a day the design leader and I are in an office, and just by getting out of the line of sight, I find that my productivity triples. And I make a note that sometimes asking for what you need turns out okay.

Even with a suitable place to work, keeping up with thirteen separate program tracks is almost impossible. In a single hour, I can switch context from information hierarchy for the aisle signage to a cute tagline for a sandwiches campaign to a recipe for Tacos al Pastor to instructional copy in the app, a space so constrained that a haiku would break it. We've gone to great lengths to make shopping the store feel "normal," but there are a few unintuitive behaviors we need customers to learn, and each one takes weeks of copy testing and iteration. And the store's components are so tightly interrelated that one small technical or design change can require language updates in five or six spots. Because the PMs can't be counted on to update me when requirements change, I resort to attending all their project meetings in person, up to thirty hours' worth some weeks. Even then, I find myself in executive reviews looking at copy I've never seen for a use case I've never heard of. Calista knows right away when the words aren't mine. "Is this meant to be final copy?" she'll ask tactfully. I try to respond with equal tact, to avoid throwing junior people under the bus. "I think the team probably has time booked on my calendar to talk through what's needed here," I say.*

"Wait, you mean you can't just write it while we all sit here and stare at you?" our SVP, Ira, jokes. I'm grateful for his support and the gentle way he models it for the rank and file. But it only calms me a little. I'm failing at a systems level, I think, the system being me. On some level I think I *should* be able to produce the perfect words out of thin air while a roomful of people watch. Everything I've come to know and respect about my work style starts to fade now that I'm back in the maelstrom. Now needing time to think starts to feel again like a career-limiting weakness.

To counteract my growing anger over being treated like an afterthought, I start dashing across the street for lunchtime

---

* By meeting's end an Outlook invite arrives.

workouts at Orangetheory, a monstrous new group-fitness concept where you fly from treadmills to rowers to weight stations over the course of an hour at the behest of an instructor saying things like "Limits are imaginary!" and "If you've given me all you've got, give me just a little more!" over pounding club music. *Why is this person encouraging me to self-destruct?* I wonder, as Amazon dudes on either side of me jump the rails of treadmills going eight miles per hour. But I only need it to exhaust me into submission for the afternoon, keep me from flipping over a conference table the next time I'm blindsided in a meeting, or when some random L5 web dev tells me I should change a line Jeff has personally signed off on because he "doesn't like it." It's the Orangetheory beatdown that stops me from saying, "I don't give a single fuck what you like."

Sometimes I think Amazon should be paying for my Orangetheory.

On better days, I'm reminded that some of what I've begun calling "being a complete fucking idiot" is actually just being really young and really, really green. One afternoon, I'm in my office writing up interview feedback when the most chaotic PM in the group stops by. "Hey!" he says. "I need to know what we should print on the shelf talkers describing heat-and-eat entrées."

"You bet!" I chirp. I dread the sight of him so much that I've taken to being extra friendly in hopes he won't know. "What's your target date?"

"Unfortunately, it's today. The printer needs the files by five." It's ten to four. ChaosPM opens his laptop and shows me an Excel list of about twenty entrées. "I thought the easiest way to knock this out is if you just tell me what to say and I'll type it directly into the file. But I could also leave you in peace to do it yourself!" he adds, presumably because of the look on my face.

You were in college when he was born, I tell myself. *Be gentle.* "Unfortunately, I have a meeting at four that I can't postpone," I say. "But either way, I couldn't write all of this by five. This is a half day's work."

"Oh, *wow*," the PM says. "I had no idea it would take that long." We have had versions of this conversation many times; my theory is that he gets a factory reset in his sleep each night.

"Unfortunately, yeah," I say.

"Totally understood," he says. "The thing is, it's for a Jeff walk-through, and I think our entrées will look even better with your brilliant descriptions on them." Big smile, as though no girl could resist the allure of showing Jeff Bezos some substandard copy she churned out under duress.

"I would never put copy in front of Jeff that I can't defend down to the letter," I tell him. "And honestly, you don't want to do that either. There's no such thing as being over-prepared for Jeff."

He looks scared at that, which wasn't my intent, but I also don't regret it. "This will actually be my first time in a room with him," he says. "It's kind of weird to think he'll be standing *right there*."

"It's super weird," I tell him. "But it'll be okay."

When my meetings wrap up at six, I text John and say I'm going for a run before I head home. From the building I jog down to First and then all the way to Pioneer Square and back, past the Market and the Seattle Art Museum and the Four Seasons and the Union Gospel Mission, where men have started their nightly lineup for a bed. I feel angry and I don't know if it's at ChaosPM or at myself for not thriving in chaos. I'm imagining what he'll write in my performance review—that I "lack hustle," maybe, or I'm not "agile" enough. He is a terrible product manager, but I've seen no evidence that he knows it, or that anyone is even trying very hard to help him get better. "I know there are issues, but I just see so much potential in him," is his manager's standard line when anyone goes to him with a tale of havoc, but nothing ever seems to change. Maybe ChaosPM thinks it's genuinely all my fault, and he'll say so in peer feedback, and some people might believe him.

All of this is on my mind because for the fifth or sixth time I'm, quote, on the promotion track, unquote. According to Josh, at least. I could probably feel Calista out about it too, but in addition to being my friend, she's my boss's boss and I'm hesitant to blur that line. One of the challenges this time around—by now I know that in a career like mine there's always some weird structural quirk or history vacuum to work around—is that I'm the only L7 Principal Writer in all of Amazon and leveling guidelines for L8 don't even exist. So at our one-on-one earlier in the week, Josh handed me a job-agnostic set of Level 8 qualifications and asked me to take a stab at customizing them for my role. "Have you read this?" I asked after a scan of the first page.

"To be honest, I have not," he says. "Why?"

"It says right up front that the bar for being a Level 8 is 'nearly superhuman talent and stamina.'" I passed the doc back to him. "*Nearly superhuman?* Really?"

"This is nuts," Josh muttered. "We should not be sending that message."

"I'd like to think I could be promoted as a person, not a lab creation," I said.

"And you will be," he said. I want to believe him. But I've seen so much by now. The directors and VPs from my last gig, moving mountains every week and still so beaten down that I'm told many of the men burst into tears during their first session with their leadership coach. A friend so worn down from months of seven-day weeks that he developed shingles in his eyes* and nearly went blind. Jobs that sit open for six months because the candidates interviewed are merely great, not perfect. I may be Amazon's highest-ranked and best writer, but that doesn't mean Amazon thinks I'm good enough.

And the thing is, I'm not going to try to be *nearly superhuman*. Not anymore. Until I got sober, I thought sobriety was something you could berate yourself into, but it doesn't work that way. To stay sober, I have to allow myself to be just a person who does her best. And it doesn't really matter that my best is still a pretty fucking lofty standard; by *Amazon* standards I will always be failing just a little bit. When Marnie and I went through leadership training, one day she told the group, "We're here because we're some of Amazon's top talent, right? But the bar for our performance gets raised every year, and so does the bar for the people Amazon hires. So at least theoretically, none of us can keep up forever. Every single person in this room will go from being top talent to getting managed out." (Glum silence ensued.)

It's conceivable that in a few years *I'll* be in that 10 percent who wash out for being really good, but not *mythically* good. And make no mistake: I *want* to be mythically good. I want to be superhuman. My ambition to work on big, loony, hard things is as ravenous as ever. It's just that I also want to be sane,

---

* So there's a new thing for you to worry about.

and that means being sober, and if staying sober means being a mild disappointment to Amazon, then that's what I'll be.

It's rush hour, cool and drizzly, and every couple of blocks I have to wait for a WALK sign, but that's okay; I love to stop even more than I love to run, and I'm listening happily to a playlist of some of the filthiest Prince songs in existence, which for reasons I have chosen not to interrogate overlap heavily with my favorites. When I hit Pioneer Square, with its buckling Victorian brick sidewalks and faint waterfront smell, I'm back in the misty, cozy city I found the day of my Amazon interview. The chance to live among these bricks and evergreens and gentle raindrops is why I said yes. I want that feeling back so badly.

I stop at the crosswalk at First and Columbia, where the guy I often see here is propping up the signpost. Sometimes he ignores me and sometimes he asks me questions: *What time is it? Have you ever seen the purple sky? Why do you run so fast?* He's never been creepy like some other guys on my route, which is enough for me to consider him a very casual friend. (Also, he is the only person who's ever said I run fast.)

Tonight, with my earbuds in, I see him gesturing at me before I hear him. "Whatcha listening to?" he asks. Prince, I tell him. "RIP," he says.

"I know, right?" I respond.

"What song?" he wants to know, at almost the exact moment the words "twenty-three positions in a one-night stand" hit my ears. I'm not going to say "Gett Off" to this man.

"'Raspberry Beret'!" I say instead.

"Love that beret," he says.

"Yeah, it's a good one," I say.

All the way back to the office, I wonder what's the worst

that could have happened. Why not just tell the man the name of the song, instead of creating a safe space for us to meet in between? So many of my interactions with men involve lies of one kind or another that sometimes I don't even notice I'm lying. Maybe it's too late for that to change.

33

NOT THE AMAZON I KNOW

I see the name on my incoming call and duck into an empty phone room. "Hey, Jodi," I say.

"Hey," Jodi Kantor says. "I just wanted to give you a heads-up that we're publishing in tomorrow's paper, and to thank you again for your help. I was able to keep you out of the story, by the way."

I wasn't consciously aware of being worried about being named in the *New York Times* story. Jodi was so deep into it by the time we met that I really didn't have much new information to offer; I mostly corroborated facts and events she'd already researched and suggested a few more people to interview. But the relief that floods my chest says my body had fears my conscious mind wasn't privy to.

"That simplifies my life. Thank you," I say, and she laughs. I'm dying to ask her all about the story, of course, but I figure she has lots of these calls to make. I can wait eighteen hours and be surprised alongside everyone else. I just need to remember to act surprised, too.

INSIDE AMAZON: WRESTLING BIG IDEAS IN A BRUISING WORKPLACE. Hoo, boy. I leave the building the next morning and grab a park bench on the next block to read the massive front-page story in peace. The first pull quote jumps out: "Nearly every person I worked with, I saw cry at their desk." She went for it. She wrote a story about how Amazonians *feel*. I've read scores of stories about how customers and publishers and other retailers feel about Amazon, and ever since the 2011 piece on dangerously hot warehouse conditions there's been a steady trickle of reporting on that part of our workforce. But this is the first piece I've ever seen on the tens of thousands of us with desk jobs.

When we met, Jodi said she was looking to write a "balanced" story on the good and bad of Amazon culture. I assumed that even a balanced piece could make us look pretty bad, but it's actually much worse than I expected, and the grimmest anecdotes focus on women. There's the one who was put on probationary status shortly after a stillbirth, and the one whose boss threw her in the bottom 10 percent because her peers had accomplished more than she did during her cancer treatment, and the one told point-blank that having kids had been a fatal career error. Human biology is a bigger problem for Amazon than I realized.

Megan passes by on her way back from the doughnut shop. "Did you see?" she says.

"Seeing it right now," I say in my best jaunty-but-also-yikes voice.

"So do you find it believable? I'm too new to tell." Megan came here from the ad-agency world, where she once flew from New York to China twice in one week to pacify a client. She's no stranger to long hours or last-minute heroics, and she's game for allowing herself to be remolded into an Amazonian. But the chaos is taking its toll. "Things will stabilize after launch, right?" she asks me sometimes, and all I can say is "Ideally."

"Yeah, it's believable," I say now. In truth, I *do* have trouble imagining the conversation where the manager of the woman who had a stillbirth tells her she's going on probation, and the conversations with HR leading up to it. I can't quite make a *human scene* out of it in my head. But I believe it. Partly because my own first thought on reading that part was, *Well, how long post-stillbirth was she off her game? Are we talking three weeks, or three months?* Straight to the place where my own skin as her boss might be at risk and I'd have to choose which one of us to sacrifice.

"I was afraid you'd say that," Megan says.

The employee email aliases are ablaze. Well, it's more of a polite simmer on women@, with comments like "made some valid points" and "must confess I nodded in agreement at times" and "thought-provoking." A while back, there was chatter on women@ about some defaced elevator posters advertising a conference for women engineers; the word "women" was crossed out on all of them. A male SVP, and not just any male SVP but the most robotically alpha one in the company, eventually chimed in to say he'd look into it. Since then, the women on that alias always write as if they were being watched.

But the highly brotastic amazon-chatter@ list has no such fears. Most days it's a mix of libertarian philosophy, tips for staying in ketosis, and complaints about paying eight dollars for lunch at the taco truck, only to be hungry again a mere five hours later, even though that is pretty much just how the human body works. But today it's all *Times* talk, a largely dude-to-dude conversation that breaks down as:

> 50 percent: I have never personally witnessed these things, and therefore they cannot have happened, because I somehow made it to adulthood without understanding that my reality is not the only reality.
>
> 25 percent: Look, this place is not for everyone. There's nothing wrong with having kids or cancer or emotions; it just means you probably should be working somewhere else.
>
> 25 percent: These allegations are horrific, and even if they're just isolated incidents, Amazon needs to make sure nothing like it ever happens again.

I'm so sickeningly grateful to the latter 25 percent that I actually hate myself *and* them. It's the same gratitude I felt to the one boy in a clique who didn't call me a dog in middle school, to the one man in a meeting who said "I don't think Kristi was finished talking, let her make her point" when I was dealing with serial interrupters.

And then a guy named Nick pipes up to tell us he's just posted a rebuttal on LinkedIn, which I click on like a big old dummy who doesn't care if she drowns in her own cortisol.

Nick is pretty darn mad about the *Times* article, and he would like the world to know that as someone with *eighteen months* of Amazon tenure he knows whereof he speaks. Nick only works weekends by choice! Nick finds it refreshing to have a desk made out of a door instead of some boring store-bought thing with drawers and sealed edges. If the *Times* had bothered asking Nick about his team's daily Nerf wars, they'd understand that morale is *just fine* at Amazon.

Nick takes special umbrage at charges of gender discrimination at Amazon. First of all, Nick has literally worked with women who outrank him, and they have earned his respect! How would these women even exist in a sexist system? More broadly, gender discrimination at Amazon *logically cannot be possible* because Amazon makes decisions based on data, and data is science, and *science is gender neutral*. In his entire eighteen months, Nick has never personally witnessed a woman being discriminated against for speaking bluntly. And even if it *did* happen, HR would put an immediate stop to it, duh.

And just so we're clear: if gender discrimination *did* exist at Amazon, Nick would be leading the charge against it, because he is—yes—the father of a daughter. But it doesn't, because it can't, because science.

Amazon-chatter@ rains praise on Nick for hitting back at those faux journalists and the lying whiners they quoted. "Thank you for speaking truth to power," he is told. I watch the hosannas fly in for a few minutes, and then I sigh and type my own contribution to the thread: "Nick, I understand you have strong feelings about the NYT story and wanted to share your own perspective. But as a man, it was not appropriate for you to explain what it is like for women to work here; you simply lack the experience to speak on our behalf. If you are interested in learning more based on my decade of experience as a female Amazonian, I'm always happy to grab coffee and chat." (I deeply, deeply do not want to grab coffee with Nick, but I feel as if I'd better end on a collegial note.)

A few women email me privately to say thanks for speaking up. But on the thread itself: crickets.

———

I'm in a park by my house a few days later, stretching after a run. My phone buzzes and I see that Jeff has sent a company-wide email, the first one in my memory, about the *Times* article. Jeff says it doesn't describe the Amazon he knows, and that anyone working in such a terrible environment would be crazy to stay. I lean back against a tree and watch two border collies chasing Chuckit! balls while I contemplate the fact that Jeff Bezos thinks I'm nuts.

His words remind me of how women are encouraged to flounce out of workplaces where they're harassed or marginalized. *They don't deserve you! They'll be sorry when you're gone!* Sure. Put your income and insurance and career momentum on ice while you look for a new job. Maybe move across the country. Pull your kids out of school. Do what you need to do to make it to a place that might be better. But don't expect them to miss you when you're gone. If they cared about women fleeing, they would try to be less fleeable. Maybe that's what keeps me at Amazon after all this time, knowing that when I finally walk away, it will be as if I never existed. At least while I'm there, I can hold out hopes for recognition.

I glance back down at my phone and notice that Jeff has also linked to the gender theory expert Nick's rebuttal and encouraged all employees to read it for "an alternate perspective."

For Jeff Bezos to make that recommendation to all Amazon workers can only be viewed as an endorsement, and it's all I can do not to tear a branch off the tree I'm leaning against and cram it in my mouth like a bit to keep from screaming. Especially when I idly click on the link again (still a dummy) and notice for the first time that Nick has paired it with a photo of two female employees waving a rainbow flag at Seattle's Pride parade. I wonder if they even know they're being used as his diversity beards.

I get home, give a few dog kisses and receive an excessive number more, and find John working on his laptop in the living room. I hand him my phone open to Jeff's email. "You know Nick's thing about Amazon and gender?" I say. (Nick has already become a household name for us.) "The richest man on earth just amplified it."

John scans the email while I hang down over my hamstrings to stretch them and also because I don't really know what else to do. "What the fuck was he thinking?" he says when he's done. "This is a complete erasure of even the *possibility* of a systemic problem."

"It's blindness," I say, pulling off my running shoes. Linus ambles over, casually picks up one of my dirty socks, and leaves the room with it. "Oh, you're very welcome," I say to his departing butt.

"Blindness?" John says. "You're setting the bar way too low."

"Maybe so, but that doesn't make it untrue. He doesn't know what he can't see, and everyone around him is a man and they can't see it either so there's no one to tell him to get his megalord head out of his ass."

"I guarantee you some of them see it and they just don't care," John says. "Anyway, what would *Amazon* tell Jeff to do first? Investigate, right? Get the data. Not go shooting his mouth off to an audience of millions based on how he *feels*. Seriously, you need to stop giving this guy the benefit of the doubt."

I exhale through my mouth. "Give me a minute," I say. "I'm getting there."

34

RAAB OR RABE OR RAPE

A few months before we open Store 1, I get the budget to hire a freelance recipe writer to work with the Meal Kits team, ending the era of my googling "how to write a recipe" and hoping for the best. For a whole two or three weeks, having an actual qualified professional on hand makes everyone's life easier. But then I start getting texts from her like "I'm at the test kitchen for the 10 am session but the door is locked and no one's answering," or "Jasper emailed at 1 AM and asked me to come in today instead of tomorrow, but I can't bump my other client with no notice." Today she showed up at the appointed time—and getting to the test kitchen south of downtown at rush hour is no simple thing—only to be told that the entire recipe development sprint had been moved out by two weeks.

The recipe writer is a former Amazonian who knows how to roll with changes. But she's a freelancer now, not on salary or stored in a little box under my desk and powered up as needed. Saying yes to us means saying no to other work, and we're routinely fucking her over. "I am so sorry. Let me see what's going on," I text back. Jasper, who runs Meal Kits, is at his desk just outside my office. He's close enough to call to, but that makes me feel like a dick, so I walk over. "Hey, Jamie just texted me from the parking lot at the test kitchen. What's going on with the schedule?" I ask.

"Oh, shoot," he says. "Did we forget to tell you?"

"I think you must have," I say. *Again*, I add silently.

"It's really best if she checks the calendar for last-minute updates."

"The calendar hasn't changed," I say, showing him on my laptop.

"I am *so* sorry," Jasper says. "I really thought I'd told you both. We're just moving so fast that these little details fall through the cracks sometimes."

"I know you're moving fast," I say. "I'm just starting to worry about losing her if we keep breaking her trust, and we don't have hundreds of other great food writers to choose from in Seattle."

"I will make absolutely sure it never happens again," he says. "These little hiccups are just the cost of innovation."

It always comes down to "the cost of innovation" with this guy. I agree that innovation has its price. Sometimes it means teams of merchandisers doubling their work while you perfect a new platform. Or randomizing book-loving editors while you try to predict the future with statistics. Even in the best of times, innovation is messy and expensive, and that's okay. What's not okay is using it as an excuse to continually blow the basics of existing in time and space. I work in Jasper's direct line of sight—how can he look at me forty times a day and not remember to at least yell out a major schedule change? I support twelve other programs, but just trying to untangle the mess caused by Meal Kit reschedules and reshoots and versioning errors and unannounced ingredient changes can suck up a third of my week.

But also, this is Jasper's first job at Amazon, not to mention his first time overseeing a whole business. He seems to have been dropped into the ocean and left to flail on his own, just as I was eleven years ago. He tosses Leadership Principles around in a way that shows he doesn't understand them but would like to. And he's obviously working his ass off. He's at his desk when I arrive and leave for the day, and emailing well into the night, even on weekends. He's kind of killing me, to be clear. But I also think he's having a pretty bad time.

So all I say is, "Thanks. I'll let her know."

But my compassion starts to slide a few weeks later, when Jasper taps on my doorway and asks if I have a second to chat about the Seared Salmon with Broccoli Rabe. "I noticed you spelled 'rabe' with a *b*," he says. "But I'm pretty sure 'rape' is the more common spelling."

"Yeah, that was a four-way judgment call. There's also 'raab' and 'rapini,'" I say, jotting them on my whiteboard. "AP doesn't list a preference, but of the big recipe websites, most use 'rabe,' so that's how I made my decision." My use of "decision" instead of "recommendation" is not accidental. "What I generally do in that case is look at some of the top online recipe sites and see if there's a consensus," I say. "Of the six sites I checked, four used 'rabe' and two 'raab.'" By now I'm accustomed to random men telling me we should change this or that word because they "don't like it," and I'm done explaining nicely that I'm not just pulling the store's vocabulary out of my ass and don't have time to argue about every little thing based on some guy's *feeling*.

"Are you sure?" Jasper asks. "Because I just really feel like I see 'rape' much more frequently."

"I am," I say. "Epicurious, Bon Appétit, Food52—they all use 'rabe.' Honestly, I was surprised myself by the strength of the consensus." That's a lie. I wasn't remotely surprised that all those sites picked the non-sex-crime spelling. I'm just trying to give him a graceful way not to die on this hill.

But he doesn't want my grace. "Well, I can see you've done your homework," he says. "I'm just concerned that *customers* will be confused. In the name of Customer Obsession and Ownership, I have to say something."

Oh, goody, is this the part where he flings around Leadership Principles he doesn't understand? I guess it is.

"Of course!" I say. "But, you know, our customers use those sites too. So I think we can feel pretty confident that they'll be familiar with the term. And frankly, I would *really* like to avoid putting the word 'rape' all over our shelves if we can help it."

"Well, it doesn't *mean* rape."

"Yes, I know that this vegetable and a sex crime are two different things," I say.

"You say both syllables. Rah-pay."

"Yes, I know," I say again in lieu of getting up and running sprints up and down the hall while screaming. "But those four letters in that order will trigger an association in a typical customer's mind that we can easily avoid by using a much more popular spelling."

"What if we put an accent on the *e*?"

I have to laugh at that. "Jasper, it isn't spelled that way. We can't just go around slapping accent marks on random words. It'll make us look stupid, which undermines customer trust."

"Here's an idea," he says, making namaste hands. "We *test* it. We survey a hundred people within the org about which spelling they're more familiar with." Nice try, buddy. You're never supposed to turn down a chance to *gather data* at Amazon. But I'm not taking the bait.

"I am not spending my time running a survey to test a simple and already well-justified editorial choice," I say. "But feel free to escalate it if you feel strongly, of course."

I mean that. If he wants to go to his boss, an eminently commonsensical man I have known for ten years, and argue that we should print "rape" on hundreds of meal kit boxes, I'm here for it. But I know he won't escalate it, and he doesn't. He *horizontalizes* it, though, bringing it up in meetings and hallway conversations for the next week, asking others what they think. "I'm just trying to Dive Deep," he says a few times, meaning stay close to the details. I wish he would apply the same energy to the details of when my expensive and increasingly disgruntled freelancer is supposed to show up, but whatever. I repeat mildly each time that we're spelling it the way the biggest food sites in the world do, and no one but Jasper has any interest in knowing more. Eventually he stops fighting with me about the names of minor crucifers.

I assume he will be promoted past me within three years.

"*What?*" Megan says from behind her monitor a few months after Rabegate. "Did you read Jasper's annual planning doc yet? Pull up page 5."

I do as told. "What the fuck," I say, wheeling my chair to the side so I can see her across our partner desks.

"I met with him *yesterday* and this did not come up," she says. The doc says next year Jasper's team will produce twice as many distinct meal kits as it did this year, which would be fine except that each one takes a week of copy and design and photography from our team, and he knows damn well that our head count is flat next year. He's assuming twenty-six more weeks of work from us with no more people to do it.

The marketing manager Simon appears in our doorway. "*How?*" is all he says before closing the door and sinking into our visitor chair, a.k.a. the floor. "He knows I don't have the head count to support this. I had coffee with him *yesterday* and he didn't say a word."

"Megan, do you want to be the one to call a meeting?" I ask. "I think he's most afraid of you."

"Already on it," she says, and sure enough, here's the invitation on my screen.

"Shall we have a friendly bet on how he's expecting us to do twice the work with flat resources?" Simon asks. "My money's on 'get creative.'"

"I'll go with 'find efficiencies,'" I say.

"I guess it's possible he's allocating money from his budget to fund the resources?" Megan offers.

"I love you," Simon tells her. "You're adorable."

"Like a fuzzy little duckling," I agree.

Megan scheduled the meeting for the design studio, which at least puts them on our turf. Jasper is waiting with the head chef, Grant, and Grant's very calming dachshund Pepper when we arrive a few days later. "Hey, guys!" Jasper says, grinning, and the way that harmless grin raises my hackles tells me I'd better watch myself today.

"Hey, guys," Grant echoes faintly, eyes cast down, like someone who actually gets it. "So!" Jasper says once we're settled (including Pepper, who lies down in my lap and stares into the middle distance). "Exciting times for Meal Kits!"

"Absolutely!" Megan says.

"Definitely!" I add.

Now that we've established what thrilling times we are living in, Megan gets down to brass tacks. "That said, there's a *lot* to discuss before we can even come close to saying we can support doubled production next year." I nod. Grant nods. Pepper licks my jeans.

"Absolutely some things to work out," Jasper says. "But I'm excited to partner with you on this amazing growth opportunity for Amazon Go!"

"Totally!" I say. "It's just that Design and Copy aren't resourced to support this number. With the efficiencies we developed this year, we think we can probably eke out 10, *maybe* 20 percent more work with flat head count. But that's all." There, that takes "find efficiencies" off the table.

"Absolutely hear you on that," Jasper says. "Let me ask you this: Have you looked into reallocating hours from other programs you support that can manage with a little less?"

"No one we support needs less from us next year," I say. "We made our allocations based on what we thought were final projections from everyone, including you."

"We thought they were final projections too," he says. "But then we saw this opportunity to innovate, and we couldn't say no." Oh, good, it's been at least a few days since I've had a chance to hear about innovation from him. "Plus, we know you love Meal Kits the best out of all your partners." Pepper turns her head to the side as if embarrassed.

Megan leans forward over her knees. "Jasper, you read our annual planning doc. You were in the review meeting. We spent weeks making very reasoned, very hard calls about what we can support next year given that we are really and truly not being given additional heads. So I have to ask, Why is this request only coming up now?"

"We've just been thinking hard about how to go big and innovate on behalf of customers," he says. "I'm sure we can work with you to find additional efficiencies."

"Efficiencies will not double our capacity," Megan says. "We can't magically make bandwidth. We *have* to be able to plan and staff for this stuff." Grant, who would clearly prefer not to be in this room, nods.

"But that's not how innovation works," Jasper says, and maybe it's the soothing, horse-gentling tone in his voice that finally makes me raise my voice for the first time in my entire Amazon career.

"Hey, look," I say. It's sort of a bark, though less than a yell. "Don't tell Megan she doesn't know how innovation works. She knows how innovation works, and it doesn't mean just making twice the stuff with inadequate resources and expecting people who are supposed to be your partners to suck it up at all costs. Okay?"

Jasper and Grant flush. Megan looks a little gleeful but more dismayed. Pepper stretches her front legs. And I wonder what the fuck I just did and how badly I'm going to pay for it.

It doesn't take long to find out. I'm leaving a totally normal one-on-one with Josh the next day when he says, "Oh, by the way, there's some chatter going around that Jasper and Grant felt intimidated by how you talked to them in a meeting yesterday." He's already turned back to his desktop monitor when he speaks.

I sigh and sit back down. "Chatter from where?"

"Just around," he says, as I knew he would. Josh's habit

is to ascribe any negative feedback to the ether, so instead of knowing whom to go have a grown-up conversation with, you get to walk around wondering which of twenty possible people are mad at you.

"It was not my finest moment," I say. "I stand by what I said, but I wish I'd said it a little more calmly." This is both truthful and not. I'm certainly not proud of snapping at Jasper, but I'd hit my limit for bullshit and didn't know how else to make him hear me. After all, we did leave that meeting with an understanding that either his projections or our head count would have to change.

"I'm hearing that Grant in particular felt emotionally unsafe," Josh says.

"Emotionally unsafe?" I say. "Nothing against Grant, but if that was enough to make him feel *unsafe*, he is doomed at this company."

"Hey, I get it," Josh said. "I'm on your side."

"Emotionally unsafe," I repeat, thinking about Mitch and Chuck and Lorna.

"I'm just telling you what people are saying because your role is so broad and so critical that it would be dangerous for the project if you're someone people are afraid to work with."

"Wow, okay," I say. "I raise my voice once in *eleven years* at one of the most notoriously brutal companies on earth and now I have a rep as scary to work with."

"It's not a big deal," Josh says.

"Are you sure?" I say. "Because I personally wouldn't be talking about fear and danger if it weren't a big deal. Those words mean something to me, Josh."

"It's just something to be *aware* of," he's saying as I leave with a wave, running late to my next meeting, where I'm distracted by memories of all the performance reviews where I was told I lacked a backbone, that I was too nice, that I should disagree more freely. Throughout the hour I'm hyperconscious of every inflection in my voice and movement of my lips. Even reaching for my coffee cup, I try to seem warm and nonchalant. I make inquisitive and encouraging faces at everyone who speaks, and I minimize my own talking. If I don't get my footing on the tightrope between spineless and spiny, I'll plummet to earth. Maybe the fall would at least be a break from the way my toes keep cramping around the rope. Maybe the landing would be less bloody than I imagine. I can't quite bring myself to risk finding out, but I'm thinking about it.

35

PROFESSIONAL HELP, SECOND REVISION

By day I learn Amazon, and at night I seek out articles and listicles and TED Talks on femaling in the business world, just in case there are tips or hacks or something that could help me do it better. This is how I know I should lean forward in my chair far enough to show warmth but not cleavage. But also sit with my shoulder blades against the chair back and my feet on the floor. That I should stand with my hands on my hips but never cross my arms. Make eye contact for at least two seconds but never more than five. Look at a man's forehead and eyes—a.k.a. the business triangle—but never his nose or mouth, the social triangle. Listen with attentive interest but without nodding or tilting my head. Speak naturally, but never end on an upswing. Speak assertively, but don't interrupt. When interrupted by a man, insist on finishing my thought, but charmingly, so he won't feel as though he did anything wrong. Don't volunteer to take meeting notes, because it will seem secretarial. But do volunteer to take meeting notes because it's the only way to make sure my contributions will be captured. Do negotiate for more money, but don't let on that money motivates me. Be an advocate for women at work plural, but not myself as a woman at work singular. Always take credit for my accomplishments, but also

~~let my accomplishments speak for themselves. Raise my hand~~
~~for new assignments to be *helpful*, not eager. Dress to embrace~~
~~my femininity but also to de-emphasize my boobs, shoulders,~~
~~waist, hips, legs, lips, and hair. And smile. But not too much.~~
~~Less. Less. Yes, like that. Now hold.~~

~~Sit in whatever way allows you to not think about your body.~~
~~When entering a room with chairs at the table and along the~~
~~wall, take a chair at the table. Speak however you speak. Your~~
~~natural speaking voice got you this job and it has not magically~~
~~gone wrong since then. Arrange your head on your neck how-~~
~~ever you like. If it tilts, it tilts. You stand fine. You walk fine.~~
~~Do consider the power of the three-inch heel, the solid kind~~
~~you can stride in. But feel free to dismiss it, too. Don't apolo-~~
~~gize for making money or wanting more of it. Don't apologize~~
~~for making decisions. Don't apologize for using your leverage~~
~~to make things happen. Don't apologize for not knowing an~~
~~answer right away. Say you will get the answer and then do it.~~
~~Don't apologize for asking a question, but try not to ask the~~
~~same question more than once. Write down what you learn,~~
~~process it later, integrate it, let it lead you to your next, slightly~~
~~upgraded question. When you *do* need to apologize, do it sin-~~
~~cerely and do it just once and move on. Never hire someone~~
~~you wouldn't be willing to work for. Never hire someone who~~
~~isn't smarter than you in at least one key way. If you're nervous~~
~~before a meeting, write the two main points you want to make~~
~~on an index card you can refer to under the table. Spend the~~
~~most time with your best people, and if you are putting off~~
~~dealing with your worst people, be aware that your best peo-~~
~~ple know it and are waiting for you to do something. When~~
~~firing someone, remember it's *infinitely* worse for them than~~

~~it is for you. Always look for ways to bring other women into the room, but be wary of creeping volunteerism: it is not your job to serve on every single committee meant to help women advance. Pick one and feel free to recommend men for the others. Without men, such programs are closed circuits anyway, and never touch the real layers of power. Worry less about actually overcoming impostor syndrome—everyone has it, even men—and more about acting in spite of it. Learn to talk sports, or not. Have opinions about the Marvel universe, or not. *Never call anyone stupid.* For God's sake, wear what you want.~~

You can't outrun it. You will always be a deviation, an alien, a guest worker, an uneasily transplanted organ. You might be tolerated, even beloved and respected, but you will never be a *citizen*, and the problem isn't how you look or talk or act. The problem is that there is no right way to be a woman. In their eyes you will always be a bit too female or not quite female enough, and trying to walk the tightrope will kill you. The silver lining: if you can't outrun your gender, you might as well live as you please. It may be the freedom of the truly fucked, but I suggest you take it.

36

THE VEAL PEN

It's as if I were on two skis that are slowly being pulled apart. Inside Amazon it's the usual lunacy. Outside Amazon, I write an essay about women and drinking, an essay I think is good enough to submit for publication. Ten or so rejections later, I decide to just publish it myself on Medium. It's bound to get at least a few hundred reads, I figure.

A week later I'm on Radio Scotland to discuss my essay and the worldwide response it has elicited. It has been translated and republished in multiple languages. Reaction pieces have run in *Slate* and *The Washington Post* and *Time* and the *New York Post*, which doesn't like me one little bit. Editors and literary agents want to talk to me and magazines want me to write for them. I get letters from every continent except Antarctica, mostly lovely ones, though because it's a feminist essay there are some rape and death threats, too. Scanning my credit card, a barista asks if I'm *the* Kristi Coulter. At work, everyone's following along giddily. At home, John alternates between exploding with pride and saying things like "You know I know people who know people in Kazakhstan who could wipe out the digital lives of these rape-threat guys in ten minutes, right? Total obliteration as soon as you say the word."

John's out of town the day I get a book offer from the

publisher of my dreams, one of the venerable clubby New York ones with lore and scandals and geniuses on its list.* I come home after the phone call, explain the terms of the deal to Linus and Ella, and then comb through my bookshelves looking for the publisher's fish-shaped insignia. I make a stack of ten books by people like Joan Didion and Lydia Davis and Jeffrey Eugenides and Michael Cunningham, take a picture of it, and text it to John with a two-word message: "And me." He calls me ten minutes later, in tears. "It's the one thing you always wanted," he says.

"I know," I say. I can't cry. All I can think is that if I hadn't quit drinking, this wouldn't be happening, because the drinking me didn't write. I feel almost afraid that time will get tricky on me and undo it all by introducing, I don't know, a wormhole or whatever to a dimension where I can't get sober. I keep that part to myself, though. "It's been twenty years since I thought I blew my last chance at being a writer," I tell him. After we hang up, I lie down on the floor and let the dogs go nuts all over me.

The only sticking point is that I actually do have to write a book now, and I wouldn't say my first book deal included a quit-your-job advance. And it seems crazy to walk away from my career just because this one thing happened. I make a detailed schedule for completing the manuscript and start devoting weekends and some evenings to it, and that works for a while. I'm always rehearsing the book in my head anyway,

---

* I should mention that in a plot twist too wild to be anything but true, the offer came from Sally, who had left Amazon after fifteen years to work at said publisher of my dreams. It was Sally who convinced me my essay had the seeds of a book in it. In fact, Sally is the editor of this book, too.

so by the time I can sit down, I have plenty to get me started. The components pile up, but as my deadline approaches, it all starts to feel jagged, as if I were in a generous custody arrangement with my book but we don't actually live together.

One day outside the cafeteria I bump into a friend from Retail days who tells me she's just back from a leave of absence. "I forgot we even had those," I say.

"You haven't taken one?" she says. "In a *decade*?" I tell her I figured they were for having babies or dealing with cancer or losing a spouse. Something that would count as an excuse for not showing up at Amazon every day.

"No," she says. "No excuses needed. All I did was sleep and hang out with my kids and now I feel like a new person. Get your ass on leave, girl."

I get my ass on leave. Well, it takes me a few months, since I'm the only writer in this organization and can't just parcel out my job to others. But with the store launched, most of the big brand-level decisions like taglines and feature names are stable for now. I put my entire brain into a wiki for the designers and marketers to refer to for the daily small stuff. My last day in the office is Donald Trump's Inauguration Day. That night, I fly with Calista and a few other old-school Amazon women to Washington, D.C., for the Women's March, where for an afternoon I have the delusion that America might be okay, even with calamity now in office. On Sunday, I arrive home with three months of time to do nothing but finish my book and be a person.

It's *weird* at first. I haven't gone more than two weeks without full-time employment in almost twenty years. I'm pretty used to a bunch of money showing up in my checking account once a month. At least my benefits are still intact and so are my stock options, as long as I'm away for no longer than three months. At three months and one day, every unvested share gets wiped out, amounting to a two-thirds pay cut that would take me years to overcome. I feel as though I were leeching off John's income, though he's quick to remind me that my steady Amazon pay is what enabled his start-up to survive its bumpy first years, and now he gets to return the favor.

What's also weird is how quickly the weirdness passes. Within a week or two, I've settled into a routine of sleeping until nine, working on my book until mid-afternoon, and then running errands at nonpeak times. "Whole Foods at 3:00 p.m. is *empty*," I marvel to John. John and I work on separate floors, so we don't trip over each other, and Linus and Ella take to napping at what seems to be the mathematically exact midpoint between us. I was fearful that having so much time to write would do a number on my brain and make writing impossible. But it's fine. At some point since my twenties I guess I learned stamina.

Best and strangest of all: I'm not anxious about Amazon. Usually I spend part of any vacation worrying that things are either falling apart without me or worse, going better without me. That's gone now. I also don't miss Amazon; nor am I relieved to be away. I just don't think about it at all. And when it's time to go back, I'm not excited *or* full of dread. My book doesn't come out for another year, so in the meantime I'm just going back to the place where I exchange time and effort for money among people whose company I mostly enjoy.

I'm not expecting much fanfare around my return, which is good because aside from Calista I don't get so much as a welcome-back email. Everyone is still running around frantically and I slip back into the stream. Now that the first Amazon Go store has opened, I hope to come back to some big new projects, something that will stretch and break and hone my brain, something that makes me smarter. But instead of building new features, the org is focused on opening more stores, which means the hard part of my job is already done and what's left is on the level of arguing over how to spell "rabe."

Soon I'm bored and poking around for extra work. The newly acquired Whole Foods business lives in our org, and during those blissful midafternoon grocery runs I noticed that the Amazon and Whole Foods brand voices aren't playing well together. One poster in the elevator lobby is a colorful paean to local farmers, and the next is a picture of an Echo with a tagline that feels bot written. I ask Josh if I might do some in-house consulting work to help them out. "I love that idea in theory," he says. "But the entire integration team is like three people, and they're just trying to keep food on the shelves. It'll be a long time before they can think about copy."

He hands over my annual performance review, the reason for our meeting, and I give it a read. My peers say the usual nice things. I'm smart, see the big picture, can write, blah, blah, blah. And for only the second time in my Amazon career, no one says I lack backbone.

Only this time, having backbone seems to be a negative. I'm intimidating, one anonymous peer says. "Can be prickly at times," says another, which is fair, though I'm pretty sure I know who this is and he doesn't know that what I *wanted* to do was pick up the conference table and heave it out a fourth-floor window. "She doesn't suffer fools gladly," says a third person, making it clear this is something I need to work on.

"Huh," I say. Josh looks up from his laptop. "I'm supposed to suffer fools more gladly?"

"Oh, ignore that. I don't think that person understands what that phrase actually means," he says, which is irritating. Josh has the power to curate which pieces of peer feedback I see, and he's supposed to omit anything he finds irrelevant or unfair. This way, the feedback stays on my record, and future hiring managers will see it.

Because I had a great year when not being prickly or scary, Josh bases our discussion around my promotion prospects. This time, the sticking point is that to reach the senior executive ranks as a creative, I need to prove that I'm influential across *all* of Amazon.

"Of course that's been impossible in this role, since the project was top secret," Josh says. "But now it isn't, so we can look for ways for you to teach and influence company-wide, and I think that just might get you where you want to be." It strikes me that I've faced that barrier before.

Amazon has over six hundred thousand employees by now, doing everything from selling books to producing TV shows to making drones. Offhand, I can't come up with a way or even a valid reason to get into all those heads, so I start closer to home. "Whole Foods *and* the physical bookstores are in this org now," I say. "What if there were an umbrella role for copy and voice across all of our brick-and-mortar businesses? I'd love to do that job." Just the thought of it gives me a stomach flutter that says the fun kind of overwhelm lies ahead.

"Well, that would require organizational changes," Josh says. "But don't worry. I'm keeping my eyes open for opportunities for you. Just hang in there and be patient." It's the same talk I had with my boss at AMG when he was at a loss for how to extend my career path. *I'm keeping my eyes open, so just trust and be patient. Just keep being patient. Patient and quiet.*

At twilight a month later, I send the final-final-final draft of my book to Sally. Now a lot of other people will take over, copyediting it and designing a cover and deciding how to market it. My main task is to wring my hands and wait to be needed again. Having hit Send, I'm unsure what to do next, and I don't even mean in the grand sense. Linus and Ella are splayed at my feet like spilled waffle batter. "What do *you* think we should do?" I ask them. No response. "Well, let's go find Dad then."

John's watching soccer in the den. "I'm guess I'm done," I say. "I turned the book in."

"*Yes*," he says. "That's my girl. How do you feel?"

"I think I feel grief that I didn't start sooner," I say. "That I spent so much time doing other things besides writing."

"Hey, everything happens in its time," he says. "You did this when you were ready."

I sigh. "You don't need to make me feel better," I tell him. "It's just *reality* that I could have written two or three books in the time I've spent working at Amazon and drinking myself to death. I'm not young. I don't know how many books I have time left to write before I die."

"So is that what you want to do?" he says. "Write books for the rest of your life?"

"I mean, it feels like the reason I was born," I say.

And yet I don't quite grasp that I can choose how to spend the life I have left. "I was thinking about taking a year off," I tell our financial adviser at our next quarterly check-in. "To promote the book and try to write the next one. I'd have to resign from Amazon, but probably I could boomerang back?"

"Why just a year?" Sean asks. "Why not take all the time you want?"

"Well, we have to live on *something*," I say, tearing the label off the bottle of water the receptionist offered me. He and John exchange a look.

"She thinks we're going to land in a literal debtor's prison," John says.

"Sean," I say, "you've been saying for *years* that the absolute best financial move I can make is to keep working at Amazon."

"Well, yes, I did," Sean says. "And you stayed for another five years of stock overperformance. It's not like you never need to work again. But you don't need to keep earning Amazon money forever, either. You've bought yourself a lot of options."

"I do really like Amazon money, though," I sort of whisper, glancing down at my new ballet-pink Prada wedges. Sally says that life after Amazon is cheaper because you no longer feel compelled to constantly reward yourself just for surviving. But I'm wary. And I really like nice shoes.

Sean laughs. "Everyone likes Amazon money," he says. "But the Amazon money is also your ticket out of Amazon."

"Maybe two more years," I say. "Two more years should be long enough to get me promoted, right?" I've been two years from promotion for more than a decade now, but hey. "Four more vesting cycles." This, at least, is solid. The future may be vapor, but the cash is real.

"Fine with me," John says. "But how do you feel when you say that?"

"Angry," I say, with a hard stop that indicates nothing more is coming.

Megan and I are in our office later that week when the team admin comes by. "So, I have news," she says. "We're running out of space, and so everyone below director level is going to be moving to high-density seating."

High-density seating means no cubes, no dividers, no boundaries at all, just a bunch of door desks crammed together. It means overheard phone calls and people on every side of you and, because sick people never stay home, round-robins of colds and stomach flus. It's the lowest deck on the *Titanic*. It's a full Ryanair flight. It's peak frupidity.

"But this is already a separate room," Megan says. "We're not adding to the space issues on the floor."

"We need to save the offices for future L8 hires," the admin explains. "I'm sorry. I know it sucks, but that's the call that got made."

Megan and I exchange a look across our desks, and then an idea occurs to me. "Hey, there," I write to Josh. "I just heard about the move to high-density seating, and have concerns about how it will impact my productivity. What would you think about turning one of the large conference rooms into a designated common quiet space people can use when they need to focus, like a study hall?" I have to override some shame to do this, a fear that I sound as if I were demanding a roomful of white orchids and blue M&M's.

He responds quickly: "Hi! I love this idea but I don't see us giving up any conference space, unfortunately. ☹ There's always Starbucks . . ."

It's not the first time I've felt as if Amazon were daring me to do my job. But I no longer believe there's any reward for winning the dare. Amazon's going to cram as many bodies into as little space as possible, and the prize for doing good work under lousy conditions will be getting to do more work under lousy conditions. I'm actually not sure I *can* produce work that will meet Jeff's standards in a fucking veal pen. But more than that, I don't think I should have to try.

Megan gives notice a week later; she's off to Facebook to run her own design lab. With her departure, I'm the only one of Josh's direct reports left from when I started more than two years ago. That's normal for Amazon. What isn't is how openly Josh disses them to me once they're gone. That one burned out her team, he says, and another never learned to do things scalably, and a third was too in love with last-minute heroics, and now the rest of us have a mess to clean up. I agree with some of what he says, but that doesn't mean I want to hear him trash these good, kind, talented people who gave it all they had. Especially because I have to assume he'll talk the same way about me if I leave.

For now, I get a lot of praise for doing things the Amazon way, unlike *some* people. Not long before one manager left, a junior person on his team passed out cold on his front porch after a week of eighteen-hour days. "That's what happens when a leader doesn't push back on unrealistic expectations," Josh says at our first post-Megan one-on-one. "*You* would say, 'Actually, we can't turn this around today. We'll deliver it on Thursday.' But Megan didn't know how to say no."

I've had it with this particular line of bullshit. I know Josh was pushing Megan and the others to learn to stand on their own feet as L7 Amazon leaders. But he was still their boss.

If they were drowning—and in turn, drowning the people on their teams—why didn't he do something about it? Why didn't *he* push back on some of the top-down demands they wouldn't say no to?

"Yeah, I know how to say no and set boundaries," I say. "And other teams hate me for it. They *loved* Megan for bending the laws of physics to get their ill-defined, last-minute shit done time after time. She enabled them to suck at their jobs without paying a price. People fainting on porches isn't *their* problem."

Josh stares at me. "Jesus," he says. "I don't like to think of this place as so mean."

"They're not mean people," I say. "They're just doing what the organism wants. If the organism wanted employees to be sane and healthy, the people would do things differently." I shrug. Lately I find myself pulling out to what Brian called the five-thousand-foot view, where Amazon's patterns look as clear and neutral as an ant farm.

"Well, Megan did a lot of great things here. But ultimately she wasn't Amazonian."

I want to tell him I'm not so sure what it means to be Amazonian anymore. If setting boundaries is Amazonian but I'm the only one on this team who'll do it, then *I'm* the cultural misfit no matter what the Leadership Principles say. I want to say that it feels as if every single one of us—him, me, superwomen like Calista, the scores of stolid men in the leadership program, even the brutal mega-alphas like Mitch—were all in service to this *one guy*. That like one of those champagne towers, Jeff's demands fall onto the Mitchs and Iras of Amazon, and from them onto the Calistas and Rons, and from them onto the Joshes and Sallys, and then onto me, and from me onto Coco and Vance and George, and then onto their people, and so on all the way to the very bottom of the pyramid, all because nobody is willing to say when enough is enough. That this entire company is built on the fear of being exposed as merely human.

But it's 1:59, so I close my laptop and stand up. "I'm happy to be on the interview loop for Megan's replacement, by the way."

"Actually, I have some news about that," Josh says. "Do you know Graham from Advertising?"

"Oh yeah, we met once last year," I say. "Nice guy." Megan and I had considered Graham's team for some in-house marketing help. The sample campaigns in his pitch deck were visually strong, but the copy was riddled with typos.

"Well, I've hired him to replace Megan. And the great thing about him is that he has experience managing *all* aspects of design, including copy. So I'm going to have you report to him, too. He's awesome. I think you're going to love him."

I sit back down. "Hang on a sec. You're layering me?"

"We should definitely talk more about this, but just to let you know, I do have another meeting in five," Josh says.

"This has a huge impact on me, and I'm honestly shocked that you waited until the literal last minute of our one-on-one to tell me about it." Under my surprise is another emotion roiling at the base of my throat and I'm startled to realize it's disgust.

"What? No," Josh says, looking genuinely taken aback. "This changes very little for you. You'll still see me all the time. It'll just be a more streamlined org structure, and Megan leaving is good timing."

I'm trying desperately to sort and triage objections as they enter my head. Given how closely tied Megan's role is to mine, I'm stunned not to have been involved in interviewing her successor, but I'm afraid saying so will just sound petulant. "A new manager is always a big change," I say. "Graham now has more sway than anyone else at Amazon over my career path." Something sickening occurs to me. "Also, he's an L7, right?" Josh nods. "So my promotion just got pushed back another two years, minimum."

"I'm not following," Josh says. "Why would his level affect your promotion timetable?"

"Because Graham can't promote me above himself."

"He doesn't have that kind of ego," Josh says. "He absolutely will promote you as soon as it's time, even if it's before he gets there himself."

I can't believe I'm having to explain this. This isn't an Amazon thing; it's an all-companies-on-earth thing. It's like having to explain what an office is. "I don't mean it that way. I mean he literally *cannot* promote me to a level he himself has not attained. He has to get promoted first, and *then* he can consider putting me up."

"Are you *sure* about that?" he asks. "It doesn't make sense to me that some minor detail of org structure would be a promotion blocker for you."

"I am overwhelmingly sure," I say. "Any HR person in the company can confirm." *Any HR person in* any *company in the galaxy can confirm*, I think. "Do you understand why I don't feel good about what this change means for my future?"

Josh is nodding slowly. "I do," he says. "Absolutely I understand. Look, let me check in with HR just for official confirmation, and then we'll talk again."

I go down to the parking garage and sit in my car and

wait to start crying. But the anger that formed in my throat, as usual, has settled into something blue and cool that feels more like lucid disappointment, and not even over Josh's decision itself so much as the lack of thought behind it. I've been through tons of Amazon reorgs, and even been layered before. And I've guided my own people through reorgs, too. You can't make someone happy about unwanted change, but you sure as hell can take five minutes to think through the impact and be ready to talk about it. And you don't wing the news at them as they're heading out the door.

Those are the thoughts of the disappointed manager inside me. The human just feels forgotten. I trusted Josh enough to take this job blind. I've talked to him almost every day for three years, about design and writing and office politics but also college and family and anxiety (mine and his) and our shared belief that *The Leftovers* is the finest television show in history. And about *my career path*. I've long since shed any illusions that I matter to Amazon the capitalist organism, which is bearable as long as I matter to the people around me. If I don't matter to Josh, I'm lost.

My problem-solving mind wakes up pretty fast. *So you'll find a new role*, it says. And yeah, I could do that. But *will* I? I can't quite see myself going through the hunt and the speed dating and the cramming for interviews and the goodbye coffees and the new cube and the fire hose of information again with anything but resignation. The fire in my belly that I've rekindled six or seven times at Amazon is going to be hard to light again. I'm just not sure it's worth it anymore. I think there are better places to strike that match.

I might have outgrown Amazon, I think, laughing silently. And I don't want to shrink myself to fit anymore.

I laugh out loud at that, and then I check the time and head back upstairs to interview some kid for his first job out of business school.

The next afternoon, Josh calls out as I pass his office. "Hey," he says. "HR confirmed that Graham can't put you up for promotion above his own level, and I just wanted to apologize for the misunderstanding. It seems obvious now. I don't know where my brain went."

"I appreciate the apology," I say. "In that case, would you consider leaving the current reporting structure in place, so my own path isn't derailed?" I'm pretty sure the answer is no. But I want to make him say it.

"Here's the thing," Josh says. "I think you're really going to like Graham. He's a great guy, and you can learn a lot from him, and he can learn at least as much from you. It's all going to work out well, and I have zero doubt you'll both get promoted soon."

"Huh," I say. "Okay. Well, thanks for the update."

"Wait, one second before you leave," Josh says. "Are *we* okay? I want to make sure you and I are okay."

"I'm fine," I say, and go.

John and I don't eat downtown very often. But Shiro's, Seattle's oldest sushi restaurant, had a freak same-day reservation and John snagged it. After work I meet him at the bar, where elderly men are slicing and stacking sashimi at speeds that would render me fingerless in moments.

"I could watch these guys all day," John says, and we do that for a few minutes until one of the chefs slides some fatty tuna over the counter.

"So I think I'm going to leave Amazon," I say. He raises his eyebrows and nods. We talked last night about Josh and his bungled reorg communication, but I needed to live with my thoughts about outgrowing Amazon a little longer before I shared them. "I need more growing room."

"Fuck yeah," John says.

"You sure?"

"Get the fuck out of there, baby."

I exhale. "I love you."

"I love you too. And I'm proud of you for leaving."

"Good," I say, using the chopsticks in my own special, desperate way to pick up some tuna and bring it to my mouth. "I'm leaving Amazon," I say again. And then we eat.

EXIT INTERVIEW

I have starred in so many films of my departure from Amazon. In the early years, they involved my retirement party, which for some reason always takes place on a boat. I'm fifty-six but look *maybe* forty-eight, and after two promotions I'm worth tens of millions of dollars. I give keynotes at conferences, some of them women's conferences, but I speak at gen-pop ones too, because even men want to know what I think. And I say what needs to be said. "Shut up about the pipeline. Keep the women who are already slogging it out alongside you. Promote them. Pay them more than they ask for, because they probably haven't asked for what they're worth." If that irks some dude, I don't care, because I will never need anything from him. I casually write big checks to good causes, because I'll never miss that fifty thousand dollars for an abortion fund or seventy-five thousand to house people on the streets who are struggling with addiction. With one donation, I wipe out the entire U.S. backlog of untested rape kits. Excellent wine is on hand at my party and I get to drink it, because in this movie I still have a functioning off switch. John is by my side, of course, looking like the most urbane version of a northwestern outdoorsman. We're about to leave for three months in Amsterdam, along with our future dogs, who will fly in whatever stratospherically expensive but low-stress way very rich people like us get their dogs to Europe. Then we'll all come home to Seattle and I'll join some boards or maybe even a start-up, because even the richest people who retire from Amazon usually have at least one new job within a year.

In later years, the film is about a war of attrition. I'm finally the right person in the right role with the right boss at the right time to get promoted, and for a month or two I'm high on approval and recognition. Then I start to validate everything friends who got there first have told me: that the pressure is ratcheted *way* up and the money isn't that much better, though at least my stock vests twice as often now. So I hang around long enough to be polite and cash in a few times, and then I ride my new director title to a senior vice president one at a different company. The celebration in this movie is just dinner with friends in the private room at Canlis. Marnie and Andy are there—in this film they've moved back to Seattle, because Seattle has mysteriously become quite sunny—and Marnie offers a toast: "To being so pigheaded that you didn't leave until you forced Amazon to admit how good you are."

Then there's a whole anthology of short films called *The Flounce*. I flounce when Mitch calls me stupid. I flounce when Lorna keeps me waiting for months to see if I still have a job, and again when Ron tells me to change the world, and again when I'm told to be happy about suffering fools. And those are just the heroic flounces: there are a hundred pettier ones, when my door desk gives me a splinter or Amazon won't let me expense a few pizzas for my team during crunch time or a man says "Just to play devil's advocate" about a topic that genuinely does not need the advocacy of the devil. In these films, the flounce itself is all the celebration I need.

Of course when it finally happens, it's anti-cinematic, not a feature, barely a GIF: a bare desk, an hourglass spinning endlessly, and then silence.

Since it's so all-fired important for Graham to be my manager, I wait five days for our first one-on-one to announce I'm leaving. It's protocol, and it's also petty. But I'm not interested in hearing Josh ask for more reassurance that *we're* okay. The only conference room I could book for the one-on-one is tucked under a staircase and so hard to find that Graham arrives late and a bit harried. "On top of the floor plan, I'm so overwhelmed with the sheer amount I have to learn about this business," he says. "I feel stupid."

"I remember that feeling well," I say. "Here's one vocab tip: 'ambient sandwiches' just means sandwiches shelved at room temperature."

"I actually did have a mental note to look that up," he says, taking a pen from the pocket of the bright suit vest he's wearing with his jeans. "So, you and I barely know each other," he says. "But your reputation precedes you, and I have to say I'm surprised you're reporting to me. I assumed you were a director."

"I mean, I've *tried*, of course, but the stars haven't aligned," I say. "You know how it goes."

"I mean, why aren't you running copy for all of physical retail? I don't get it."

"Yeah, I tried to at least start a conversation about that too," I say. "The timing wasn't right."

"Well, obviously the new reporting structure is a bottleneck for your growth, which I feel kind of bad about," he says. "But we can still work on expanding your scope, right?"

He's saying all the right things with such sincerity that I hate having to do this to him. "I really and truly appreciate that," I say, "but you're actually off the hook. I'm leaving Amazon." I slide a document across the table. "I wrote up this job description for my replacement, and of course while I'm here, I'll do what I can to help you recruit and screen."

He stares at me for a moment. "Shit," he says. "I hope this isn't because of me."

"Oh no," I say. "Not you *specifically*, at least. Really. It's just time."

Graham nods. "I understand," he says.

There's so little involved in leaving. All my stuff still fits in one tote bag, and my whole brain is still documented on the wiki from my pre-sabbatical preparations. There's not a lot of explaining to do to my co-workers, either. The ones who know I have a book coming out tease me that I'm leaving to go be famous, and I laugh and let them think it's just that simple, though in reality it's the solidity and routine of my Amazon life that's been keeping my book terrors barely at bay. The rest don't ask for an explanation. People leave here every day, after all. I'll go, Josh will vent about all the ways I wasn't good enough, and then someone new will fill the gap and it will be as if I never existed.

I think a lot in my last two weeks about the difference between leaving and quitting. I long to feel the punctuation of quitting, as if a sentence were ending. But what I feel instead is more that I'm just not going to be coming here and doing things anymore. I'll be four miles away, not *at* Amazon, but still *of* Amazon, for the foreseeable future. I've been warned by friends who've left to expect bad dreams and random cortisol spikes as long as a year out. Mid-afternoon adrenaline surges that I don't know where to direct. See an endocrinologist, one friend tells me. Another passes on the name of a trauma therapist. He won't laugh at the idea of Amazon as trauma, she assures me. *He's worked with a lot of us.*

I also think about what to say in the exit interview. I know not everyone gets invited to do one in person, that a lot of employees just get a form to fill out. But I'm in the ninety-eighth fucking percentile. I've worked across five different organizations and had a hand in hiring many hundreds of people. Plus I'm a woman in leadership, that population Amazon keeps saying it's trying to grow. Of course I'll get a real exit interview, right?

I do not. I get a link to a form, with instructions to submit it within two days of my departure. I know I could pitch a fit, demand an in-person meeting. But I also know I won't.

I spend my last two hours filling out the form. I write hundreds of words about the thrill and the damage, about never feeling bored and also never feeling safe. I write about being the only woman in so many rooms, and about all the ways Amazon made me smarter and all the ways it damaged me. I express gratitude for being allowed to reinvent myself at will, to make wild career moves that wouldn't fly in the straight world. I say I expect to know and love some of the people I've met here for the rest of my life. I say I'm leaving with no more understanding of how to get promoted than I had the day I arrived. I say that Amazon set the stage for my addiction, but that sobriety has been manageable here, too.

The final question is yes/no: "Would you recommend Amazon as an employer to others?" I stare at the choices for several minutes before clicking no.

At ten to five, I figure I've said enough and hit the Submit button. The page hangs. The hourglass spins and spins. *Amazon is being Amazon to the end*, I think, but maybe I've already started to shed my Amazonness, because despite all the docs and notes I've lost to the intranet void, I didn't think to save my exit interview on my hard drive.

Finally, in panic-induced thoughtlessness, I hit the Back button. "This form must be resubmitted to be refreshed." I hit Refresh and nothing happens. I hit Cancel and the page hangs for another second and then it's blank and everything I had to say to Amazon is gone.

Except wait—the email that accompanied the form said I had to submit it within two days of my departure, meaning the link should work until Sunday at 5:00. It's a pain in the ass to type it all out again, but at least I'll have my say.

It's 4:58. I email the form link to my home address, pull my personal laptop out of its bag, and click the link, just to make sure it works. "You do not have permission to access this server." I get the same message on mobile. By now it's 5:03 and my network access has vanished on my work laptop, too.

I read the email that came with the form again and realize the most likely explanation is that whoever built the form and wrote the email had a different understanding of the word "within." And then I laugh out loud. Well, what would *you* do? I laugh out loud and then I leave my laptop on my desk, hit the restroom to change into my running clothes, drop my tote bag of wordly possessions in the car, and slip quietly out of the building, hanging a right onto Bell Street at a light jog. A man on a bench looks up from his phone. "Is this the ending you envisioned?" he asks.

"I used to think there would be a party on a boat," I say as I pass.

At the corner of Bell and Third, my parents are waiting for a cab. "But how will you support yourself now?" my mother asks.

"Plasma," I say, and hug her. "I know how much you liked having jobs, Mom. I wish you could have had more of them."

My father is shaking his head. "Let me guess: men are jerks."

I hug him too. "I love you. I wish we hadn't had to pretend my world would be like yours."

At First Avenue I see a cop on horseback. "Did Amazon make you a drunk?" he asks.

"No," I say, "it just let me map the edges."

"What did you find at the edges?" asks the horse.

"The erasure of all my traits," I say, a sugar cube on my open palm.

A woman with an employee badge and a clipboard steps into my path outside Le Pichet. "These questions were not on the form, you know."

"Yes, but the forms belong to me now, too," I say, and hang my own badge gently around her neck.

By the bridge to 99, the wino wants to know what Prince song I'm listening to. "'Pussy Control'!" I say, and we high-five. "I was always afraid to tell you," I say.

"I know," he says, "I know."

Across the street, the Hammering Man statue peers down at me outside the art museum. "Will you always feel like a failure?" he asks, which stops me in my tracks.

"I hope not," I say, nearly tipping over backward to meet his gaze. "But if so, at least I know how."

I start jogging again, Jeff Bezos beside me. "Didn't you promise to never let me down?" he asks.

"I did," I say. "But I want you to know I won't be laughing at your sexting scandal next year."

"My *what*?"

"I'll be thinking how *human* you sound," I say as we round the corner. "I'll wonder how Amazon might have felt if you'd been that human all along."

"Sexting?" he says, but I'm already jogging backward away from him.

"I promise I don't look at the dick pic," I say, and wave as I turn my back.

Suddenly I'm too tired to go on. I stop and hang down over my legs outside the Irish knits store.

"Were you successful?" asks the shopkeeper, folding her sidewalk sign as she closes for the day.

"Only in tiny moments," I tell her. "But there were a lot of tiny moments."

The light changes. I step into the crosswalk, where midway I meet a beautiful old woman who looks a lot like me. "What will you do with all those tiny moments?" she asks with a smile, and tears come to my eyes.

"I guess I'll turn them into a glitter ball," I say, and she nods.

"Good work," she says.

ACKNOWLEDGMENTS

Thank you to Daphne Durham, editor and friend, who walked so much of this road with me. Can you believe we made it to the other side? Thank you to the wonderful Sarah Burnes, who believed in this book even before I was sure I did. Thank you to Sean McDonald, Sarita Varma, Claire Tobin, Devon Mazzone, Alex Merto, Hannah Goodwin, and Brianna Fairman at MCD / Farrar, Straus and Giroux for taking such splendid care of my work.

It turns out that a global pandemic, punctuated by political upheaval and a couple of significant personal crises, is not my ideal setting for productive creativity. Who knew? If not for Miranda Beverly-Whittemore, Claire Dederer, and Tova Mirvis, I'd still be staring into the middle distance with half a book to show for it. Joanna Rakoff also provided valuable feedback early on. Thank you all for your friendship, expertise, and cheerleading. Many thanks also to the Mineral School residency, where parts of this book were revised, and to Caveday, the virtual coworking space that did mysterious, almost surreal wonders for my productivity.

I grew up taking it for granted that work could and should be not just a means of paying the bills, but also a place to channel my passions and find new ones. For that I thank my dad, Neal Coulter, who modeled how to turn intellectual curiosity into a long and distinguished career. My mother, Ann Copeland Coulter, worked equally hard at home to make my dad's career sustainable. She was also a great reader, and I wish she were still here to read this book.

Amazon employees are a brilliant, creative, stouthearted bunch. I learned so much from you, and you made me laugh so hard. I love far too many of you to list by name, and I also want to protect your privacy. But thank you for making the bad days survivable and the good days exhilarating.

I wish I could remember the name of the woman who ran the gift shop in Los Alamos, New Mexico, and gave me my very first job at age fourteen. I still have the hand-painted wooden trinket box I bought with my employee discount, and every time I see it I recall the satisfying *kathunk* of the manual credit card device. Thank you for taking a chance on my weird teenage self.

Linus, you were a Dog of Great Character and I miss you so much. Prince and Bowie, thanks for looking after him up there; I owe you one. Ella, you are a good girl and your resilience and glee inspire me every day.

John, my Big Love: I could thank you for thirty years of adventures, but the truth is that *you* are the adventure of my life. The rest is anecdote.

A NOTE ABOUT THE AUTHOR

Kristi Coulter is the author of *Nothing Good Can Come from This*, which was a finalist for a 2019 Washington State Book Award. She holds an MFA in creative writing from the University of Michigan. She is a former Ragdale resident and the recipient of a grant from the National Foundation for Advancement in the Arts. Her work has appeared in *New York* magazine, *The Paris Review*, *Elle*, and *The Believer*, among other publications. She lives in Seattle.